The Best Distance Learning Graduate Schools

Earning Your Degree Without Leaving Home

1999 Edition

Praise for
The Best Distance Learning Graduate Schools

"A most exceptional guide to distance learning and virtual graduate schools...This book is a must for 21st century graduate school degree seekers unable or unwilling to leave home for the outmoded, traditional campus residence.... A gem of research."

> *Stephen A. LeMah, Ph.D., Distance Learning Division Chairperson, The Association of Management and International Association of Management*

"Phillips and Yager have provided an excellent roadmap...to a graduate degree in cyberspace. They correctly point out that neither distance nor work nor family obligations are, any longer, necessarily obstacles to obtaining that graduate degree."

> *Dr. Jodi Servatius, Professor of Education and Director, On-Line Teaching Certificate Program, California State University, Hayward*

"Life-long learning is the new key to the American Dream, and this book places that key within everyone's reach."

> *Peter D. Weddle, Author, National Business Employment Weekly's "Web-Site Review"*

"Recommended reading for serious learners who refuse to put their lives 'on hold' while pursuing a graduate degree."

> *Ted Christensen, Assistant Vice President for GW Television, George Washington University*

"A must-read for anyone contemplating a non-traditional graduate education. It is comprehensive in providing the facts needed to make a wise decision as to not only which university to select, but in determining the readiness of the reader to enroll in any of its well selected listings."

> *Thomas L. Russell, Director, Instructional Telecommunications North Carolina State University*

"Distance Learning is one of the powerful tools of the Internet Age. Being able to attend the graduate school of your choice, from anywhere and in the time format of your choice opens new career opportunities. This is a valuable guide for citizens around the world as they continue their education."

> *Elliott Masie, President, The MAISIE Center, and Author, Living in the Digital Age*

The Princeton Review

The Best Distance Learning Graduate Schools

Earning Your Degree Without Leaving Home

Vicky Phillips and Cindy Yager

Random House Inc., New York
1999 Edition
www.randomhouse.com

Princeton Review Publishing, L.L.C.
2315 Broadway
New York, NY 10024
E-mail: info@review.com

ISBN: 0-679-76930-7

Editor: Gretchen Feder
Production Editors: Amy Bryant and Kristen Azzara
Designer and Production Manager: Robert McCormack

Manufactured in the United States of America on partially recycled paper.

9 8 7 6 5 4 3 2

CONTENTS

CHAPTER ONE

Back to School at Your Age: You Are Not Alone

THE DESKTOP UNIVERSITY

If you're in your late twenties, thirties, forties, or older, and considering earning a higher degree or career credential, you are not alone. College is not just for kids anymore. These days a less boisterous crowd is occupying the front row of America's collegiate lecture halls. In the case of distance learning, adult learners are seating themselves in front of computer keyboards and cable TV channels in record numbers. This new distance learning collegiate crowd comes with as much academic enthusiasm and mental muscle as ever, but with different expectations and attitudes from that of the traditional 18- to 21-year-old college student.

This new collegiate crop typically has years of career experience, less time to philosophize on what *might be*, and a more immediate career interest in what *is*. The average age of today's distance learning college "kid" runs anywhere from 35 to 47, depending on the studies or programs one cites. If you're older than 25 and thinking of attending college again as the next century dawns, you are part of an emerging college majority.

For instance, on average, students in the Duke University distance MBA program are in their thirties (a whopping 59 percent of the enrollment). Learners in the 40 to 49 age range represent 27 percent of the Duke distance learning student body, while those older than 50 account for 7 percent of the incoming class each year. Only 7 percent of the Duke distance MBA student body are younger than 30. Similarly, Purdue University's low-residency Executive Master of Science in Management program supports a diverse student body whose average age is 35, with students ranging from 25- to 50-years-old in each new "freshman" class.

Adults are returning to college in record numbers to acquire new skills, sharpen old career competencies, and keep abreast of changing technologies. Careers today require more specialized skills than ever before. In addition, career-climbing has become an increasingly competitive activity as more and more Americans have earned their college degrees. The number of people who hold bachelor's degrees has grown tremendously in the last three decades. In 1970, 12 million Americans held bachelor's degrees. Today, 36 million are four-year college graduates. Having a graduate or professional career credential can help set you apart from the well-educated competition, resulting in greater long-term career mobility and financial advantages.

Because most adults can't afford to relocate themselves and their families to receive the continuing education required in today's knowledge-based economy, universities are beginning to defy campus boundaries. Adult students are abandoning the traditional ivy halls, going to class in their homes via surface mail, videotape, fax, and modem. What's different for adults considering graduate or professional school in this decade is that many of them will not go to the campus—instead the campus will come to them.

People sometimes imagine distance learning as a lonely process—long hours spent studying alone with no sense of class companionship and no chance to see or meet fellow learners. But as more and more programs use interactive delivery via the Internet, students experience enriching online classroom environments where they can kick back, meet in real-time chat rooms, see scanned photos and biographies of their classmates and professors, and socialize at virtual campus cafes and union halls.

Real people—people like your sister or your neighbor or your boss—are using online distance learning to meet, socialize, and establish classroom rapport and friendships. To help combat the myth that distance learning is a solitary endeavor that is perhaps best suited to computer nerds and asocial types, we have included photo-enhanced profiles of real-life distance learners in this guide. These photos and personal commentaries should help demystify the process of distance learning and help you understand that distance learning is something that is suited to *anyone* who needs greater access to continuing professional education, rather than a phenomenon that is best suited to certain solitary types.

Today's College Kids: Older, Wiser, and Online

Meet two adult students who commute to college via the Internet—

Name: Bob Clune

Age: 47

Home: Endwell, New York

Occupation: Coordinator of Program Development for a Northeastern Utility

College of Choice: Boise State University

Program: Master of Science in Instructional and Performance Technology

Why are you earning your graduate degree?

As a Coordinator of Program Development for a Northeastern utility, I wanted to learn more about working with adult learners. In addition, I aspired to create more effective instructional and performance interventions, and to be at the top of my field within the company. Given the current competitive utility climate, our employee population needs to meet new job challenges and demands through improved job performance. They also require more knowledge in their jobs than ever before. My graduate degree in the field of Instructional and Performance Technology will provide me with the skills to aid in the development of these employees.

Why are you earning your degree through distance learning?

As important as the field of adult learning is, the opportunity to learn these skills does not exist here at my local university. I work full time, have a wife and two children, and am deeply involved in the community. To drive 100 miles to attend an evening program with a similar curriculum would have been prohibitive without changing family and lifestyle options. This program allowed me to balance work, my life, and an education, without excessive personal sacrifices.

Do you think the quality of the education you're receiving is equal to what you'd have received by attending a program on campus?

I would recommend a distance learning environment to anyone looking to extend his or her education who is faced with circumstances that otherwise would prohibit them from doing so. Without a doubt, a learner faces different challenges and experiences when working at a distance, but considering the rigors and demands of the virtual classroom, the Boise State Instructional Performance Technology faculty and staff are excellent. They have provided wonderful guidance, transforming the distance learning environment into a great and challenging learning adventure. The camaraderie I have built with fellow students facing similar learning situations has been wonderful. I wouldn't hesitate for a minute to call on one of my fellow classmates for an answer to a question or a piece of advice. It's been great!

Name: Susan Mary Smith
Age: 39
Home: Brookfield, Connecticut
Occupation: Computer Systems Manager
College of Choice: Nova Southeastern University·
Program: Master of Science in Management of Information Systems

Why are you earning your graduate degree?

My primary reason is to learn. Though I have worked in the systems field for thirteen years, I need more knowledge of current technology. I believe the only way to get this is to study seriously. Stephen Covey's "Law of the Farm Principle" says that "there is a natural order process. When it comes to the mind, the ability to think analytically, creatively, the ability to communicate orally and in writing, to rise above outmoded practices and solve problems in newer, better ways comes from following a natural systematic process." You must cultivate your mind with deep study to truly integrate both practical and theoretical knowledge. I am a computer person. I thrive on computers making life and work better for people. The more I understand, the more I have to offer.

Why are you earning your degree through distance learning?

I am using distance learning as a solution to the work/family dilemma. I am a single parent of a teenager, and I have a full-time career. I want to be available to my son. The program at Nova is accelerated. I can go full time, while still working, and receive my master's degree in eighteen months. Since I am a systems professional, I want to experience the effectiveness of the online environment in education so I can later utilize the technology and principles in the business sector. Telework is one of my areas of research.

Do you think the quality of the education you're receiving is equal to what you'd have received by attending a program on campus?

Absolutely equal, if not better. Access to students and teachers is almost immediate. When I have a question, I just E-mail my professors or colleagues. So far, they have all responded within twenty-four hours—usually within a few hours. The program requires a lot of research, so we become proficient with online information access. Like virtual organizations and communities, a lot of nontraditional social communication also occurs.

CHAPTER TWO

Distance Education Earns an "A"

One of the most frequently asked questions about distance learning goes something like this: "If there is no classroom and no instructor physically present, how is it that anyone learns anything?" This is a fair question given that for most of us formal education has been based on a model where we listened to a lecture by an expert twice a week, read a companion book, and were then tested on the material.

This model of formal education assumes that listening to a "sage on the stage" is the bona fide way to learn. The sage on the stage model is still used in many universities and formal educational settings, but other models have also recently emerged. These newer models have been tested and found to be *as* effective, *if not more so*, than the approach that single-mindedly dominated the academic lecture halls of yesteryear.

THE WORLD AS A UNIVERSITY WITHOUT WALLS

We are learning all the time. Informal learning, learning on-the-job, learning by trial and error and with the unofficial helping hand of a co-worker accounts for much of the learning that happens after graduation. You have probably acquired an amazing amount of knowledge this way—even more than you did in the lecture room.

Distance learning borrows from the longstanding philosophy that the world is a university without walls. In fact, one of the earliest organized university movements toward rigorous degree-based correspondence study in the United States was dubbed the University Without Walls movement. One of the key tenets of the American distance learning movement is that the professor is less a sage on the stage and more of a "guide on the side." In distance learning, a professor's role is more often that of a mentor or an evaluator than that of an expert who stands and broadcasts data and analysis. However, in some distance learning programs professors still deliver lectures—albeit via mailed videotapes, rather than face to face as was once the norm.

For Adults Only

What is unique about some of the distance learning programs in this book is not just the instructional delivery mode, but the educational philosophy that supports the nature of the learning itself. In reviewing the programs in this book you'll see a model of learning emerging that is designed for a more mature student in that it puts the learner into a more dynamic role in planning and executing her own program of study. Often, the resulting curriculum and course requirements include not just exposure to classic textbook theory but hands-on projects, simulations, and team strategy sessions that encourage the integration of career and college in rather unique ways.

At some schools, like the Union Institute, based in Cincinnati, Ohio, no established curriculum exists. Learners must work to design their own program of study based on their final educational and career goals. Faculty mentors and advisors, as well as degree committee members, help structure the learning and approve the final degree plan, but they are not the ones who determine what is to be learned. That decision is in the hands of the learner—within acceptable limits.

At other schools, like George Washington University's Executive Leadership Doctorate program, cohort study groups are charged with team work and the completion of work-related projects. In the past, such projects would have been completed by isolated scholars working alone among dusty reference books. Concepts that were once restricted to think-tank settings or skills training seminars now appear in academic degree programs. Team-based learning and assessment are replacing the solitary scholar model, just as projects demonstrating excellence and work-based case studies and management simulations are replacing or augmenting the footnoted thesis in some programs.

But Can I Really Learn This Way?

Educational researchers, themselves skeptical at first that distance learning and structured self-study could rival the traditional lecture hall method, have several times set out to see if distance learners are as well educated as their on-campus peers. The results have consistently surprised even the educational experts.

Researchers John R. Verduin and Thomas Clark reviewed the literature from different distance delivery systems, including print, TV, video, audio, and computer-assisted systems. Verduin and Clark concluded in their book, *Distance Education*, that there are no significant differences in learning achievements or program satisfaction when learners in accredited residency programs are compared to their no-residency (no campus visits required) or low-residency (some campus visits required) program peers. The "no significant difference phenomenon," as it is now called, has held up across time and multiple types of comparative analysis.

The most recent—and still ongoing—comprehensive review of distance learning studies is by Dr. Thomas Russell, director of the Office of Instructional Telecommunications at North Carolina State University. After reviewing 248 research reports, summaries, and academic papers, Russell concluded that there are no significant differences in learning when traditional face-to-face classroom methods are compared to distance delivery means. Dr. Russell's study, "The No Significant Difference Phenomenon as Reported in 248 Research Reports, Summaries, and Papers," is available online at http://trnb.mta.ca/phenom/phenom.html

For anyone who doubts that much can be learned outside the walls of a university lecture hall, look at the alumni of some of the simplest mail-based correspondence programs that have operated for over a century in the United States. Ben Cohen and Jerry Greenwald, founders of Ben & Jerry's Ice Cream, the Vermont-based company that revolutionized the gourmet ice cream market in the early 1980s, learned how to make their famous ice cream by completing a $25 non-credit, mail-based correspondence course from Pennsylvania State University's distance learning program. Ben and Jerry completed the ice cream manufacturing course out of curiosity when they were thinking of starting a business, but were uncertain what kind of business might be best. The course was a direct result of Penn State's efforts in the 1880s to develop correspondence courses that would extend business know-how to Pennsylvania's rural dairy farmers looking to enhance their product lines and incomes. The continuing education mail-based correspondence program that Penn State set into motion more than 100 years ago is one of the ideological grandparents of the more than 190 professional degree and career credential programs profiled in this guide. Today, according to a 1997 report by the National Center for Education Statistics, more than 750,000 students are enrolled in university-sponsored distance learning courses.

Today's Distance Learning College Kids: Acquiring Invaluable Career Skills Through Distance Learning

Name: Ben Mazza
Age: 26
Home: New York City
Occupation: Madison Avenue Advertising Executive
College of Choice: New York University
Program: Advanced Professional Certificate in Information Technology

Why are you earning your career credential?

Young people like myself need to manage their careers like an investment portfolio. If you want to stay ahead of the ever-changing technology you need to make investments in your career at an early age. I'm using the professional certificate program to make myself more marketable to future employers and stay ahead of the technological curve. NYU's program in Information Technology allows me to acquire valuable long-term assets for my career portfolio.

Why are you studying through distance learning?

NYU's Information Technology program is the most advanced in the country. It was almost necessary that the program be taught through distance learning because the best way to truly understand information technologies—what the program is all about—is to use them. At NYU, hands-on study means using NYU's proprietary network via an ISDN line from your home computer with Lotus Notes—a powerful groupware application tool used for group learning and communication online. The program not only taught us about information technologies, but allowed us to experience the technical and human psychological effects associated with technology and distance learning.

Do you think the quality of the education you're receiving is equal to what you'd receive by attending a program on campus?

Greater than attending class! I have excellent reading, writing, and comprehension skills along with a good work ethic—enabling me to fully take advantage of a distance learning program. This type of learning is not for everyone. You have to ask yourself if you can feel comfortable not seeing classmates or professors, and if you have the discipline to rely on yourself to spend an enormous amount of time researching, writing, and reading from your computer.

CHAPTER THREE

Getting Admitted:
Some Honest ABCs

If you're considering graduate or professional school you may have questions about policy, procedure, and career-related concerns. In this chapter you will find answers to the following questions:

- What special entrance exams will I have to take?
- Do I need an undergraduate degree to be admitted to a graduate program?
- Can I get degree credit for my career experience?
- Can I take undergraduate course prerequisites through distance means?
- If I hold a bachelor's degree in one area and now want to attend graduate school in another area, do I have to earn a second bachelor's degree with a new major first?
- What are Continuing Education Units (CEUs) and who needs them?

To make it easy for you, we've prepared this chapter in question and answer format. It addresses the most common questions our clients and those who have visited our Adult Education & Distance Learner's Resource Center online (http://www.geteducated.com) have asked us over the last few years.

ARE THESE PROGRAMS EASIER TO GET INTO THAN ON-CAMPUS PROGRAMS?

One misconception people sometimes have about distance learning is that because these programs use nontraditional methods of instruction they also use nontraditional admission requirements. This assumption can lead you to think that distance learning programs are easier to get into than their on-campus counterparts. Nothing could be further from the truth.

Most of the programs listed in this guide are *at least as competitive* as your local university. Some of these programs are *more competitive* than your local university. For example, the Fielding Institute, a private professional school offering doctorates, recently accepted only 85 of the 254 applicants who completed their intensive admissions process for doctoral study in clinical psychology and psychotherapy. The Colorado State University Master of Business Administration program is ranked among the top 25 percent of business schools in America. Their requirements for admission are higher than those maintained by most universities. The University of Idaho offers top-notch engineering and computer science training through their Video Outreach division, but warns applicants that admission is granted on a competitive basis.

In most distance learning programs applicants are held to the same standards as on-campus learners. They are often using the same texts, taking the same exams, even being graded at the same time and in direct comparison to their on-campus cohorts. As with campus-based programs, admission requirements vary widely among distance learning programs. Study the "Admission" sections of each institutional profile for a detailed listing of criteria. Although a few programs will admit most who apply, the majority of these programs, like campus-based programs, maintain selective standards.

WHAT SPECIAL ENTRANCE EXAMS WILL I HAVE TO TAKE?

The "Admission" section of each institutional profile in this guide lists required entrance exams. Many graduate schools require applicants to take standardized exams in addition to submitting transcripts from all undergraduate work, letters of professional reference, and an admission essay. If you find that you need to take any of these exams, contact the test administrators to request a free explanation and registration information. All testing agencies outlined in this section also send free information on the books and software programs they have developed to help learners self-study for their exams. The Princeton Review offers a full line of test-prep books, courses, and software that will help you sharpen your test-taking acumen as well. They're definitely worth checking out.

One entrance criterion that is not an exam but is commonly employed by distance programs is the stipulation that applicants already have career experience or employment in their chosen study area. Most distance programs attract experienced adults and have accordingly established curricula that assume an ability to carry out advanced learning practicums, internships, and projects in the work environment. Your chances of admission to, as well as the suitability of, any distance program may rely heavily on your ability to use your workplace as a part of the extended university experience.

Below, you'll find a guide to the standardized tests that graduate schools commonly require:

Graduate Management Admission Test

Many business management and administration programs require applicants to submit scores on the Graduate Management Admission Test (GMAT). Contrary to what the name implies, the GMAT will not directly test your knowledge of management or business issues. Instead, the GMAT will test your verbal, mathematical, and analytical reasoning aptitudes. The quantitative section of the GMAT tests mathematical skills, including basic math and applied algebra, geometry, and first-level calculus. The verbal section will test your ability to read and comprehend complex written passages. The analytical section will test your ability to analyze situations critically and communicate complex ideas in writing.

As of October 1997, the GMAT abandoned the old paper-and-pencil version of the exam, and now only offers the computer adaptive test, or CAT, for a hefty $125 registration fee. For a free copy of the GMAT Bulletin and Registration Form, contact:

Graduate Management Admission Test
Educational Testing Service
P.O. Box 6103
Princeton, New Jersey 08541-6103
609-771-7330
E-mail: gmat@ets.org
URL: http://www.gmat.org

The bulletin explains the exam and gives sample questions. It also provides registration information for applicants who are in the military or living abroad

Programs rarely rely solely on the GMAT to determine admission. More commonly, as with Colorado State University's MBA program, admission is determined by an integrated analysis of scores on the GMAT, undergraduate grade point average, and letters of reference, as well as evidence of career-relevant business ability.

Graduate Record Examination—General Test

The Graduate Record Examination (GRE) is commonly required for those applying to graduate programs in areas other than business administration. The GRE has three sections: verbal, quantitative, and analytical reasoning. Some universities do not use the scores on the analytical reasoning section but all applicants must take all three sections of the exam once registered. Both the paper and pencil and CAT versions cost $96. Higher fees apply to exams taken outside the United States.

A free Information and Registration Bulletin and General Test Descriptive Bulletin can be obtained from:

Graduate Record Examinations
Educational Testing Service
P.O. Box 6000
Princeton, New Jersey 08541-6000
609-771-7670
E-mail: gre-info@ets.org
URL: http://www.gre.org

GRE Subject Tests

In addition to the GRE general aptitude test discussed above, you may also be required to take a single-subject GRE, which tests your depth and breadth of knowledge in a single subject. For an additional $96 each, the GRE subject exams are available in biochemistry, biology, chemistry, computer science, economics, education, engineering, geology, history, literature, mathematics, music, physics, political science, psychology, and sociology.

A free Information and Registration Bulletin and a free Subject Test Descriptive Bulletin can be obtained from:

Graduate Record Examinations
Educational Testing Service
P.O. Box 6000
Princeton, New Jersey 08541-6000
609-771-7670
E-mail: gre-info@ets.org
URL: http://www.gre.org

Miller Analogies Test

The Miller Analogies Test (MAT) is a timed, 100-item test of one's ability to think and reason in analogies. An analogy is simply a comparative thought paradigm. The statement "cat is to kitten as dog is to puppy" is a very simple analogy. The analogies given on the MAT are somewhat more sophisticated and require a sharp comparative ability. The MAT is most commonly used by education, psychology, and human resources programs as a general admission indicator. The MAT registration fee is $40.

A free Information Bulletin and List of Testing Centers can be obtained by writing to:

Psychological Corporation
Miller Analogies Test Information
555 Academic Court
San Antonio, Texas 78204-2408
210-299-1061 or 800-622-3231

Test of English as a Foreign Language

The Test of English as a Foreign Language (TOEFL) is often required for applicants whose first language of instruction is not English. The exam will test your ability to read and comprehend English instruction. The ability to read and write formal English is important because although many of the programs listed in this guide actively recruit and enroll international learners, all of the programs in this guide use English as the instructional language. A score of 500-600 is commonly required on the TOEFL to be admitted to an English-based instructional program in the United States. The TOEFL is given at designated testing sites in more than 180 countries, twelve times a year. The exam fee varies by testing site.

For a free registration bulletin on TOEFL, and its related exam, the Test of Written English (TWE), contact:

Test of English as a Foreign Language
P.O. Box 6151
Princeton, New Jersey 08541-6151
609-771-7760
E-mail: toefl@ets.org
URL: http://www.toefl.org

College Level Examination Program

The College Level Examination Program (CLEP) administers 29 subject exams designed to test undergraduate-level knowledge in specific subjects such as algebra, accounting, and business law. Each exam lasts for 90 minutes and must be taken at a proctored testing site, usually the testing center of your local college or university. Each exam costs $43, plus an additional administration fee (generally $10) if you take the exam at a small testing center.

Some graduate programs listed in this guide will accept passing scores on selected CLEP exams in lieu of passing grades on formal undergraduate prerequisite courses. For a free copy of CLEP's Information for Candidates and Registration Form and CLEP Colleges, a directory of colleges that maintain public CLEP testing sites, contact:

College Level Examination Program
P.O. Box 6601
Princeton, New Jersey 085441-6601
609-771-7865
E-mail: CLEP@ets.org
URL: http://www.collegeboard.org/clep/html/indx001.html

Do I Need an Undergraduate Degree to Attend Graduate School?

In the United States, one is expected to have an undergraduate degree, commonly a four-year bachelor's degree, prior to admission to graduate study in any area. Some programs listed in this guide will *sometimes* consider applicants to graduate study who do not hold an accredited bachelor's, but who have achieved a notable amount of success in their chosen study areas.

Universities that will accept petitions from applicants not holding conventional qualifying credentials are clearly indicated in the "Admission" section of each institutional profile. For example, ISIM University, a Distance Education and Training Council (DETC) accredited university that offers no-residency master's degrees in business administration and management, will waive the bachelor's degree requirement for candidates who have at least twenty years of business experience.

> Most graduate programs in the United States do *not* have a general policy of accepting applications from those who do not hold accredited bachelor's degrees. When such a policy does exist, it is most likely to be in areas where a professional portfolio can be submitted for review, such as the creative arts, and less likely to exist in professional areas that are more heavily regulated or dependent on specialized knowledge, such as engineering. It is possible—though not widely practiced—for professionally accomplished applicants to petition American graduate schools for admission if they do not hold the traditionally expected credentials.

Colleges operating out of Great Britain and Canada have slightly different policies. It is not unusual to seek admission to a British or Canadian professional school without having earned a traditional bachelor's degree. Herriot-Watt University, a Scottish university, for example, offers a no-residency MBA. That program routinely admits applicants who do not hold bachelor's degrees or who have not completed a required course of undergraduate study. You can find more information on European trends and international programs in chapter 6—"International Options"—on page 31.

Can I Get Degree Credit for My Career Experience?

As more adults return to college, universities are exploring the issue of what to do with learners who have already mastered topics at an advanced level without academe's assistance. Although not yet common policy, a few universities listed in this guide will allow applicants to document their advanced expertise for graduate degree credit. An established process—known as a portfolio process—is usually followed to allow learners to petition program faculty for a review of their accumulated career accomplishments.

The California College for Health Sciences, Antioch University, Skidmore College, the Rochester Institute of Technology, and the Union Institute are among the universities in this guide that will consider awarding limited academic credit for documented career expertise. The few colleges that *do* have an established process for recognizing career expertise for academic credit also limit the number and kinds of credits they will award. It is not possible to earn an entire graduate degree through documented career experience at any accredited university listed in this guide. Policies on awarding credit for career expertise can be found in the "Notes" section of each institutional profile.

CAN I TAKE UNDERGRADUATE COURSE PREREQUISITES THROUGH DISTANCE LEARNING?

In most cases, if undergraduate course prerequisites are enforced they may be met through independent study or distance learning. Many of the graduate schools listed in this guide offer both graduate and undergraduate courses and degrees via distance learning. Saint Joseph's College, based in Standish, Maine, is one example. It offers both graduate and undergraduate programs of study in health services and business. The New York Institute of Technology offers undergraduate courses and bachelor's degrees online in addition to supporting an online MBA. The Colorado State University MBA program offers most of the undergraduate courses it requires for MBA entry. It also refers learners who need additional preparatory study to other regionally accredited undergraduate distance learning programs.

If the program you're considering does not offer its own undergraduate prerequisites, ask the program advisor for help in locating your needed prerequisites through distance learning. Many programs have a prepared sheet that will tell you where you can acquire preparatory courses conveniently through distance learning.

I HAVE A BACHELOR'S DEGREE IN ONE AREA AND WANT TO ATTEND GRADUATE SCHOOL IN ANOTHER AREA, DO I HAVE TO EARN A SECOND BACHELOR'S DEGREE FIRST?

It is not a good idea to earn a second bachelor's degree unless doing so is absolutely required. In most cases, instead of earning a second bachelor's degree it will be quicker, less costly, and more helpful if you simply take the selected undergraduate prerequisites for advanced study in your new subject area.

For example, most graduate business programs listed in this guide do not require applicants to hold a bachelor's degree in business. More commonly they do require applicants without a bachelor's in business, or with outdated college studies in business, to take a selected cluster of undergraduate business courses to prepare for advanced business study. A preparatory undergraduate cluster might consist of microeconomics, macroeconomics, statistics, college algebra, calculus, introductory accounting, business law, and introductory marketing.

Most colleges will grant students a second bachelor's provided it is in a different subject area than the first bachelor's. The reason we do not recommend taking a second bachelor's is that this process usually entails repeating some general education courses as well as taking new university-specific requirements. It is usually better to concentrate your efforts on the foundation studies that will most quickly prepare you for your real goal of earning a higher professional degree.

Cases where a second bachelor's will be required are almost always related to careers where a specially regulated professional first degree must be earned to comply with state or national licensing or certification needs, such as pharmacy graduate programs. A pharmacy bachelor's degree is a special kind of bachelor's degree, one that is highly regulated to include both laboratory work and a standardized clinical program of study. To attend a graduate school in pharmacology using distance learning an applicant must hold a special first professional degree in pharmacy and be a practicing pharmacist with prior clinical experience.

WHAT ARE CONTINUING EDUCATION UNITS AND WHO NEEDS THEM?

Continuing Education Units, or CEUs as they are commonly called, are special kinds of credits that you normally cannot apply toward a degree. CEUs are measures of learning contact hours. If a course awards one CEU it is assumed that it took at least ten contact hours to complete that course.

CEU study is often undertaken by professionals to meet requirements for keeping professional licenses current. Legal assistants, engineers, psychologists, pharmacists, lawyers, nurses, allied health professionals, accountants, and real estate and financial professionals often must engage in a certain number of continuing education hours to keep their licenses current. Some programs listed in this guide award only CEUs. Be aware that while the CEU is a widely recognized award for professional continuing education, it is not the same as a regular degree credit.

CHAPTER FOUR

Mail, Video, or Internet: Selecting the Best Delivery Method for You

People tend to think of distance learning as a phenomenon of the 1990s and the computer age, but it isn't. As long as communication across time and space has been possible distance learning or "educational correspondence" programs have operated. The first organized system of distance learning in the Western world was tied to the emergence of a reliable horseback postal system in the United Kingdom and the United States. In both countries the postal system was enlisted to deliver teaching texts and lessons to rural learners looking to acquire trade skills not readily taught in the public institutions of the time. Sir Isaac Pitman offered business shorthand training through postal exchange of assignments from his offices in Bath, England in 1840. Lessons consisted of having students copy passages from the Bible—the most publicly accessible book of the time—and therefore an excellent textbook choice—in shorthand. Students then mailed these shorthand lessons back to Pitman for grading and competency certification.

In the United States during the late 1800s, a major issue taken on by land grant universities operating in rural areas was how to deliver agricultural instruction about emerging agricultural science to farmers that would help increase productivity. Pennsylvania State University launched a postal correspondence program to deliver noncredit agriculture courses in the 1890s. The University of Wisconsin, also concerned about agricultural efficiency, began a similar statewide effort at about the same time.

Today, these federal land grant university systems operate degree and noncredit training programs at a distance, using advanced technologies that allow for more interactive study than the mail delivery system of the late 1800s did. The University of Wisconsin operates impressive statewide course and degree delivery programs using every conceivable distance delivery system. Wisconsin also now offers a first-class, no-residency professional certificate program in distance education that offers educators and trainers a chance to systematically study emerging issues in the field of distance learning.

TV GAINS GROUND AS A DISTANCE TEACHER

In the 1950s and 1960s, television became the dominant way to deliver information to audiences across a wide area. University lectures were broadcast on a growing cable TV system in the 1960s and 1970s. Some campuses built internal television or cable systems and began piping lectures from large lecture halls to smaller classrooms around the campus or around the region. These closed-circuit TV and cable systems allowed universities to extend their offerings regionally through a system of TV-equipped extension sites.

Several programs in this guide are offered through a private, national cable system called Knowledge TV, formerly the Mind Extension University. Cable subscribers can choose Knowledge TV as a cable service in the same way that they would subscribe to The Learning Channel or HBO. Subscribers can then sit in on lectures for the price of a cable channel subscription. To earn college credit or degrees, however, you must be formally admitted to the degree program, complete all course requirements—including exams—and pay the required tuition for transcriptions and academic services.

Knowledge TV does not award its own degrees. The instruction and the degrees come from regionally accredited universities. Knowledge TV is simply an electronic delivery platform that pairs with universities to help them deliver their instructional programs worldwide. A growing number of private electronic delivery companies are pairing with universities to help them deliver their degree programs. These delivery companies, namely the Electronic University Network and Connected Education, are mentioned throughout this guide. Both Connected Education and the Electronic University Network develop and maintain virtual campus environments. These delivery companies attend to details such as mailing out program materials, processing registrations, and teaching faculty to develop and teach their courses in an online environment. They do not commonly provide degrees themselves, however, because they are not accredited universities.

Videotapes and the Net Achieve Dominance

In the 1970s and 1980s, satellite broadcasts of lectures became popular, followed immediately by the dominance of videotaped lectures, which could be mailed directly to learners and replayed at home at any hour on the ubiquitous home VCR. Thus, Knowledge TV, for example, was no longer limited to those with access to that cable channel. Learners without cable access could receive videotaped lectures in the mail.

In the 1990s, programs began using a hybrid approach, combining the various delivery systems to provide richer, more interactive programs as well as more certain access from all corners of the world. Knowledge TV and its parent company JEC College Connection currently use cable, surface mail, voice mail, satellite, fax, the World Wide Web, and videotapes to extend degree instruction to learners worldwide who might otherwise be limited in their access to higher education because of their lack of access to cable technology.

Despite its interactive multimedia power delivering desktop video and audio lectures across continents via the Internet has been a challenge. The College Connection project of Knowledge TV uses an Internet and Web instructional design system to deliver degrees from International University, America's first private, completely Internet-based university (no physical teaching campus exists) to have achieved candidacy for regional accreditation. (See page 26 for more information on regional accreditation.)

How Does Distance Learning Work?

Most programs in this guide use a hybrid delivery approach. Printed textbooks and study guides are used in all programs, with their delivery still accomplished largely via surface mail. (A few programs may also post special readings and assignments to a site on the World Wide Web that can easily be downloaded by Internet-connected learners.) How students receive and participate in their courses after the textbooks are delivered varies widely, however.

A few of the programs in this guide rely largely on surface mail, fax, and the telephone for interaction between faculty and students. Students receive their textbooks and their course study guide—a booklet or three-ring binder that typically lays out class procedures such as how to drop a course—along with weekly reading and writing assignments.

Most, but not all, programs are semester-based, with defined beginning and ending dates that parallel those offered on-campus. In semester-based or time-structured programs, students complete a lesson each week, just as they would on-campus. They then mail in their assignments to instructors or tutors for grading or assessment feedback. They may also fax in their assignments in some cases or, increasingly, transmit them directly to instructors via E-mail.

When examinations are used, commonly at the end of a course, they are almost always taken in a proctored setting to ensure that the distance learner registered for the course is indeed the one taking the exam and to ensure that the learner takes the exam without any outside assistance. Programs that require a thesis may also require students to come to the campus to defend or present their theses to a faculty committee just as their on-campus peers are required to do.

Locating an approved proctor to take exams is usually not difficult. Most local universities have testing centers that will proctor exams for another college for a small fee. Many distance learning programs will also accept public librarians, high school officials, and corporate human resources department officials as proctors. Members of the military may take exams under the eye of ranking or educational officers. Religious academic programs will often accept ministers or other church officials as exam proctors. International or corporate training programs may arrange for their learners to take exams either at an approved nationwide system of private sites—like the Sylvan Learning Centers—or at embassy outreach posts. Proctored exams are an important part of most degree-granting distance programs.

Though Internet access remains optional for some programs, it is mandatory for study with the International University, and increasingly for other multiplatform programs, like Colorado State University's MBA. The Colorado MBA program originally used mailed videotapes of on-campus lectures coupled with printed textbooks as their primary instructional system. Learners in the Colorado program still receive weekly videotapes of on-campus lectures but they also retrieve assignments and special readings from Internet sites and participate in classroom discussions by visiting online bulletin boards to post their comments on weekly readings and assignments.

Many of the Internet-based programs profiled in this guide use "asynchronous computer conferencing" or "electronic bulletin boards" for online classroom discussions. Asynchronous conferencing is a technique that allows learners to log on to the Internet, visit a class site that generally looks like a large bulletin board, and read the comments that have been posted by their instructor and fellow students. Then, while still online, they can compose and post their own contributions to the discussion.

Asynchronous classroom discussions are free of time constraints. You may log on at 6:00 a.m. Sunday to read that week's question and comments and post your own, or you may log on and contribute your ideas during your lunch break on Monday. Most instructors specify a day and time by which everyone must have read and contributed to each week's discussion and questions—say, by Thursday at 7:00 p.m.—but the exact day and time that one actually "attends" an asynchronous classroom discussion is generally left up to each individual learner.

After they have read the weekly assigned section of the textbook, students often visit these electronic bulletin boards to read new class discussion questions and to post their own comments. In this way, learners who are geographically distant from each other can create a written bulletin board of their thoughts and ideas. These electronic bulletin boards serve as ongoing transcripts of issues and ideas. Electronic bulletin boards and asynchronous conferencing allow students and instructors to meet online and engage in a kind of back and forth commentary that mimics the traditional classroom discussion. The difference is that online no one talks—instead everyone writes down his or her contributions to the discussion.

In contrast to asynchronous conferencing, a few distance learning programs use live chat rooms. In live chat rooms everyone logs on to a central meeting space at the same time—say, Tuesday night from 7:00 p.m to 9:00 p.m. Everyone types in their ideas or comments live, into the virtual conference room. Ideas and comments scroll on your computer screen like ticker-tape lines of text. Students and instructors can type queries and ideas to each other and receive immediate responses.

If a live chat sounds chaotic, it sometimes is! This method is most commonly used when the class is scheduled to have a guest speaker or presenter. Say you are taking a class on constitutional law. You have read this week's textbook chapter on the First Amendment. A judge has agreed to appear online at 7:00 p.m. on Tuesday to let members of the class question her about her papers and ideas. At 7:00 p.m., everyone in the class logs on to a central Internet chat room. One by one you and your fellow students type in your individual questions. The judge then types back her answers. The questions and answers go back and forth just as they would in a live classroom until it is time for the class to end. Though live chats are used less often than asynchronous discussions, they do have their special uses and advantages in distance learning. They are also often very effective for small teams of learners who are geographically far apart to convene and actively brainstorm about group projects and ideas.

The exact kind of discussion or chat software used varies by college program. Colorado MBA students use a software and conferencing system called "e.mbanet" to communicate. Other programs use the online conference and chat rooms of commercial services, like America Online, or other types of proprietary or Internet software to connect their learners. The University of Phoenix Online, one of America's largest enrollees of adult distance learners, and one of America's first no-residency virtual degree programs, connects students online each week through their own computer systems as well as through a central administrative site on the World Wide Web.

WHICH DELIVERY METHOD IS THE BEST?

Studies have shown that most students learn equally well using distance learning regardless of the technology used to deliver instruction. For a quality education, the kind of delivery system should not be an immediate concern. Personally, you may prefer one kind of system to another. Many learners love the videotape method because they like receiving a weekly lecture—a way of learning that is familiar to them—and they feel that viewing videotapes gives them a helpful visual way to absorb the reading material on their own.

Learners using Internet-based programs that incorporate tools that mimic the classroom discussion or teamwork groups—tools like online discussion boards and real-time chat rooms—often report that group conferencing gives them a feeling of camaraderie with their·classmates that helps them stick to the learning process. Students tend to learn more as they borrow or springboard from their classmates' ideas and experiences.

> One common fear is that if a program requires access to the Internet, and you're not a natural tech-head, then the technology may overwhelm you. This fear is generally unfounded. Most of the educational tools used in an online learning environment are fairly easy to master. Computers and the online world are rapidly becoming a point-and-click universe that anyone can readily feel comfortable in. Many of the degree programs in this guide that have an online component require little more than learning to use E-mail to send and receive assignments.

Programs that operate electronic campuses always provide orientations in how to use the necessary online tools. A hands-on introduction to online learning is included in every student's orientation to the low-residency degree programs at Walden University, which is based in Naples, Florida. Learning to use E-mail and online conferencing systems is a part of the mandatory campus residency that each Walden learner must complete to launch his program of study. The New York Institute of Technology's Web-based MBA begins with a mandatory stint in a short course called Introduction to Online Conferencing. This course gives learners a chance to try out online learning tools, hopefully getting any technical assistance that might be needed out of the way before classes commence.

THE BENEFITS OF STRUCTURE

One feature of a degree program that may make a difference in student completion rates is how structured the program itself is and how often feedback is provided by an instructor or a tutor. People do better with more structure rather than less. Programs that begin and end on a set date, following a semester or quarter calendar, with weekly reading and work assignments, generally experience less student dropout rates.

A few of the programs listed in this guide are completely self-paced. These programs allow you to register at any time and to proceed through courses at your own pace. These types of programs, while inviting on the surface for their promise of flexibility, are often the most difficult to stick with. People respond well to a more structured learning approach in which required activities given out each week serve to bump them along, making procrastination—a very human characteristic—much less likely.

CAMPUS VISITS

The programs in this guide have been selected because they offer the best no-residency or low-residency options. They represent the most flexible accredited programs available for those seeking to extend their knowledge and skills without uprooting their lives and livelihoods. The "Campus Visits" section of each profile clearly indicates residency and attendance requirements.

An increasing number of programs require no campus visits. In these programs, learners usually have the option of attending graduation ceremonies on campus, but many will graduate without ever seeing their alma mater. Other programs require a few days on campus, often as a part of a general orientation to the program and the delivery system, or for the presentation or defense of a thesis. A few programs require one semester on campus, or an intensive summer session.

High-residency, site-based distance learning programs are not profiled. High-residency programs often operate by broadcasting live lectures to special reception sites within a geographically restricted area. Some state university systems use local high schools and community colleges as reception sites for weekly lectures that are broadcast live from their main campus. These programs require weekly classroom attendance at broadcast sites inside a small geographical radius. Many are Interactive Television (ITV) programs. If you are interested in site-based or ITV distance learning programs, universities that sponsor them generally advertise these programs in a local paper.

Programs that restrict delivery or enrollments to corporate subscribers or special populations like the military, and that do not take enrollments from the public, are not fully profiled in this guide. If you work for a corporation or specifically the human resources and training department of a corporation, chapter 10 may interest you. This chapter discusses special university programs that develop and deliver educational courses to corporate reception sites.

CHAPTER FIVE

Accreditation:
How to Avoid Scams,
Rip-offs, and Diploma Mills

Distance learning in the United States has been around since the 1800s, so too have mail-order diploma mills. Fly-by-night "correspondence colleges" are big business. What surprises most people is that so many fraudulent degree institutions operate in the United States and abroad—many of them virtually indistinguishable in their outreach materials from accredited universities.

Make no mistake about it, scores of unaccredited universities freely operate distance learning programs in the United States today. New ones crop up on the Internet and in advertisements in the back of magazines almost every week. With the rising popularity of distance learning has come a rising number of unaccredited universities offering "fast-and-easy" no-residency degrees. Surprisingly, many well-educated professionals register with these universities each year not understanding that the degrees they are about to "earn" will not be recognized later by other colleges, professional colleagues, or their employers.

How could this happen? How could well-educated people not be able to tell the difference between an accredited distance learning university and one that is not accredited or is accredited by a bogus agency? In the United States the term "university" can be legally used by a wide variety of educational operations. The term itself is not regulated under national law. If you want to open an educational institute and call yourself Bertha's University of Good and Great Causes, in most states you are free to do so without having to meet any special requirements to use the term "university." Much confusion begins with the fact that the term "university" can be legally used so widely by so many kinds of institutions.

To make matters even more confusing, in the United States there is no one national government agency that oversees the academic integrity of degree-granting institutions. Instead of one national agency, six independent regional boards have historically been responsible for reviewing and granting accreditation status to degree-granting colleges and universities. These six regional agencies recognize each other's accreditation standings and operate under similar laws and regulations to ensure consistency in curriculum and program offerings, but the regional agencies are not regulated by any one master agency.

To help you understand what accreditation is—what to look for and what to avoid—let's look at the kinds of accreditation that exist. Let's look also at what it means to attend an accredited university from the perspective of a consumer or someone who wants to earn a degree that is above reproach—a degree that will be recognized widely by other colleges and future employers.

REGIONAL ACCREDITATION

If someone asked you if you earned your undergraduate degree at an accredited college you'd probably say, "Well, I must have!" Few of us ever stop to think what the term accreditation means. Fewer still can name the accreditor of our undergraduate alma mater—though we're sure we attended a duly accredited college!

> Accreditation exists as an attempt to ensure that degree-granting institutions provide a standardized program of study, delivered by a qualified faculty, using generally approved-of means, within a solid business structure. Although the true quality of what you learn at college is ultimately up to you and your study efforts, accreditation exists to provide broad standards of good practice for degree-granting institutions.

That assumption is usually correct. In academia, and the world at large, when someone refers to an "accredited" college they generally mean a "regionally accredited college." Regional accreditation is the most widely recognized standard in accreditation for degree-granting colleges in the United States. Harvard University is regionally accredited. Indiana University is regionally accredited. The University of Nebraska is regionally accredited. Unless otherwise specified as being accredited by the Distance Education & Training Council (DETC), or operating outside the United

States, every university listed in this guide is regionally accredited. Following are the six recognized regional accreditation boards:

MSA	Middle States Association of Colleges & Schools
NASC	Northwest Association of Schools & Colleges
NCA	North Central Association of Colleges & Schools
NEASC	New England Association of Schools & Colleges
SACS	Southern Association of Colleges & Schools
WASC	Western Association of Schools & Colleges

What Does It Mean to Hold a Degree from a Regionally Accredited University?

To hold a degree from an accredited university can mean a lot from a consumer perspective. Although all of us can learn a great deal without ever entering the university environment, there are advantages to having our learning certified by a recognized third party. Regionally accredited universities are the bodies that are widely recognized as being these kinds of third-party certifiers.

Regionally accredited universities recognize each other's degrees and programs as acceptable. Hence, if you earned your bachelor's degree at an SACS regionally accredited college, a WASC-accredited graduate school will, without question, accept your SACS accredited bachelor's degree as valid preparation for entering their graduate program of study. On the other hand, a bachelor's degree earned at a college that is not regionally accredited will rarely be accepted by a regionally accredited college at face value as adequate preparation for graduate-level study. From a consumer's perspective, not earning your degree at a regionally accredited university may ultimately mean limited acceptance of your degree by regionally accredited institutions, professional colleagues, and future employers.

DISTANCE EDUCATION & TRAINING COUNCIL

The Distance Education & Training Council (DETC) is the oldest national nongovernmental agency in the United States dedicated specifically to accrediting programs that are delivered through distance means. Originally known as the National Home Study Council, DETC began operation in 1926. Historically, the DETC has regulated home study or correspondence programs, many of them related to skills acquisition in the trades and vocations.

In the United States, distance learning has a much longer history as a means of providing vocational training than it does as a means of earning a professional higher degree from a regionally accredited college. Many of the schools that belong to the DETC and assist in its operations and ongoing efforts to bring quality to distance learning are true pioneers in the development and delivery of programs at a distance. Their historical emphasis on teaching career skills is now a trend that is much more prevalent in regionally accredited degree programs than it was a decade ago.

A few of the programs listed in this guide are not regionally accredited, but are accredited by the DETC. With the rising popularity of distance learning and concerns about acquiring solid career skills, DETC professional degree programs will probably expand at a fairly rapid rate in the next decade.

From a consumer's perspective, the one drawback to attending a DETC-accredited program rather than a regionally accredited one is that degrees and credits earned at DETC schools are not universally accepted by regionally accredited universities. Some regionally accredited universities will accept DETC degrees as on a par with their own offerings, but most will not. Remember: Most programs listed in this book *are* regionally accredited.

A special program operated by the American Council on Education (ACE), the Program on Non-Collegiate Sponsored Instruction (PONSI), evaluates DETC and corporate courses and makes recommendations about the equivalency of these courses to those offered at regionally accredited graduate schools. If the DETC graduate courses you complete have been approved by ACE/PONSI this will increase their acceptability in the eyes of most regionally accredited universities, but it will not guarantee full acceptance of them later by any single regionally accredited university.

This lack of universal acceptance will cause problems if you earn your master's at a DETC school, then later decide to attend a doctorate or other professional degree program at a regionally accredited university. In our experience, however, most employers and corporate tuition programs, including ones operated by the U.S. government, do widely recognize and reimburse for DETC-accredited study. The United States Department of Education nationally recognizes the DETC as an accrediting agency.

PROGRAMMATIC ACCREDITATION

In addition to accreditation, which is granted to an institution as a whole—like regional and DETC designations—special programmatic accrediting agencies accredit or approve only one specific program or department within a college. We list some of the more popular and important programmatic accrediting agencies below.

American Psychological Association (APA)
Accrediting Board for Engineering & Technology (ABET)
National League for Nursing (NLN)
National Council for Accreditation of Teacher Accreditation (NCATE)

Throughout this guide you will find mention of the above accrediting agencies in the "Admission" and "Notes" sections of program profiles. The above programmatic agencies are the ones most commonly asked about by adult learners in relation to finding programs that meet specific career needs.

In engineering, for example, admission requirements may include holding a bachelor's degree in engineering that was awarded by an engineering department that was accredited by the Accrediting Board for Engineering & Technology (ABET). This is referred to as an ABET-accredited bachelor's degree. Bear in mind that a regionally accredited university may award an engineering degree, yet the engineering department of that school may not have operated under ABET standards of accreditation.

Why and when should you care about programmatic accreditation? In most cases you will need to pay attention to programmatic accreditation if the career you are studying for is regulated by a state or national licensing or certification board. In such cases, you may be required to attend a school that has a programmatically accredited degree department. For example, certified or licensed public school teachers should always check to see what requirements they need to meet in order to satisfy state-specific teacher certification regulations. They may need to take a degree or course of study from an NCATE-approved program to meet licensing requirements in some states.

If you intend to pursue a degree that will qualify you to practice mental health counseling, most states regulate this profession closely and may require that you follow a set course of study or attend a state-approved counseling program. Always check with both your state licensing/certification boards and the college you are considering to see if a program of study taken through distance means will qualify you for your final career goal. This is especially crucial if you intend to follow a career path that may be dependent on post-degree, state-specific licensing—a process entirely separate from earning your degree.

Unrecognized Accreditors

A favorite trick of distance universities that are not accredited by the regional agencies or DETC is to advertise that they are "accredited worldwide," or "fully or nationally accredited." They then simply neglect to mention whom they are accredited by. You need to be very careful that a university is not only accredited, but accredited by a recognized agency. In the United States, the Council for Higher Education Accreditation (CHEA) is the agency that recognizes and works with legitimate accreditors. There are no shortage of "nationally accredited" distance learning universities that are accredited by impressive sounding but unrecognized agencies. If an accreditor is not recognized by CHEA, it is not going to be recognized by the higher education community in general. The CHEA website (http://www.chea.org) lists the names of recognized accreditors in the United States.

How about a college that is accredited by the National Association of Higher Educational Standards (NAHES). That sounds impressive, right? Well, it does sound impressive, but there is no such agency recognized by the United States Department of Education or CHEA. A degree earned from a university accredited by the NAHES— a completely bogus agency—might impress your great-uncle Charlie, but it will not hold up to scrutiny when examined by the academic and professional world at large.

> Be careful when looking at distance learning universities. Only programs accredited by the regional agencies or the DETC are listed in this guide. If a university tells you they are accredited by some other agency, proceed with caution. Last we counted, there were well over twenty-five bogus accrediting agencies associated with fly-by-night "distance learning universities."

FULLY AUTHORIZED AND STATE-APPROVED PROGRAMS

There is currently a big boom in "state-approved" or "fully authorized" schools offering degrees through distance learning, especially from California. Many states regulate private training and trade schools by putting them through a state-approval process. This process is not the same as accreditation. Sometimes it simply means that a license to do business has been granted.

A "state-approved" distance learning school may meet your career needs; it may provide very sound training, but degrees earned from unaccredited universities are not widely accepted in the academic and business worlds. No state-approved programs are listed in this guide unless they also hold regional or DETC accreditation.

INTERNATIONAL ACCREDITATION AGENCIES

Some of the programs listed in this guide do not operate from the United States. This being the case, they generally do not hold regional or DETC accreditation (though an increasing number of international programs are seeking DETC review as they look at recruiting learners from the American market). Most countries have a process of academic standards monitoring that is similar to regional or DETC accreditation in the United States. For example, the Canadian programs listed in this guide operate under the standards of the Association of Universities and Colleges of Canada (AUCC). AUCC universities are commonly recognized as the international equivalents of regionally accredited universities in the United States. The best programs from the United Kingdom are likewise included in this guide if they operate under a Royal Charter, an internationally recognized equivalent to American regional accreditation.

CHAPTER SIX

International Options: The Pros and Cons of Studying Abroad While Remaining at Home

Most of the programs listed in this guide are physically located in the United States yet actively recruit learners worldwide. For example, Nova Southeastern University's field-based educational doctorate program supports an international study cluster. The international cluster brings together learners from Canada, Europe, Latin America, and the Far East into geographically convenient study groups.

A few of the programs listed in this guide are not located in the United States but freely admit learners who reside in the United States while offering programs of high academic caliber. Athabasca University, Canada's provincially sponsored university without walls, enjoys a student body composed of electronically connected learners in the United States, all the Canadian provinces (themselves quite culturally diverse), and Mexico. The University of London External Programme operates several no-residency master's degree and postgraduate diploma programs, which are open to learners worldwide.

By freeing universities from the confines of a physical campus, distance learning is creating a new international educational melting pot. Indeed, one of the things many distance learners value about their learning cohorts is the exciting cultural diversity that distance learning has almost accidentally brought to the learning process.

LIVING ABROAD AND STUDYING THROUGH A U.S. UNIVERSITY

Learners residing abroad—U.S. citizens or not—often have specific questions about attending a distance learning university that operates out of the United States. If you're not a U.S. citizen, or you have an undergraduate or first degree from a college not accredited by a U.S. agency, you may have questions about these issues. In designing this guide, we've tried to include in the "Admission" and "Notes" sections of each profile details about qualifying issues for learners who reside abroad.

Most—though not all—of the programs listed in this guide accept learners living abroad regardless of their country of citizenship. Some programs, because of foreign tariffs or custom clearances on items like videotapes and books, do not accept distance learners residing outside the United States or North America. We indicate in each profile geographic restrictions related to admission.

If in doubt about a program's ability to accommodate you from your country of residence, query that program directly. In some cases learners can be accommodated through special circumstances, like the delivery of course materials to U.S. embassies or military outposts. However, in some countries, learners cannot be accommodated at all because of programmatic regulations, customs, or limited Internet or broadcast access.

It's worth noting that the military and large corporations sometimes arrange for special closed study groups or cohort classes for their personnel. These special programs may not be mentioned in a university's distance learning general outreach material, but your military educational officer or corporate training division would have information about such programs. In considering your options, if you are a member of the military or a large corporation, check directly with your in-house resource person about special distance learning programs that may be available to your unit or division.

In some cases, U.S. distance learning programs maintain special administrative or study sites abroad. Antioch University, for example, whose U.S. location is in Ohio, maintains a site in Germany that serves European-based learners of American and non-American citizenship alike. Although located in Renton, Washington, City University maintains a series of European and Eastern European learning extension centers for foreign students. Vermont College of Norwich University in Montpelier sponsors fourteen regional study locations within the United States for centralized meeting with faculty advisors, and the university also supports twice-yearly study colloquia in Germany and Israel for learners who reside in Europe, the Middle East, or Africa. The best way—sometimes the only accurate way—to find out if a program can accommodate you from your country of residence is to query that program directly.

Evaluating International Academic Credentials

Most American universities will use a standardized review process to evaluate the equivalency of your undergraduate degree or educational credentials relative to the standards used by regionally accredited American colleges. Individual programs will provide information about how you can determine the equivalency of your past education to the education you are expected to have to enter their program. In most cases, distance learning programs will refer you to a special private agency in the United States that translates and reviews the equivalency of foreign transcripts and credentials into American academic terms.

Fees for this type of service can vary, costing up to several hundred dollars in complicated cases that involve translation as well as unusual or rare foreign credentials. In simple cases, fees are less than $100. Certain universities will only accept recommendations and translations from selected agencies, so before you pay to have your records translated or certified for American equivalency, make sure you are dealing with an agency that is acceptable to the universities you are considering attending. Transcripts or records from English-speaking and Canadian universities may not need any special treatment and may be reviewed free of charge for equivalency by the registrar or program director of the admitting American university.

In almost all cases, to enter a program of graduate study in the United States, you will be expected to hold the equivalent of a four-year American baccalaureate (bachelor's degree) with graduation in the top third of your class. Exceptions to this standard are noted in the "Admission" and "Notes" sections of each institutional profile. Typical international equivalents of the American bachelor's degree are the British or Canadian Honors Bachelor's, the South American four-year Licenciatura or its equivalent, the German Diplomgrad, Staatssexamen or Magister Artium, or the French Maitrese or its equivalent.

One last question—and a fairly frequent one—is whether attending a U.S. distance learning university will qualify a foreign learner for a special student entry visa into the United States. In most cases, since learners either do not have to come to the United States, or will be here only for a few days or weeks over a several year period, the answer is generally no. The student visa is a special visa that allows for extended periods of stay in the United States for study reasons. As such, it is generally not the kind of visa that distance learning programs will support. The student visa is generally restricted to foreign citizens who are required to attend long campus-based residencies in the United States. Foreign citizens who will need to come to the United States should discuss the visa question directly with each potential program.

Benefits for American Learners Studying Abroad

Interestingly, because of differing funding procedures, it is sometimes less expensive, or at least no more expensive, for a U.S. resident to attend a distance learning program that operates out of the United Kingdom or Canada. Though Americans tend to think of distance learning as an American phenomenon, its strongest antecedents can be found in early efforts by the United Kingdom, once a sprawling colonial empire, to develop outreach and educational opportunities to serve its expansive military, foreign service, and frontier populations. These target populations needed educational systems that would come to them across great distances.

While American distance learning programs might maintain an outreach or assistance center in one or two European locations, it is not unusual for programs from the United Kingdom—like Henley Management College's MBA—to maintain affiliated associates and support centers in more than twenty different countries. If you travel extensively abroad or can foresee relocating to several international sites while pursuing your degree, an international university that maintains worldwide support centers may be best for your needs.

The University of London's External Programme is one of the best known and longest standing distance degree systems profiled in this guide. The London Federation of Universities was founded in 1836 (the External Programme came along in 1858) to allow learners to study via postal correspondence with university-appointed mentors and tutors. The London program currently supports more than 25,000 distance learners worldwide. Already extensive in its offerings, the London program plans to add more no-residency graduate and professional degree options in the next few years.

London external or distance degrees were awarded then as they are now. When a learner thought she had mastered the subject material she sat for comprehensive examinations. The scores on these examinations determined the pass status of the distance learner. Indeed, the British have such a longstanding tradition of mentoring and tutoring learners on an individual basis that many American distance learning programs have borrowed this model and refer to themselves as mentor-based, tutorial programs modeled after the scholarly tradition of Cambridge and Oxford.

Studying through a foreign university can offer American learners several distinct advantages. If you work in the international arena or value cultural diversity and awareness, studying your subject matter—whether it be economics or human resources—from a new cultural perspective can be very enriching. Many American students are surprised to discover that different countries vary so widely in their philosophical and hands-on treatment of key academic issues. Discovering and exploring these differences can be a rich education unto itself.

One reason that some American learners have turned to foreign graduate schools is that admission requirements are often more flexible. In the United States it is rare for a learner without a bachelor's or first college degree (a "first degree" means a bachelor's degree in American educational argot) to be admitted to a graduate or professional school. It is not so rare for this to happen in other university systems. In the "Admission" sections of the profiles of some of the British and Canadian programs listed in this guide, you will see that admission is based on possession of "a first degree or its equivalent." What "its equivalent" means can vary widely.

While the American university system tends to award degrees based on seat occupancy or the fact that one registers for and shows up for class, completing classroom projects and assignments along the way, the British educational system and its derivatives in Canada and abroad tend to use what is called a competency-based model. Whether or not one actually attends courses has historically been of less consequence than how one performs on the final examination. In the competency-based model, how one learns something—by attendance at class lectures or by independent reading—is much less important than the fact that something was learned and that the student proves that learning occurred by earning passing scores on exams. For this reason some of the world's best scholars, such as Charles Darwin, graduated from British universities like Cambridge, though in fact they rarely attended the classroom lectures that traditionally make up such an educational experience.

A consequence of the competency-based model is that admissions reviewers are less concerned with whether or not an applicant has earned a formal first degree and more concerned about whether or not the applicant is truly prepared to enter advanced professional study. Some of the British and Canadian programs profiled in this guide do not require applicants to hold formal bachelor's degrees. Some are willing to accept evidence of preparation in the form of career achievement, professional credentials, or by fact of sheer application. It is fairly common, as in the Athabasca University MBA program, for applicants without a bachelor's to be admitted to study the first set of courses, or to study at what is called the Diploma level, initially. If the applicant passes this first set of Diploma courses, he is then allowed to continue on to earn the MBA or other graduate degree proper.

The downside of this unusual rule is that applicants sometimes mistakenly assume that, since a bachelor's is not required, neither is the level of knowledge that generally comes with earning that degree. That assumption is a mistake. Even if a program does not require a bachelor's degree for admission, the program still expects applicants to have somehow acquired the knowledge equivalency of that degree.

Assuming that programs that do not require bachelor's degrees are easier, academically speaking, is also a serious mistake. Remember that these same programs also generally use the competency-based final examination method to determine pass or fail. These examinations are often more rigorous than anything most Americans have encountered within the American university system. The competency exam system makes for a sink or swim situation. You can't ask for extra credit papers or cheat on your projects or papers along the way to inflate your grade. You either make the grade or you do not and are asked to either leave the program or retake your exams.

If you decide to attend an international university, explore the program in as much detail as possible. At one end, some programs provide almost no structure or contact with faculty, mentors, or fellow students. You register for a course and after you've read all the text and the study material, you register for and take the comprehensive examination. While this type of study is the most flexible, it is also the most difficult to complete on your own. The less structure, feedback, and peer/faculty interaction a program offers, the less likely your chances of staying motivated and focused in your efforts to complete a degree.

On the other end, some international programs provide a highly structured approach in which you enjoy a weekly or biweekly connection to faculty and fellow learners (often electronically, via the Internet). In these programs you can complete assignments and receive feedback on a regular basis as you master small units of your course or module material. Your final grade may still depend on one exam, but you will receive a lot of structure, support, and feedback while you acquire the knowledge necessary to pass the final.

One last word: In reviewing foreign options you will notice a slightly different language for describing degrees and the educational process. After a while you will realize that a programme is simply a program, that a module is often a yearlong course, and that if you are invited to "taste a course" you are literally being offered an educational appetizer—a chance to audit a course to see how you like it and the program (or programme) before committing to the entire degree.

Today's Distance Learning College Kids: Crossing International Boundaries

Name: Rebecca Chan Allen

Age: 47

Home: Calgary, Canada

Occupation: Organizational Consultant

College of Choice: The Fielding Institute—Santa Barbara, California

Program: Doctor of Philosophy in Human and Organizational Development

Why are you earning your doctorate?

When I completed my first master's in 1983, I went on to do my doctorate. I quit after one month, choosing to accept a job offer instead. After I started my consulting practice, Delta Learning Organization, I decided that I wanted to do Fielding and was able to afford it from my consulting income. I enrolled in the fall of 1991. My objective was primarily to have an opportunity to make more sense of the learning I was gaining from my professional practice, as well as making sense of my self and my life as a whole. My second objective was to complete what I set out to do in 1983. I also liked the idea of having Ph.D. behind my name.

Why are you studying through distance learning?

I had a full-time consulting practice, so distance learning made sense. I was attracted to the program at Fielding. Fielding is a distance learning program, but mainly I loved the adult-orientation, the self-directness, and the beautiful location in Santa Barbara, California [where I get to go for brief study residencies each year].

Do you think the quality of the education you're receiving is equal to what you'd receive by attending a program on campus?

Better. I was given scholarships to do my doctorate on campus by two universities. I decided against a conventional program. I wanted a program that would help me integrate the scholarly and the practical. Fielding was a great choice. A perfect choice. I love the self-paced holistic emphasis.

CHAPTER SEVEN

Master's in Business Administration or Master's in Management: Which Is Really Right for You?

In the 1980s the Master's in Business Administration (MBA) gained popularity in American business circles. The MBA is still a very popular professional degree, and is now one of the most common degrees earned through distance learning. But it is not the only degree available to business students, nor is it necessarily the best degree for all managers or executives. If you're considering advanced business study, a variety of degrees might best suit your career needs. An MBA is not your only option. Master's in Management, Leadership Studies, and Executive Management are other degree options. No two business administration or management master's are identical, so before you register for an MBA, consider carefully your study options in light of your long-term career goals.

THE MBA

The traditional MBA takes a strong two-prong approach to the study of business. These two prongs are people administration and quantitative administration. In support of the higher study of finance and economics, the MBA has traditionally required students to master a quantitative base that includes algebra, statistics, and some applied calculus. For this reason the MBA is known as a degree that stresses the quantitative approach to the study of business instead of the people, or leadership, approach. For this reason virtually all MBA programs require learners to take preparatory work in undergraduate-level mathematics, economics, and finance, and to achieve acceptable scores on the quantitative as well as verbal and writing skills sections of the standardized Graduate Management Admission Test (GMAT).

Many MBA or Executive Management programs follow the curriculum and faculty standards issued by the American Assembly of Collegiate Schools of Business (AACSB). The AACSB is a voluntary, nongovernmental agency that oversees the standardization of business and accounting programs. The AACSB has used peer review and self-evaluation to watchdog business administration and accounting programs since 1916. Some of the best known universities in this guide—Duke University, Purdue University, Syracuse University, Colorado State University, and Auburn University—operate AACSB-accredited business programs. Other business programs also hold AACSB accreditation, as specified in the Notes section of each profile.

If your long-term career goal is to obtain a tenured faculty position teaching business administration, you should seriously consider attending an AACSB-accredited business program. Outside of academia AACSB accreditation is less crucial. Universities do not need AACSB programmatic accreditation to offer the MBA or any other advanced business degree. Several first-rate, regionally accredited business programs listed in this guide do not follow the peer standards of the AACSB, and therefore are not AACSB-accredited; others do follow AACSB guidelines but for their own reasons have not sought AACSB peer review of their curriculum or faculty development programs.

Many regionally accredited graduate business schools have opted for approval by the AACSB as a public mark that they adhere to a standardized curriculum and rigorous program of faculty hiring and development. AACSB accreditation is not an absolute mark of program quality, however. A non-AACSB accredited MBA may follow the same curriculum as an AACSB-accredited MBA, or it may show innovation when compared to a traditional AACSB-accredited program. Indeed, because non-AACSB accredited programs do not pledge to follow a prescribed curriculum model, they are ideal for those seeking more flexibility or individualized input in their degree program.

For more information on the AACSB, its standards, and its accredited member colleges, visit the AACSB online at http://www.aacsb.edu or contact them for a roster of current member colleges and standards at the American Assembly of Collegiate Schools of Business, 600 Emerson Road, Suite 300, St. Louis, MO 63141-6762.

Other Business Degrees—But Which One Is Best?

What if you neither need nor want to study higher level finance, economics, and quantitative management? What if your approach to business is not in crunching numbers or financing enterprises, but in motivating people and building an organizational structure that optimizes human performance? In this case the MBA may not be the best degree for you. Other degrees—Master's in Human Resources, Management, Leadership, or Organizational Behavior—might better fit your interests and aptitude.

Several newer kinds of management degrees rely less on quantitative skills in favor of developing people and leadership competencies. Those employed in career areas such as human resources, training and development, advertising, or sales and service may favor the non-MBA approach, while those in accounting, finance, economics, information technology, engineering, and quality control may feel most at home within a traditional MBA program.

Whether you ultimately decide on an MBA, an AACSB-accredited MBA, an Executive Management degree, or another kind of management or leadership degree, is entirely up to you. In considering graduate study in business, compare programs carefully. You cannot always tell what a degree will require of you or which curriculum standards it follows based on its title alone. In addition, some programs require a host of prerequisite or foundation study in undergraduate business areas like economics, finance, and calculus, while others admit applicants with little or no management preparatory work. Undergraduate preparatory work, particularly in finance and math, can lengthen a graduate program of business or management study considerably.

To see how widely program requirements vary, study the actual course requirements of the business and management programs below. Purdue University's Executive Master of Science in Management program follows AACSB standards, and consequently requires extensive study in economics, finance, and the quantitative aspects of business. On the other hand, Thomas Edison State College's Master of Science in Management is a newer type of applied management and leadership degree. Notice that unlike the standard MBA offered by Colorado State University or the Purdue Executive Master's in Management, the Edison program emphasizes leadership and people management.

COLORADO STATE UNIVERSITY

Master of Business Administration (MBA)

Students must complete a minimum of 33 semester credits. The degree represents a traditional MBA curriculum and is designed to emphasize both people management and quantitative management.

Required Courses
3 credits
Managerial Accounting
Information Technology Management
Financial Management: Theory & Case Studies
Business Policy
Marketing Strategy
Production Administration
Management
Advanced Business Statistics

Electives
Students choose any 3 additional business courses to complete the program. They may also choose to complete a 3-course traditional concentration in Finance, Management, Marketing, or Quality Management.

THOMAS EDISON STATE COLLEGE

Master of Science in Management (MSM)

Students must complete a 42 semester credit program of study. The main emphasis of this degree is on the development and management of people within an organization. Leadership seminars are required. Students can take statistics if they wish, but the study of higher level mathematics is not a required part of this degree.

Required Courses
3 credits
Human Resource Management
Economic Issues in Organizations
Finance & Accounting for Managers
Organizational Environment
Organizational Research
6 credits
Organizational Theory & Behavior

Electives (Choose One Course at 3 credits each)

Ethics, Statistics, Marketing Management, or Management of Information Systems

Required Leadership Seminars

3 credits

Professional Leadership Development 1

Professional Leadership Development 2

Required Thesis:

6 credits

Thesis

PURDUE UNIVERSITY

Executive Master of Science in Management (MSM)

Students must complete a 48 semester credit program of study. The following courses, which cover both people management and quantitative concerns, are all required.

Required Courses

2 credits

Economics & Social Policy

Financial Management

Human Resource Management

Macroeconomics

Organizational Behavior

4 credits

Accounting for Managers

International Finance

International Marketing

Legal Environment of Business

Marketing Management

Microeconomics

Operations Management

Strategic Management

Quantitative Methods

Today's Distance Learning College Kids:
Truly Portable Business Programs

Name: Jan Shelton
Home: Lake Mary, Florida
Age: 29
Occupation: Telecommunications Manager
College of Choice: Purdue University
Program: Executive Master of Science in Management

Why are you earning your graduate degree?

I reached a level in my career where I had learned a tremendous amount through experiences on the job, but wanted to expand my knowledge of global business and management. Specifically, I wanted an opportunity to enter a formal program that would enable me to apply new textbook, case study, Internet, and classroom knowledge while I was learning. In addition, I wanted to attain a master's degree to support my career goals and remain competitive in business.

Why are you earning your degree through distance learning?

I was working in International Strategic Business Planning, and traveling extensively, when I began investigating opportunities to achieve a master's degree. I wanted to continue my international career, however I knew that my schedule would limit my options regarding school. Purdue's program fit my needs perfectly. I was able to study and participate in conference calls from anywhere that had a telephone connection. Distance learning allowed me to continue to pursue my career goals— that included a relocation from New Jersey to Florida—while successfully participating in an aggressive master's program.

Do you think the quality of the education you're receiving is equal to what you'd receive by attending a program on campus?

I graduated this spring and thoroughly enjoyed my experience at Purdue University. I believe there are positive and negative aspects associated with any degree program. Personally, I enjoyed the diversity of people, geographic areas, and industries represented in the Purdue program, and feel that the program enabled me and each student to grow personally and professionally. Working via the Internet, learning to utilize new technologies, further enhanced the educational experience. Discipline and self-motivation are essential to be successful with distance learning but the rewards are immense!

CHAPTER EIGHT

Financial Aid: Real-life Strategies to Make Your Educational Costs Manageable

At the present time, the system of financial aid for graduate and professional studies is far from perfect. University tuition rates have risen an average of 6 percent a year for the last decade—more than twice the rate of inflation. Though distance learning will save you money on items like commuting and childcare, most distance learning programs are not less expensive than their on-campus counterparts. Some, in fact, cost more, due to the emerging tendency for universities to charge "technology fees" to help cover the costs they are incurring while building the technological infrastructure needed to deliver their programs at a distance.

The majority of distance learners are adults who attend college part-time, relying on a combination of their own savings, loans, and corporate tuition benefits to pay their educational bills as they continue to work on their careers. Surprisingly, the number one source of financial aid for adult learners is not government-backed student loans, but their own savings or a combination of their own savings and a company tuition benefits plan.

If the thought of paying for continuing education keeps you from pursuing a higher degree, you will find comfort in the fact that, inflated prices aside, continuing education remains one of the best investments you'll ever make in your long-term earning potential. According to the 1992 U.S. Census Bureau's analysis of wage differentials by educational level, a person with a master's degree can expect average lifetime earnings of $1,619,000, compared to $1,421,000 for bachelor's degree holders, and $2,142,000 for those who achieve a doctorate. Put another way, if you hold a bachelor's and decide not to earn a master's, it could conceivably cost you $198,000 in earnings over your lifetime. With this in mind, a master's degree that costs $20,000 is perhaps best seen as an investment rather than an expense.

FEDERAL GOVERNMENT AID

The federal government does not sponsor direct grant, scholarship, or "free money" programs for graduate-level learning. What the government does offer graduate-level learners is a series of guaranteed student loan programs. Not all distance learning programs participate in these student loan programs. The United States Department of Education maintains an online resource center (http://www.ed.gov) for government aid. The "Student's Guide to Financial Aid" is a free publication that explains government aid, types of student loans available, and how eligibility for government-backed loans is determined. You can download a copy of the free and helpful "Student's Guide" online at http://www.ed.gov/prog_info/SFA/StudentGuide/ or receive it in the mail by calling 800-433-3243. Address inquiries by surface mail to Federal Student Aid Information Center, P.O. Box 84, Washington, D.C. 20044.

FEDERAL GOVERNMENT LOANS

The federal government sponsors several student loan programs to help graduate learners finance their education. Student loans vary in interest rates and repayment terms. The federal Perkins loan has the most favorable interest rate. Perkins are available at a 5 percent rate to those with exceptional financial need. Federal subsidized Stafford loans of up to $8,500 per year are available to learners with financial need at variable interest rates that currently cap at 8.25 percent. Federal unsubsidized Stafford loans are available to learners with less financial need under terms that are the same as the subsidized loans except that the borrower is responsible for the interest that accrues while the borrower is still in school.

To be eligible for a government-backed student loan you must meet the following basic criteria:

♦ Be a United States citizen or eligible noncitizen. Those with alien registration cards, special asylum status, or temporary resident cards may not be eligible.

♦ Attend a college that is approved for the government loan program. Not all universities or distance learning programs participate in government loan programs.

- Be enrolled in a degree or certificate granting program. Individual courses taken outside a degree or certificate program are not covered.
- Make satisfactory academic progress. Take and pass a set number of courses each semester. Usually you must be enrolled at least part-time or taking at least two courses each semester of your enrollment.
- Demonstrate financial need (except for the unsubsidized Stafford loan). Financial need is determined by a standardized annual analysis of your income, assets, and liabilities versus the cost of the college you wish to attend as determined by the data you provide on the Free Application for Federal Student Aid (FAFSA) each year of your enrollment.
- Be in good standing with the government aid program, with no defaults on previous loans.

How Federal Aid Eligibility Is Determined

Level of financial need, as determined by the government, is a complicated matter. The level of your need will be officially calculated each year by the government using a special form called the Free Application for Federal Student Aid (FAFSA). The FAFSA is a form that all learners must file each year so colleges can determine the amount of their aid eligibility using a standard formula. You can access the FAFSA online at the government aid resource center (http://www.ed.gov/offices/OPE/express.html) or you can receive a print copy by calling 800-4FEDAID.

Level of aid eligibility will vary with annual income, number of dependents, asset holdings, and the specific cost of tuition at any one degree-granting school. The higher the tuition at any one school, the higher your level of need will be at that one school. After analyzing your FAFSA, the government will send you and the universities you are thinking of attending an official Student Aid Report (SAR). The SAR will be used by the aid officer at your university to determine your final eligibility for aid.

Even if you think your income is too high to qualify you for a student loan, you should always complete a FAFSA if the university you are attending has an aid program. State aid agencies and private scholarship programs use the data from the FAFSA/SAR to determine eligibility for all types of aid and loan programs.

STATE GOVERNMENT AID

In addition to federal government aid, individual states operate their own financial aid programs. Supplemental loans or grant programs may be available for residents of certain states, especially if they attend distance learning programs in state. Some states are educationally rich in their adult aid programs—New York State, for example, has a special tuition assistance grant program for part-time learners who attend college in New York State—while other states provide little or no economic incentive for adult or part-time learners. Adult learners in New York State enjoy some of the best state benefit programs. New York administers several programs for part-time, usually older, learners: Tuition Assistance Program (TAP), Aid for Part-time Study (APTS), the Vietnam Veteran's Tuition Awards (VVTA), and the Empire State Scholarships of Excellence, are some of the awards that residents of New York can qualify for through their state financial aid programs. New York also supports a number of distance learning universities.

How do you find out about state-aid programs? All colleges will send financial aid information and application forms if you request them. That information usually includes both federal and state guidelines and forms. Every state maintains a State Office of Financial Aid, which acts as a clearinghouse for all state-initiated programs. If you can't locate that information on your own, call your college's financial aid office and ask for it. Because state aid is administered separately from federal aid, and programs vary widely from state to state, always investigate aid possibilities with your state office of financial services to see if you qualify for any special aid programs.

WHY GOVERNMENT AID IS NOT ALWAYS AVAILABLE

Having outlined the government student loan programs, we caution that not all distance learning programs participate in these student loan or state incentive aid programs. Why not? The most compelling reason for not participating is that government aid programs were never meant to be used by working adults, most of whom study part time. They were designed for dependent, unemployed, full-time learners, for use as supplemental aid by their parents. Why does this make a difference?

Government-aid programs have many requirements attached to them. They are most beneficial to full-time students. "Full-time" students are those who typically complete at least four courses each semester. Most adult learners work full time and study part time. Full-time work income routinely disqualifies adult learners from any aid but the higher interest government loans.

Some distance learning programs do not participate in government-aid programs because these programs are not well-suited to alternative learning formats. To qualify to participate in government loan programs universities must design programs that recognize and meet a complex set of laws and regulations that deal with correspondence and distance learning programs differently than they do with on-campus programs.

You will encounter all combinations of aid from universities listed in this guide. Some of the programs listed in this guide offer no form of organized aid to learners at all. They leave it entirely up to you to fund your educational undertakings. We've heard learners declare up front that if a university doesn't offer government student loans, then they won't attend that program. However, in our experience, government aid and loans are really not all that desirable, especially for adult learners.

Just because a program doesn't offer government loans doesn't mean you're out of luck. National statistics reveal that only 11 percent of all part-time, post-baccalaureate learners use student loans for their education. There are alternatives to government aid, and in reality most adult and distance learners rely heavily on these alternatives.

CORPORATE TUITION BENEFITS

According to a recent study by the International Foundation of Employee Benefit Funds, as reported by the National University Continuing Education Council, more than 90 percent of American companies offer tuition reimbursement as a benefit to their employees. Eighty-eight percent of these companies will pay for graduate-level studies, while 63 percent will pay for vocational or technical training. Yet less than 5 percent of the money earmarked for employee education in the United States is used each year. Find out if your company has an aid program, then find out if you are eligible.

Some companies will pay 100 percent of your university tuition provided it is work-related. Many companies will pay a minimum amount each calendar year, often up to $2,000. Even small companies will often pay a part of the tuition bill if approached with the notion that an investment in your knowledge is actually an investment in the knowledge base of the company as a whole. Never assume that your company won't pay at least some of your tuition bill. Try to negotiate for such benefits if they don't already exist. If your company does not pay for college degrees, ask them to pay only for specific courses, ones that are directly related to your role at work.

Most employers will gladly pay for continuing education that has an immediate payoff for them in terms of increased productivity. It is in their best interest to help improve an employee's ability to design or use a better computer data entry program, for example. Many of the programs listed in this guide require work-based project completion or case studies. Approach your employer and ask her to pay for any course that could result in a study or an application that will help the company as a whole.

On the flip side, be aware that as this book went to press tax laws were being changed to make graduate educational benefits granted by employers taxable as a type of noncash income. Talk with your benefits manager to determine how much tax you would owe on graduate tuition payments if your employer makes payments on your behalf. Pending legislation could make graduate tuition benefits tax-exempt once again, as well as provide for better student loan programs for working adults and distance learners. To find out more about the changing nature of taxes and tuition aid, speak with your accountant or request "Publication 508: Educational Expenses" free from the Internal Revenue Service hotline at 800-TAX-FORM.

Family Loans

If the university you want to attend offers no student loan program, or you don't qualify for a student loan, look around for other possible bankers. In 1997, 5 percent was a good return on a bank-guaranteed Certificate of Deposit. If the bank will pay your mother 5 percent for use of her money for three years, why don't you up the ante and offer her 7 percent for the same privilege? One word of advice: Treat a loan from a relative just as you would one from the bank. Agree in writing to the terms: amount loaned ($3,000), interest (7 percent), repayment schedule (begin January 1, 1995, end January 1, 1998, for a total of 36 monthly payments of $92.97).

Finance not your best talent? Anyone can figure loan repayments. Your public library or bank loan officer will have an "Amortization Handbook." This handbook reveals in clear tabular form what your monthly payments would be for any amount you borrowed for any length of time at any interest rate.

Home Equity Loans

Home sweet home is the greatest piece of equity owned by most working adults. Home equity loans usually carry a lower interest rate than other lines of commercial credit, and most home owners easily qualify. Call several banks in your neighborhood and ask to speak with their Home Equity Loan officers. Banks will vary in what they offer but usually a bank will loan up to 80 percent of your paid equity at rates competitive with those offered by Uncle Sam on a bona fide student loan. One benefit of a home loan over a government-backed student loan is that, oddly enough, for most people the interest on a home loan or second mortgage is tax-deductible, whereas, at present, the interest on a government-backed student loan is not.

Education as a Business Deduction

If you are self-employed your education may be deductible as a business expense, just like your office supplies. This deduction is commonly taken on income tax "Schedule C: Profit or Loss From Business." Not all educational expenses, however, are allowable deductions for the self-employed. Uncle Sam has shifting rules about the kinds of education or training that are allowable deductions. Current *nonallowable* deductions include education to change your career—that is any education not directly related to the work that currently yields income for you. If you are a self-employed educational consultant, you will not be allowed to deduct educational expenses related to becoming a certified financial planner—unless of course a part of your business income is derived from helping people use financial planning techniques to achieve their educational goals. But if you take a course to learn how to do the bookkeeping for your home-based business, that expense is probably fully deductible.

If you work for someone else, your educational expenses may also be deductible. If you meet the eligibility criteria, and you itemize your deductions, you can currently include educational expenses as deductions on "Schedule A." To deduct your educational expenses you have to meet a lot of qualifying conditions. For one thing, you usually must be employed, and your education must be related to your current career, not as a means to change your career.

Tax laws are complicated and protean. It is possible that all adult education—including education that will help you to change your career—could become deductible in the near future. Check with your accountant about your personal situation and contact the IRS for their latest publications before assuming that you qualify for any educational deductions.

PENSION PLAN BORROWING

If you have a pension or retirement plan at work and you need cash for your continuing education, explore the possibility of tapping your pension or 401K assets. Some pension or retirement funds allow borrowing from these funds at a reasonable interest rate of from 6 percent to 9 percent. Use reason when considering such borrowing. Make sure you understand any tax liability that might accompany your decision as well as the terms of repayment. You will have to replace the money you borrow. It is still a loan. But it may be a valuable loan option that will allow you to return to school under a reasonable low-interest repayment plan of your own making.

Similarly, many adult learners are able to borrow against their life insurance or other investments that they thought were untouchable. Take a good look at your whole financial situation when considering how to finance your continuing education. You may have more borrowing capacity than you imagined. Most adults do.

MILITARY AID—ACTIVE DUTY

Military aid programs are as complicated as any form of government aid. There are many rules to qualifying for military aid—even more rules to using that aid for distance learning. If you are on active duty, meet with your educational benefits advisor. Get a complete orientation to your benefits package. Benefits can vary with branch of service, rank, dates of enlistment, and terms of active duty. Your military aid advisor can assist you in interpreting your benefits package regarding any one distance program.

Your military educational advisor can also guide you to Service Members Opportunities Colleges (SOCs)—colleges that work with the military to maximize credits already earned through the American Council on Education (ACE) or other specialized military in-service training programs. Ask your advisor to provide you with a directory of all independent study or distance learning programs that are preapproved for military benefits under the DANTES program. Using a DANTES or SOCs program may make your military tuition reimbursement process less cumbersome in the long run.

Military Aid—Veteran's Aid

If you are a veteran your educational entitlements probably expire at a preset date. If you are a veteran contemplating distance education and training, start by contacting your local Department of Veteran's Affairs (DVA) and speaking with the Educational Benefits Officer (EBO). If you don't know where your closest DVA is, ask your local librarian for help, or check the local yellow pages for a phone listing under "Government—Federal." Only your DVA can check your service record and determine your official eligibility for aid.

If you have already decided on a college, speak with a financial aid officer at your college about whether they will accept Veteran's benefits for your studies. All the programs at any one college may not be approved for Veteran's tuition benefit payments. Most universities have at least one person who specializes in processing military aid. Ask to speak with your chosen college's military aid advisor for the most helpful assistance.

Again, only the DVA can report on how much and what kinds of aid you might be eligible for. Only the DVA can issue a financial aid eligibility report based on your service records. Individual universities can help you understand military aid as it may apply to your tuition and fees if you study with them, but individual universities can't tell you if you are eligible for veteran's educational aid and for how much. All the programs listed in this guide are not preapproved for veteran's tuition benefits. Shop around accordingly for academic programs that can maximize the use of any aid you may be entitled to under your military benefits plan.

PRIVATE LOANS

With inflated tuition rates, universities have begun to give consideration to making education more financially accessible for adults. Realizing that government-backed student loans are not always the most accessible credit lines for working adults, more universities are instituting their own form of aid through low-interest payment plans or by contracting with outside firms to provide accessible private educational loans for working adults. Private educational loan companies are appearing on all horizons. Their rates and terms vary, but usually an 11 percent to 13 percent rate is offered with reasonable repayment terms.

Tuition "sales" or "discounts" are sometimes offered today by bona fide colleges to entice adults back into the ivy halls. Lynchburg, Virginia's Liberty University, for example, offers a standing spouse discount, a program that lowers tuition considerably if both a husband and wife enroll. While not quite a two-for-one sale, it is a price break in an area that a decade ago was never subjected to such "markdown tactics."

PRIVATE SCHOLARSHIPS

Private groups award millions of dollars for college study each year. Unfortunately, most private scholarship programs accept applications only from high school seniors or promising youth younger than 21. Many scholarship programs further restrict awards to regular on-campus programs. Be aware of these common restrictions before you hire a private scholarship search firm to generate a special report for you. In our experience you will not find scholarship search firms helpful in locating aid that is specific to adult learners in distance education programs. Even more bogus scholarship search companies are out there than bogus mail order colleges. Read the Latin on the wall. Caveat emptor!

One of the best free resources for adults looking for scholarship aid is the booklet published by the American Association of Retired Persons (AARP), "The Back-to-School Money Book: A Financial Aid Guide for Mid-life and Older Women Seeking Education and Training." "The Back-to-School Money Book," authored by financial aid expert Gail Schlachter, is an especially good primer for military personnel, military spouses, and women older than 30 seeking special scholarships that have been earmarked for career change or enhancement. Order this free book from AARP Fulfillment, 601 E Street, NW, Washington, D.C. 20049. Request publication D16245.

If you have online access, the Internet is rich in free financial aid information. Below, find the best free online databases to use in searching for aid that fits your study plans and financial situation.

FASTWeb
http://www.studentservices.com/fastweb
This is the best free, searchable database online. It archives listings and content information on over 185,000 scholarship, loan, and gift aid programs.

Reference Service Press
The scholarship guide publisher, Reference Service Press, maintains a free searchable database of scholarship and aid award programs on the commercial online service, America Online. Use keyword RSP to access the database on America Online.

Scholarship Research Network Express
http://www.rams.com/srn/index.htm
The Scholarship Resource Network maintains this free searchable database of 7,000 privately awarded, primarily non–need-based awards and loan programs.

CHAPTER NINE

When, Where, and How to Design Your Own Degree

One of the greatest opportunities that distance learning offers is the chance to actively participate in the design of your own degree. If you're considering distance learning but don't see a program exactly like one you'd like to study, consider attending one of several programs that encourage learner-designed majors or emphasis areas. These types of programs are listed under "individualized" in the index of your guide.

One of the best known and longest operating design-your-own-degree program is operated by the Union Institute in Cincinnati, Ohio. Since 1964, Union has allowed learners to design doctorate degrees in any one of thirteen broad special interest areas: creative arts and communication, educational administration, environmental studies, health and health care, literature and creative writing, multicultural studies, organizational behavior, peace studies, philanthropy and leadership, professional psychology, psychoanalysis, public policy, racial and ethnic studies, or sociology and social work.

Learners at the Union Institute do not register for predesigned courses. Instead, they work with Union faculty and local advisors to develop their own courses and practicums around unique, career-related interest areas. Self-designed courses or academic inquiries often begin with a learning contract or a self-designed degree plan between the learner and the evaluative faculty or degree committee. Corinne Gerwe, profiled in this chapter, could not have attended a distance doctorate program that offered a formal major in her career specialty area—biological psychology—because no such program exists. However, Corinne was able to design a program in her chosen career specialty area through the Union Institute.

At the Union Institute, as at many individualized degree programs, instead of following course syllabi designed by faculty, learners develop learning contracts that address their personalized learning goals. A self-written learning contract typically outlines the goals and objectives of a learning activity, identifies key readings, outlines projects that are to be included in the learning activity—things like attendance at local lectures, seminars, or special events—and identifies the type of assessment that will be used by the degree committee to determine that the prescribed learning has been completed to academic satisfaction.

Though the Doctor of Philosophy degree is awarded by the Union Institute a research thesis is not required. Instead, Institute learners complete their degrees by engaging in self-designed Projects Demonstrating Excellence or PDEs. The PDE may be a research thesis, a biographical case study, a creative or artistic master project, a social action project, or an analytical inquiry. The Union Institute operates one of the most far-reaching, learner-centered degree programs in the world. Learners from more than fifteen countries and several Canadian provinces register with the Institute each year because of its uniquely flexible program of study.

LIBERAL STUDIES AND INTERDISCIPLINARY DEGREES

A second option that can allow flexibility in degree design is the Liberal Studies or Interdisciplinary degree. The Master of Arts in Liberal Studies (MALS) and Master of Liberal Studies (MLS) are degrees that have been gaining favor in the last decade as professional degrees that allow for broad advanced study in the Liberal Arts culminating in a career-relevant final thesis or integrative project. School teachers in particular have been using the Liberal Studies format to meet state licensing requirements for advanced learning and study for several years.

Many learners don't investigate liberal studies or interdisciplinary degree options because they are not familiar with this type of degree, or because they do not immediately recognize how such a degree might allow them to study within their career interest area. If you don't investigate liberal studies or interdisciplinary programs you could be overlooking some of the best and most cost-effective degree programs.

The University of Oklahoma, for example, sponsors one of the least costly master's programs in this guide. That program also allows for an increasing number of career specialty options within the Liberal Studies model. Specialties or emphasis areas exist in administrative leadership, health care, or interdisciplinary education. Other areas may also be designed, as in the case of Stephen Bennett, a Radio News Director, profiled in this chapter. Stephen used the Oklahoma low-residency Liberal Studies program to study computer-assisted journalism.

The most flexible of all liberal studies programs is operated by Skidmore College. Skidmore is a well-known, private liberal arts college, located in Saratoga Springs, New York. For more than twenty-five years, Skidmore College has offered a self-designed, distance bachelor's degree program. The newer MALS program is based on the college's experience and success providing self-designed, undergraduate degree options to adult learners.

Skidmore invites learners to design their own thirty-credit (about ten courses or learning activities) MALS. Learners can study any area as long as it blends or crosses the traditional three Liberal Arts classifications: the humanities, the social sciences, and the natural sciences. Many career areas, like environmental studies, women's studies, race relations, family counseling, or corporate communication and public relations, rely on a blending of the three Liberal Arts classification areas. You can readily study these areas, as well as many others, through Skidmore's program.

The Skidmore program begins with a mandatory five-day entrance and degree planning seminar. Here, learners are introduced to the interdisciplinary study method and the two faculty advisors who will assist them in designing their degrees. Off campus, learners begin to work on their twenty-four credit individualized concentration. The concentration can consist of formal graduate courses taken at other universities, independent study and readings, internships, or prior graduate-level experiential learning, which needs to be documented for faculty review. (A maximum of 6 credits can be earned at Skidmore for prior, documented, graduate-level, experiential learning.) The degree program concludes when the student completes a final 3-credit, integrative written project or thesis. To help clarify the process, look at a sample plan of the kind of degree a learner might design through Skidmore.

SKIDMORE COLLEGE
Master of Liberal Studies—Corporate Communication

1. Entrance & Orientation Seminar, 5 Days On-Campus—3 credits
2. Individualized Concentration, Corporate Communication, Off-Campus—24 credits
   a. Graduate Course at Local University—Nonverbal Communication
   b. Independent Readings & Study—Verbal Communication & Successful Management Style
   c. Independent Readings & Study—Corporate Culture & Group Identity
   d. Independent Readings & Study—Worker Personality Types & Corporate Cultural Congruency
   e. Assessment of Prior Learning—Women & Effective Communication Styles
   f. Assessment of Prior Learning—Women & Non-Effective Communication Styles
   g. Internship—Designing Print Communication for a Specific Corporate Culture
   h. Internship—Designing Multimedia Communication to Change a Corporate Culture & Identity
3. Final Project—3 credits
   Developing & Enhancing a Corporate Culture for a Small Technology Company

The Downside of Designing Your Own Degree

While the idea of designing your own degree may seem appealing, there are factors to consider before launching a less structured approach to your education. The first factor is that those who use a less structured approach must be willing to take on tremendous responsibility for the design and execution of their own learning. It takes a lot less research and effort to attend a structured course where the texts and assignments are given to you each week than it takes to research what you want to study and then outline how you will study it using the flexible learning contract model.

> Studies show the less structured a distance degree program is, the greater the likelihood that procrastination or other human factors will cause learners to get sidetracked or drop out along the way. If you use a self-designed degree program, be prepared to spend as much time researching and outlining your degree program, as you will eventually spend studying the curriculum you have created.

To study the areas that are most relevant to your degree, you should already have a significant amount of exposure or career experience in your chosen study area. Most programs that allow self-design require learners to have an established career record in their chosen specialties. Those who lack adequate theoretical knowledge or career experience in their desired study area often find that they cannot adequately research and create the kind of advanced curriculum or study experiences that a graduate curriculum requires. Learners seeking an advanced degree in a new theory or career area may need to take a series of undergraduate preparatory courses or spend extended time volunteering or working in their new career area before they can adequately make use of a design-your-own-degree program.

If you choose to use a liberal studies or interdisciplinary degree program, compare the various programs for flexibility. Skidmore allows for the most flexible self-design, whereas other liberal studies programs require learners to complete a broad set of established liberal core or critical thinking courses or seminars before specializing by designing a final individualized, integrative project or thesis.

Finally, certain subject areas are unable to be accommodated by the faculty or study programs at individualized programs. Antioch University's low-residency Individualized Master of Arts (IMA) program offers learners tremendous flexibility in designing their own degrees across several subject areas. However, Antioch, like many other programs, lacks the distance learning faculty and facilities to support the study of the pure medical or lab sciences or professional disciplines like engineering or law that are specially regulated by state or national licensing boards.

If you need a specialized degree to meet state or national licensing requirements in a particular professional area, like a Master's of Social Work (MSW), a self-designed degree might not meet your career needs. If you're not sure if a self-designed or liberal studies degree would meet your career needs, call the university you are considering and ask to speak with an advisor or counselor. The counselors at these programs are experienced in translating how everyday career concerns can be turned into academically sound and feasible degree plans.

Today's Distance Learning College Kids: Designing Their Own Degrees

Name: Corinne Francis Gerwe
Age: 49
Home: Saluda, North Carolina
Occupation: Clemson University Counselor/ Research Associate
College of Choice: Union Institute
Program: Doctor of Philosophy emphasis in Biological Psychology

Why are you earning your doctorate?

I am entering a doctorate program in order to continue my work on issues concerning the problem of chemical addiction, with a focus on the chronic condition of addiction and addiction-related criminal recidivism. Since my research has begun to gain attention, it is even more necessary that my academic credentials provide a context in which my ideas and hypotheses can be acknowledged and respected. It is also an effort to continue growing both personally and professionally in my abilities and interests.

Why are you earning your degree through distance learning?

My previous undergraduate experience through distance learning introduced me to the idea. While my on-campus university experience was rewarding, the idea of being educated with a broader perspective is more personally appealing. The Union Institute philosophy has taught me to think as a world citizen. I have also found that my creativity is more able to thrive in an environment like Union that values innovative thinking.

Do you think the quality of the education you're receiving is equal to what you'd receive by attending a program on campus?

The quality of the education I have received through distance learning is excellent. When I first entered the on-campus graduate program at Clemson University after completing a distance learning undergraduate program, I was able to excel in my graduate program as a continuous full-time student and research associate. I was also nominated by my fellow students for a Profiles in Excellence Award.

Name: Stephen C. Bennett
Age: 43
Home: Oklahoma City, Oklahoma
Occupation: Radio News Director
College of Choice: University of Oklahoma
Program: Master of Liberal Studies—Computer-Assisted Journalism

Why are you earning your graduate degree?

I earned my undergraduate degree more than two decades ago. There have been incredible changes in information gathering and reporting since then. Earning my graduate degree is an effort to stay abreast of the changes, to stay ahead of the wave, so to speak. My focus is on news dissemination and the evident paradigm shift from the top-down delivery of news and information to the bottom-up, unfiltered model created by the World Wide Web.

Why are you earning your degree through distance learning?

I first undertook some additional undergraduate studies in computer science. Graduate studies seemed the next logical step. Traditional programs were not feasible options. I am employed as the news director of two radio stations, and share child-rearing duties with my wife, which requires me to be a stay-at-home father when I'm not at work. Distance learning is the perfect format for me to continue my research.

Do you think the quality of the education you're receiving is equal to what you'd receive by attending a program on campus?

The program certainly requires a great deal of initiative on my part. There is no "hand-holding" involved. This is not a handicap, however, and has, in fact, forced me to sharpen my research skills rather than relying on someone else to "spoon-feed" what I need to know to me.

CHAPTER TEN

Corporate-sponsored Distance Learning

The need for lifelong continuing education has prompted many large corporations to partner directly with universities in the design and delivery of special distance degree programs. These types of distance degree programs are often referred to as "subscriber-supported." Corporations subscribe to them directly, generally by paying development and delivery fees to the sponsoring university. In return, employees of sponsoring corporations are able to "attend" classes that are broadcast to their work sites via cable or satellite television or videoconferencing. Corporate-sponsored distance degree programs are not fully profiled in this guide because they are not accessible to the public (see list below of well-known universities that offer such courses). To qualify for admission to these special degree programs you must be employed by the sponsoring corporation.

Historically, subscriber-sponsored distance degree programs relied on satellite and cable broadcasts for their delivery. Corporations built special reception studios—massive electronic classrooms—where learners congregated weekly to receive live or "real-time" broadcasts of remote classroom lectures through either satellite or cable means. These types of distance degree programs are also known as "site-based" because learners must go to the broadcast sites where the programs are received.

A new generation of corporate-supported programs is now available via compressed desktop video over high-speed Internet lines. Classes are typically held one evening a week for approximately two hours. Learners can talk "live" with their remote instructors during the interactive broadcast of their distance learning courses and workshops. They can ask questions, participate in class discussion, and present ideas.

Newer programs, like the Master of Business Administration from the University of Notre Dame, are broadcast and received using special videoconferencing room systems. Videoconferencing systems allow learners and remote faculty to see each other and to interact in real-time with audio questions and answers while the class is actually in session at the school in Indiana. These programs are also described as "two-way video" and "two-way audio" because remote faculty and students use desktop videoconferencing technology to see and hear each other during live class sessions.

Corporate learning centers that are equipped with PictureTel, VTEL, or other advanced videoconferencing room systems can arrange to subscribe to and receive programs like the University of Notre Dame's award-winning Master of Business Administration. Learners "attend" the Notre Dame courses weekly via VTEL, seeing and participating in the same lectures and classroom discussions as their on-campus MBA counterparts.

Videoconferencing systems are not yet perfected for home instructional use. The best videoconferencing systems require more powerful graphic and audio reception capabilities than most home phone systems can accommodate. Even in corporations, most videoconferencing for instructional means is displayed through specially built and equipped videoconferencing classrooms where learners sit next to each other to view live broadcasts on a central auditorium screen, or on specially equipped high-powered desktop units.

In the future, advances in home phone reception and the ability of the Internet to send and receive compressed video, graphic, and audio information, may make home desktop videoconferencing and distance-degree reception a viable reality. Below are examples of some of the most well-known, subscriber-based distance learning programs. Corporations can contact these programs directly for further information. If you work for a large corporation or the military, ask your human resources office if your company subscribes to or supports any special distance-degree programs.

BOSTON UNIVERSITY

Department of Manufacturing Engineering
15 Saint Mary's Street
Boston, MA 02215
617-353-4622
E-mail: mailto:jpilton@bu.edu
URL: http://eng.bu.edu/MFG

Boston University's engineering department develops and delivers degrees and training programs in manufacturing engineering to subscribing corporations. An interactive PictureTel videoconferencing system is used to deliver educational programs.

GEORGE WASHINGTON UNIVERSITY

GWU-TV
801 22nd Street, NW, Suite 350
Washington, DC 20052
202-994-8233
E-mail: N/A
URL: http://www.gwu.edu/~gwtv

GW Television offers a full range of professional production services including video production, videoconferencing, and distance learning. Efforts are underway to develop multimedia capabilities using the Internet, World Wide Web, and computer-assisted learning. GW Television's three broadcast studios are equipped with high-speed Internet access for broadcast-quality computer imaging, C- and Ku-band satellite signal reception capability, a four-channel microwave ITFS network, and connections to uplink facilities for national and international distribution of satellite programming. GW Television has full remote production capability and access to compressed video systems. Partnerships with other universities and corporations facilitate tailoring degree and certification coursework to suit specialized audiences. Currently GW offers distance learning corporate programs in management, technology, and the health sciences.

GMI ENGINEERING & MANAGEMENT INSTITUTE

Video-Based Off-Campus Programs
1700 West Third Avenue
Flint, MI 48504-4898
810-762-7494
888-GMI-GRAD
E-Mail: bbedore@nova.gmi.edu (Betty Bedore, Coordinator)
URL: http://www.gmi.edu/official/acad/grd

GMI was established in 1919 as a night school program for industry workers in Flint, Michigan, who wished to improve their technical skills. In 1945 they awarded the first academic degrees. Until 1982 GMI was a wholly-owned educational subsidiary of General Motors. GMI operates today as a private university, offering several on-campus undergraduate and graduate engineering programs. GMI also offers a distance, video-based Master of Science in Engineering/Manufacturing Systems

Engineering, a Master of Science in Engineering/Mechanical Design, and a Master of Science in Manufacturing Management. Companies are invited to contact GMI directly about establishing in-house learning sites. Foreign corporations may apply for learning center status. Learning centers already exist in Mexico, Canada, and other sites abroad.

MASSACHUSETTS INSTITUTE OF TECHNOLOGY

Systems Design & Management Program
77 Massachusetts Avenue
Cambridge, MA 02139-4307
617-253-0254
E-Mail: sdm@mit.edu
URL: http://web.mit.edu/sdm/www

The Massachusetts Institute of Technology delivers real-time broadcasts of courses and a certificate program in systems design and management for practicing engineers. Instructional broadcasts can be received via a Picture-Tel desktop videoconferencing system. MIT supports a range of collaborative learning programs with industry partners nationwide.

NATIONAL TECHNOLOGICAL UNIVERSITY

700 Centre Avenue
Fort Collins, CO 80526
970-495-6400
E-mail: mailto:doug@mail.ntu.edu (Doug Yeager, Vice President of Marketing)
http://www.ntu.edu

NTU has been broadcasting advanced courses and master's programs in engineering, computer science, and advanced business and technology to subscribing corporations since 1984. Forty-six accredited universities participate in the development and delivery of NTU's professional distance learning programs. NTU contracts with member corporations to design and deliver new curricula and courses as demand warrants.

RENSSELAER POLYTECHNICAL INSTITUTE

RSVP Program
Office of Continuing Education and Distance Education
CII Suite 4011
Troy, NY 12180-3590
518-276-8351
E-mail: rsvp@rpi.edu
URL: http://rsvp.rpi.edu

Rensselaer Polytechnical Institute develops and delivers computer science, engineering, manufacturing, management, and management and technology courses, certificates, and master's degrees via satellite television, videoconferencing, and the Internet to the workplaces of partner corporations. In 1993 Rensselaer was named "Best Distance Learning Higher Education" by the United States Distance Learning Association (USDLA). In 1996 RPI received another award from the USDLA for its partnership with General Motors in developing and delivering a master's degree in the management of technology.

STANFORD UNIVERSITY
Center for Professional Development
Durand Building #401
Stanford, CA 94305-4036
650-725-3000
E-mail: N/A
URL: http://www-scpd.stanford.edu/scpd

Stanford University has been working with industry partners in engineering, technology, and computer science to develop and deliver quality curricula via distance learning means for almost thirty years. Master's degrees and professional training courses in engineering and computer science are delivered via videoconferencing, satellite, and the Internet to subscribing corporations worldwide. More than 5,000 engineering and computer science professionals study through Stanford's distance learning network each year.

STEVENS INSTITUTE OF TECHNOLOGY
Corporate Distance Learning
Castle Point on Hudson
Hoboken, NJ 07030
201-216-5234
E-mail: thegradschool@stevens-tech.edu
URL: http://attila.stevens-tech.edu/gradschool

Master's degrees, a doctorate degree, and professional certificates in engineering, management, and computer science are delivered via videoconferencing, television, and the Internet, to subscribing corporations.

UNIVERSITY OF DALLAS
Graduate School of Management
1845 East Northgate Drive
Irving, TX 75062-4736
972-721-4009
1-800-UDAL-MBA
E-mail: admiss@gsm.udallas.edu
URL: http://gsm.udallas.edu

In partnership with Wescott Communications, a national distance delivery company, the Graduate School of Management at the University of Dallas satellite broadcasts real-time Master's in Business Administration, Master's in Health Services Management, and professional certificates to subscribing corporations.

UNIVERSITY OF MICHIGAN

Academic Outreach
837 Green Street
Buhr Building Room 1210
Ann Arbor, MI 48104-3297
313-764-5300
E-mail: mailto:ao-courses@umich.edu
URL: http://www.outreach.umich

The University of Michigan sponsors several educational outreach programs in partnership with industry and the United Auto Workers Union. Projects include the UAW Ford Motor University and the Michigan Virtual Automotive College.

UNIVERSITY OF NOTRE DAME

Executive MBA Program
Room 126 College of Business Administration
P.O. Box 399
Notre Dame, IN 46556-0399
219-631-5285
800-631-3622
E-mail: CBA.execprog.1@nd.edu
URL: http://www.nd.edu/~execprog

The University of Notre Dame offers a real-time, interactive two-way audio and two-way compressed video Executive MBA program using the VTEL Smart Videoconferencing system. The program is delivered to corporate sites in Indiana and Illinois.

COLLEGE PROFILES

Alphabetical List of School Profiles

American College
American Military University
Andrew Jackson University
Antioch University
Athabasca University—MBA
Athabasca University—MDE
Atlantic Union College
Atlantic University
Auburn University
Azusa Pacific University

Baker College
Bath College of Higher Education
Bellevue University
Berean University of the Assemblies of God
Bethel Theological Seminary
Boise State University
Brunel University

California College for Health Sciences
California Institute of Integral Studies
California State University
California State University
   Dominguez Hills—QA
City University
Clarkson College
College for Financial Planning
College of Saint Scholastica
College of Saint Scholastica—DE
Colorado State University—MBA
Colorado State University—SURGE
Columbia International University
Columbia University—AEGIS
Columbia University Teacher's College
Columbia University—Columbia Video
   Network (CVN)
Concordia University Wisconsin
Covenant Theological Seminary

Duke University
Durham University

East Carolina University
Embry-Riddle Aeronautical University
Empire State College—SUNY

Fielding Institute
Florida State University
Frostburg State University

Garrett-Evangelical Theological Seminary
George Washington University—ELP
George Washington University—JEC
George Washington University—PM
Georgia Institute of Technology
Goddard College

Goucher College
Goucher College—MFA
Graceland College
Graduate School of America
Grambling State University
Grand Canyon University
Grand Rapids Baptist Seminary

Henley Management College
Heriot-Watt University—EUN

ICI University
Idaho State University
Indiana University
Indiana University—IUPUI
Indiana University of Pennsylvania
Indiana Wesleyan University
Institute of Transpersonal Psychology
International University
Iowa State University
Iowa State University—Engineering
ISIM University

John F. Kennedy University
Johns Hopkins University
Johnson Bible College

Kansas State University

Lakehead University
Leicester University
Lesley College
Liberty University
Loma Linda University
Loyola Institute for Ministry Extension

Mankato State University
Marygrove College
Marywood College
McGill University
Michigan Technological University
Montana State University—Bozeman

National-Louis University
New Hampshire College
New Jersey Institute of Technology
New York Institute of Technology
New York University
North Carolina State University—
   Engineering
North Carolina State University—IT
North Carolina State University—TOTE
Nova Southeastern University—FCAE
Nova Southeastern University—MA
Nova Southeastern University—SBE
Nova Southeastern University—SCIS

Ohio University
Open University of the United Kingdom
Ottawa University

Pepperdine University
Pepperdine University—EdTech
Prescott College
Purdue University
Purdue University—Krannert Graduate
  School

Reformed Theological Seminary
Regent University
Regent University—MBA
Regents College of USNY
Regis University
Regis University—MBA
Rochester Institute of Technology

Saint Joseph's College
Saint Mary-of-the-Woods College
Saint Mary-of-the-Woods College—ELM
Saint Mary's University of Minnesota
Salve Regina University
San Francisco Theological Seminary
Saybrook Institute
Skidmore College
Southeastern University
Southern Christian University
Southern Methodist University
Southern Polytechnic State University
Southwest Missouri State University
Spertus Institute of Jewish Studies
State University of New York—
  EngiNet
Stephens College
Syracuse University

Texas A&M University
Texas Tech University
Texas Wesleyan University
Texas Woman's University
Thomas Edison State College
Trinity University

Union Institute
United States Sports Academy
University of Alabama
University of Alabama—Huntsville
University of Alabama—QUEST
University of Alaska—Fairbanks
University of Arizona
University of Arizona—Extended University
University of Bridgeport
University of Colorado
University of Colorado—CATECS
University of Colorado—JES

University of Colorado—MBA
University of Guelph
University of Idaho—Engineering Outreach
University of Illinois at Urbana-Champaign
University of Illinois at Urbana-
  Champaign—CCEE
University of La Verne
University of London—Birbeck College
University of London—CIEE
University of London—King's College
University of London—Wye College
University of Louisville
University of Maryland University College
University of Massachusetts
University of Memphis
University of Minnesota
University of Missouri—Columbia
University of Nebraska—CHRFS
University of Nebraska—Lincoln
University of New England
University of North Carolina—Chapel Hill
University of North Dakota
University of Oklahoma
University of Phoenix—CDE
University of Phoenix—Online
University of San Francisco
University of Sarasota
University of South Carolina
University of St. Augustine
  for Health Sciences
University of Surrey
University of Surrey—Ed.D
University of Tennessee
University of Tennessee—PEMBA
University of Victoria
University of Washington
University of Washington Extension
University of Washington—Pharmacy
University of Wisconsin—
  Distance Education
University of Wisconsin—
  Engineering Outreach
University of Wisconsin—Professional
  Development in Engineering
University of Wisconsin—
  Graduate School of Banking
University of Wisconsin—Stout

Vermont College of Norwich University
Virginia Commonwealth University

Walden University
Warren Wilson College
Warwick Business School
Western Seminary
Wheaton College Graduate School
Worcester Polytechnic Institute

THE AMERICAN COLLEGE

Graduate School
270 South Bryn Mawr Avenue
Bryn Mawr, PA 19010
610-526-1377
E-mail: n/a
URL: n/a

Campus Visits

Certificate programs or individual courses taken for personal or professional enrichment require no campus visits. The master's requires two one-week residency sessions on campus.

Admission

The American College's programs are designed for applicants with experience in financial services but not necessarily limited to those employed in financial services. Applicants without a bachelor's degree are eligible to enroll in single courses and certificate study. Successful certificate candidates may be admitted to the master's program if they have a college degree. Individual courses are open to nondegree learners to meet the continuing education needs of Chartered Life Underwriters (CLUs) and Chartered Financial Consultants (ChFCs). No special exams are required for admission. International learners are welcome.

Programs

12 credits
Certificate in Advanced Management
Certificate in Estate Planning and Taxation

9 credits
Certificate in Pensions and Executive Compensation
Certificate in Portfolio Management and Asset Allocation

36 credits
Master of Science in Financial Services
Master of Science in Management

Tuition & Fees

Basic Tuition:	$490 per course
Certificate Tuition:	$1,470–$1,960
Master's Tuition:	$6,920
Financial Aid:	None

Notes

The American College is an independent, nonprofit, accredited institution founded in 1927 that offers professional certification and graduate-degree distance education to individuals seeking career growth in financial services. Resident faculty at the Bryn Mawr, Pennsylvania, campus develop the courses that thousands of students across the nation and abroad take. Learners study independently or in local classes and earn credits toward a designation or degree by passing computer-administered course examinations given at exam centers throughout the U.S. and abroad.

AMERICAN MILITARY UNIVERSITY

Graduate Admissions
9104-P Manassas Drive
Manassas Park, VA 22111
703-330-5398
E-mail: amugen@amunet.edu
URL: http://www.amunet.edu

Campus Visits

No campus visits are required. Applicants are required to meet with faculty online or via the telephone for twenty minutes at least four times each semester.

Admission

Applicants should hold a bachelor's degree from a nationally recognized, accredited college with a minimum 2.7 GPA in the last 60 semester credits of study. International applicants are welcome with TOEFL. A computer and modem with access to the Internet will facilitate studies and communication with faculty and staff.

Programs

36 credits

Master of Arts in Military Studies/Land Warfare
Master of Arts in Military Studies/Air Warfare
Master of Arts in Military Studies/Civil War Studies
Master of Arts in Military Studies/Naval Warfare
Master of Arts in Military Studies/Defense Management
Master of Arts in Military Studies/Intelligence Studies
Master of Arts in Military Studies/Unconventional Warfare

Tuition & Fees

Basic Tuition:	$200 per credit
Master's Tuition:	$7,200
Financial Aid:	DANTES military aid, veteran's benefits, National Alliance for Education Scholarships

Notes

The American Military University is a private distance education school founded in 1991 to provide higher education in military studies. The university operates exclusively through distance means, serving a primary audience of military service people in the United States and abroad. The university does not maintain a residency degree program. Degree programs are accredited by the Distance Education and Training Council (DETC). Learners and faculty communicate using surface mail, phone conferences, and the Internet. Learners receive course packages via surface mail and follow a self-paced schedule, completing their courses within a traditional fifteen-week semester format. Up to fifteen credits of military-related study will be considered for transfer toward the degree. Credits reviewed and approved by the American Council on Education (ACE) or earned through military career experience will be considered. In exceptional cases, credit may also be awarded for documented career experience. Individual courses in military history and tactics are open to non-degree learners. Individual courses may be audited for a modest fee. The school charges $5.00 for a catalog of course offerings.

ANDREW JACKSON UNIVERSITY

Andrew Jackson University
10 Old Montgomery Highway
Birmingham, AL 35209
205-871-9288
800-429-9300
E-mail: enroll@aju.edu
URL: http://www.aju.edu

Campus Visits:

None

Admission

The requirement for admission to a master's program is a bachelor's degree from an institution accredited by an institutional accrediting agency recognized by the United States Secretary of Education or the Council for Higher Education Accreditation (CHEA).

Programs

36 credits
Master of Business Administration
Master of Public Administration
Master of Science/Criminal Justice

Tuition & Fees

Basic Tuition: $4,950 flat degree fee
Financial Aid: Tuition payment plan, veteran's benefits

Notes

Andrew Jackson University (AJU) is a private, independent university founded in 1994. The university was first accredited to award bachelor's and master's degrees by the Distance Education and Training Council in 1998 and offers all degrees via distance means. Primarily, instructors mail printed materials to students, but plans are underway to integrate Internet delivery in the near future. To be adequately prepared for advanced study at the master's level at AJU, applicants are expected to bring an appropriate core body of knowledge with them from undergraduate study or workplace experience at the decision-making level. Students can make up any deficiencies by completing preliminary course work for an additional fee and without graduate credit in addition to the courses required in their degree programs. Thirty-six credits are required for all master's degrees. Transfer credits will not reduce the program tuition.

ANTIOCH UNIVERSITY

McGregor School
800 Livermore Street
Yellow Springs, OH   45387
937-767-6325
E-mail: admiss@mcgregor.antioch.edu
URL: http://www.antioch.edu

Campus Visits

A five-day orientation seminar is required for those who reside in the United States or Canada. A five-day thesis seminar is required to complete the degree. Applicants to the conflict resolution program must attend mandatory three-week session on campus each of the first two years of the program. Applicants to the intercultural relations programs must attend one- to two-week seminars at the Intercultural Communications Center in Portland, Oregon. European applicants may apply to and attend residencies at: Antioch Germany, Waldstrasse 3, 72805 Lichenstein/Traifelberg, Germany; Phone: 07129-3275.

Admission

A bachelor's degree from a regionally accredited college is required for non-provisional admission. Applicants should be at least twenty-five years old and have some professional experience in their chosen study area, as well as access to local learning resources to undertake internships or applied practicums. In unusual circumstances, applicants who don't have bachelor's degrees from regionally accredited colleges but who have significant career experience in their chosen study area may petition for provisional admission. Writing samples or significant evidence of professional work in the intended area of study will be required for learners in the creative or studio arts. Applicants to the conflict resolution program must have a computer and modem to participate on "ConflictNet," an international computer learning network.

Programs

60 quarter credits
Master of Arts/Individualized
Master of Arts/Art & Art History
Master of Arts/Communication
Master of Arts/Counseling & Applied Psychology
Master of Arts/Creative Writing
Master of Arts/Education
Master of Arts/Environmental Studies
Master of Arts/Fine Arts
Master of Arts/Heath Care
Master of Arts/History
Master of Arts/Journalism
Master of Arts/Literature
Master of Arts/Management
Master of Arts/Organizational Development
Master of Arts/Media Arts
Master of Arts/Philosophy
Master of Arts/Playwriting
Master of Arts/Rural Development
Master of Arts/Theater Directing
Master of Arts/Studio Arts
Master of Arts/Women's Studies
Master of Arts in Conflict Resolution
Master of Arts in Intercultural Relations

Tuition & Fees

Basic Tuition: $1,305 per quarter
Master's Tuition: $7,830–$13,050
Financial Aid: Government loans, conflict resolution scholarships

Notes

Antioch is a comprehensive, private liberal arts college founded in 1852. Antioch has sponsored field-based distance learning programs for adult learners since the 1970s. Within the Individualized Master of Arts (IMA) degree option, Antioch offers no predesigned courses. Learners work with Antioch faculty and local advisors or mentors to write learning contracts, which outline their desired program of study. Counseling degrees can sometimes be designed to meet state-specific licensing requirements. Education degrees may sometimes be designed to meet state-specific public school teacher licensing requirements. Antioch welcomes ideas for individualized degrees but cannot support studies in the lab sciences (chemistry, physics), advanced mathematics, technical studies (engineering, computer science, speech pathology), or medicine (radiology, nursing) through the distance program. Though applicants may design degrees in numerous academic areas, such as counseling, business, and the fine arts, the degree awarded will be the Individualized Master of Arts (IMA), not the MFA, MBA, MSW or any other specially designated degree. Up to fifteen quarter credits (ten semester credits) of career experience may be documented toward the master's or transferred from other colleges. The conflict resolution and intercultural programs begin with a common core of study. Learners in the conflict program may individualize their studies to explore conflict resolution in regards to organizational development, labor relations, multicultural and international relations, or peace studies. Learners in the intercultural program may individualize their studies to cover cultural diversity in the workplace, teaching or counseling from a multicultural perspective, or race relations. Transfer credits are accepted only if not previously used toward another degree. Regardless of transfer credits or career experience all learners must complete at least eighteen months, or six quarters, of study through the Antioch program to earn a master's degree. Most learners take from eight to ten quarters to complete their degrees.

ATHABASCA UNIVERSITY—MBA

Centre for Innovative Management
Electronic MBA Program
Suite 301, Grandin Park Plaza
22 Sir Winston Churchill Avenue
St. Albert, Alberta
Canada T8N 1B4
403-459-1144
800-561-4650
E-mail: aumba@cs.athabascau.ca
URL: http://www.athabascau.ca

Campus Visits

No campus visits are required for the diploma. All degree applicants must attend one seven-day summer session and two intensive weekend sessions. Weekend and summer schools have been held in Alberta and Ontario.

Admission

Applicants should hold a first degree in any subject from an accredited college and have from three to five years of supervisory, professional, or managerial work experience. Applicants without a bachelor's or first degree may enter the graduate diploma program. If the graduate diploma program is successfully completed entrance may be granted to MBA study. Applicants must have a computer and modem and Internet access, as the program is delivered online. The GMAT is required for admission to MBA study but not required for admission to the diploma program. International applicants are welcome.

Programs

13 course modules
Master of Business Administration
Advanced Graduate Diploma in Management

Tuition & Fees

Master's Tuition: $19,950
Diploma Tuition: $9,250
Financial Aid: None

Notes

Athabasca University, founded in 1970, is a provincially chartered distance learning university. The university is a member of the Association of Universities and Colleges in Canada (AUCC), the Canadian national organization that accredits universities. The MBA electronic program began in the early 1990s and welcomes learners worldwide. Online interactive communication and collaborative learning are essential parts of the degree program. The GMAT is required, but it is not used to determine program entry, only to help isolate academic problem areas that may need to be addressed prior to entering graduate-level study. Learners are assigned to study groups with from eight to fifteen participants. Study groups may cross national boundaries to facilitate international learning. Summer school sessions focus on the applied collaborative solution of real and current management dilemmas. A final comprehensive applied research or consultancy project (formally an MBA dissertation) is required.

ATHABASCA UNIVERSITY—MDE

Masters in Distance Education
Box 10000
Athabasca, Alberta
Canada T9S 1A1
403-675-6179
E-mail: mde@cs.athabascau.ca
URL: http://www.athabascau.ca/html/programs/masters.htm

Campus Visits

None

Admission

Applicants must hold a bachelor's degree from a recognized post-secondary educational institution. Students will need an IBM compatible PC and modem with full-service Internet access. The program is supported with Computer Mediated Communication for E-mail, file transfers, computer conferencing, as well as for accessing electronic databases. Applications are accepted from applicants outside of Canada. No admission exams are required. Applicants must ask for an "application package" (see address above). Applications must be received by March 1 for consideration for a September intake.

Programs

42 credits
Master of Distance Education

Tuition & Fees

Basic Tuition:	$700 per 3-credit course (Canadians)
	$1,400 per 3-credit course (others)
Master's Tuition:	$9,800 (Canadians)
	$19,600 (others)
Financial Aid:	None

Notes

Athabasca University, founded in 1970, is a provincially chartered distance learning university. The university is a member of the Association of Universities and Colleges in Canada (AUCC), the organization charged with accrediting Canadian universities. Once an applicant is admitted to the program, the MDE program committee will review his/her request for advanced standing and will consider transfer credit or "not-to-take" status for those graduate courses taken that have not been applied to another credential. Individual courses are open to non-degree students, as space permits. Tuition and fees are stated in Canadian dollars.

ATLANTIC UNION COLLEGE

Adult Degree Program—Master of Education
338 Main Street, P.O. Box 1000
South Lancaster, MA 01561-1000
508-368-2300
800-282-2030
E-mail: enroll@atlanticuc.edu
URL: http://www.atlanticuc.edu

Campus Visits

Attendance is required at three three-week summer seminars.

Admission

Most applicants are licensed or credentialed school teachers, K-12. Applicants with bachelor's degrees in areas other than education will be required to complete the following undergraduate work prior to being admitted: developmental psychology, philosophy of education, psychology of teaching and learning. A minimum 2.75 GPA is required for all bachelor's work. All applicants should have competencies in computers, statistics, and writing prior to entry. The GRE is required.

Programs

33 credits
Master of Education in School Administration
Master of Education in Special Education
Master of Education in Curriculum & Instruction

Tuition & Fees

Basic Tuition: $295 per credit
Master's Tuition: $9,735
Financial Aid: Government loans, Grants, Scholarships

Notes

Atlantic Union is a private Christian college founded in 1882 and run by the Seventh-Day Adventist Church. Atlantic Union College has operated an external bachelor's degree program for two decades. The distance master's program was launched in 1996. The program is intended for those involved in teaching in private or public schools and may meet teacher licensing requirements in Massachusetts. Applicants from other states interested in public school licensing should inquire directly.

Atlantic University

At-A-Distance Master's Program
Building 3300, Suite 100
397 Little Neck Road
Virginia Beach, VA 23452
757-631-8101
E-mail: n/a
URL: n/a

Campus Visits

No attendance is required for the certificate. Attendance is required for the last semester of study for the master's degree. Atlantic University is considering abolishing all campus attendance requirements for future academic years. Inquire directly about on-campus requirements.

Admission

Applicants should hold a bachelor's degree in any subject from an accredited college with a minimum 2.5 GPA.

Programs

33–36 credits
Master of Arts in Transpersonal Studies
Master of Arts in Transpersonal Studies/Archetypal Studies
Master of Arts in Transpersonal Studies/Holistic Health
Master of Arts in Transpersonal Studies/Intuitive Studies
Master of Arts in Transpersonal Studies/Transpersonal Counseling
Master of Arts in Transpersonal Studies/Visual Arts

7 noncredit courses
Certificate in Transpersonal Studies

Tuition & Fees

Basic Tuition: $480 per 3-credit course
Certificate Tuition: $295 per course
Master's Tuition: $5,280–$5,760
Financial Aid: Payment plans

Notes

Atlantic University is a private, independent college founded in the 1930s and revitalized to offer academic degrees in the 1980s. The university specializes in holistic learning according to the tenets of transpersonal psychology. Atlantic University is accredited by the Distance Education & Training Council to award degrees. The distance learning program is an extension of on-campus offerings. Transpersonal studies, as defined by Atlantic University, is an interdisciplinary endeavor, which includes psychology, philosophy, sociology, history, literature, religion, and science. Those interested in Jungian psychology, holistic healing, alternative art therapies, and spiritual development in modern times would be interested in the transpersonal approach. Atlantic University follows the tenets of Edgar Cayce and encourages a holistic approach to learning. Although developed courses are available, applicants may design their own courses if they wish. Individual courses are open to non-degree learners. Up to six credits may be transferred in toward the master's degree.

AUBURN UNIVERSITY

Graduate Outreach Program
202 Ramsay Hall
Auburn University, AL 36849-5336
334-844-5300
888-844-5300
E-mail: durrocl@eng.auburn.edu (Latisha Durroh, Marketing Coordinator)
URL: http://www.eng.auburn.edu/department/eop/eophome.html

Campus Visits

Master of Engineering degrees require only a two-hour final exam on campus. Master of Science in Engineering (MSE) degrees require one quarter on campus to complete the thesis. Business master's degrees require from two to three days on campus for final exams and may require a three-day, intensive on-campus visit to complete team-based case analyses. Engineering doctorates typically require at least three years of study beyond the bachelor's degree, with at least three consecutive quarters of doctoral study completed on campus.

Admission

Applicants to business study without a bachelor's in business may take the required undergraduate business prerequisites through Auburn. Differential calculus and statistics are required to enter the business program. The GMAT is required of all business applicants. Applicants to engineering study should hold a bachelor's from ABET-accredited engineering schools or a bachelor's degree in a closely allied field, such as math or physics. The GRE is required for admission to all engineering programs. International applicants are welcome with the TOEFL.

Programs

58–87 quarter credits (67 credit average)
Master of Business Administration/Finance
Master of Business Administration/Marketing
Master of Business Administration/Management Information Systems
Master of Business Administration/Management of Technology
Master of Business Administration/Operations Management
Master of Aerospace Engineering
Master of Civil Engineering
Master of Chemical Engineering
Master of Computer Science & Engineering
Master of Electrical Engineering
Master of Industrial Engineering
Master of Materials Engineering
Master of Science in Aerospace Engineering
Master of Science in Civil Engineering
Master of Science in Chemical Engineering
Master of Science in Computer Science & Engineering
Master of Science in Electrical Engineering
Master of Science in Industrial Engineering
Master of Science in Materials Engineering

45–48 quarter credits
Master of Mechanical Engineering
Master of Science in Mechanical Engineering
Doctor of Engineering
Most master's majors listed above may be earned at the doctoral level (80–120 quarter credits)

Tuition & Fees

Basic Tuition: $210 per quarter credit
Master's Tuition: $12,180–$18,270 (Business)
                      $9,450–$10,080 (Engineering)
Doctorate Tuition: $16,800–$25,200
Financial Aid: DANTES military benefits

Notes

Auburn is a land grant university founded in 1856 that offers a variety of undergraduate, graduate, and professional degrees on campus. The university has delivered graduate programs through distance learning since 1984. The business program is accredited by the American Assembly of Collegiate Schools of Business (AACSB). The engineering program is accredited by the Accreditation Board for Engineering and Technology (ABET). The distance program enrolls about 450 learners from thirty-eight states. Classes are recorded on videotape and sent to either private homes or corporate sites. Applicants without a business undergraduate degree generally must complete the longer eighty-seven-quarter credit MBA, which includes graduate preparatory courses such as calculus. A significant portion of the engineering doctorate may be done at a distance in some major areas with only three consecutive quarters on campus. Some engineering and business courses are open to non-degree students. Though the program is primarily VHS video-based, learners may use E-mail to submit assignments for some courses. No prior commitment is made concerning whether transfer credit will be accepted. A student must earn at least thirty-five quarter hours, or half of the total hours required for a master's degree, whichever is greater, at Auburn University.

AZUSA PACIFIC UNIVERSITY

Operation Impact
901 East Alosta Avenue
P. O. Box 7000
Azusa, CA 91702-7000
818-815-3846 or 3848
E-mail: mhart@apu.edu or gbarnes@apu.edu
URL: n/a

Campus Visits

Studies begin with a two-week concentrated summer session. Three summer sessions are typically required to complete the master's degree. Overseas applicants may attend sites in Latin America, Europe, Africa, and Asia.

Admission

Applicants should hold bachelor's degrees from regionally accredited colleges, with at least twelve credits having been earned in any social science area. Undergraduate GPA should be at least 3.0. Applicants with GPAs in the range of 2.5–2.99 may be provisionally admitted. Applicants should be experienced professionals, occupying positions of agency leadership. International applicants are welcome with TOEFL at 550 or above.

Programs

39 credits

Master of Arts in Social Science with an Emphasis in Leadership Studies

Tuition & Fees

Basic Tuition:	$115 per credit
Master's Tuition:	$4,485
Financial Aid:	None

Notes

Azusa Pacific is a private Christian university established in 1899. Campus programs include undergraduate and professional studies. The Impact Master's program incorporates Christian leadership values and is designed for leadership professionals who are dedicated to organizational change. Human resource professionals, adult trainers and learning specialists, and managers of Christian social service agencies attend the program. The international program allows a focus on Christian mission management. Individual courses are open to non-degree learners and to audit by non-degree, noncredit learners. Tuition is lower for a noncredit option. Up to six credits of graduate work may be transferred toward the master's degree through a petition process.

BAKER COLLEGE

Online MBA
1050 West Bristol Road
Flint, MI 48507
810-766-4390
800-469-4062
E-mail: gradschl@baker.edu
URL: http://www.baker.edu

Campus Visits

None

Admission

To qualify for admission, applicants should have a bachelor's degree from a regionally accredited college with a minimum 2.5 GPA. Applicants with a 2.0–2.5 GPA will be individually considered. Applicants should have at least three years of full-time work experience. Applicants may submit scores on the GMAT or GRE, but this is optional. Applicants need a computer, modem, and Internet access, as the program is offered in an online format. International learners are welcome with a TOEFL score at or above 500.

Programs

50–60 quarter credits

Master of Business Administration/General Business
Master of Business Administration/Leadership Studies
Master of Business Administration/Human Resource Management
Master of Business Administration/Industrial Management
Master of Business Administration/International Business

Tuition & Fees

Basic Tuition:	$210 per quarter credit
Master's Tuition:	$10,500–$12,600
Financial Aid:	Government loans, scholarships, veteran's benefits

Notes

Baker College is a private, independent college founded in 1888. Baker operates four extension sites and eight campuses across Michigan. On-campus offerings include more than seventy-five certificate, associate, bachelor's, and master's programs. Distance programs operate as extensions of on-campus offerings. Distance MBA courses are delivered online, using asynchronous classroom discussion boards, E-mail lessons, and paper submissions. Instruction occurs via BakerNet, a UNIX-based operating system connected to telephone lines via MICHNET and a direct modem pool. Fax and phone communication may also occur with faculty. Courses are accelerated, lasting only six weeks each quarter. Learners may choose from a longer (sixty-quarter credit) traditional MBA program or a shorter (fifty-quarter credit) MBA program. The traditional MBA is designed for learners with less life and career experience who are seeking more grounding in classical business theory. The executive MBA is designed to accommodate learners who have significant career experience in management and business and who wish to combine the best of academic learning with the best of field-based learning. Baker will assess a maximum of sixteen-quarter credits completed in the last seven years to transfer toward a Baker MBA. In addition to the online program, Baker operates a distance delivery system for corporate partners with site-based delivery of customized programs in business and technology to more than twenty-five corporations across Michigan.

BATH COLLEGE OF HIGHER EDUCATION

C/O Connected Education, Inc.
65 Shirley Lane
White Plains, NY 10607
914-428-8766
E-mail: tvozick@compuserve.com (Tina Vozick, Vice President)
URL: http://www.cinti.com/connect-ed/welcome

Campus Visits

None

Admission

Applicants should hold a recognized bachelor's degree and have a computer, modem, and Internet access.

Programs

2 modules (12 credits)
Postgraduate Certificate in Creative Writing
4 modules (24 credits)
Postgraduate Diploma in Creative Writing
Master of Arts in Creative Writing (4 modules, plus double dissertation module (36 credits)

Tuition & Fees

Basic Tuition:	2,000 British Pounds Sterling per module ($3,200 US)
Certificate Tuition:	4,000 British Pounds Sterling ($6,400 US)
Diploma Tuition:	6,000 British Pounds Sterling ($9,600 US)
Master's Tuition:	12,000 British Pounds Sterling ($19,200 US)
Financial Aid:	Veteran's benefits, government loans (pending approvals)

Notes

Bath College of Higher Education, located in Bath, England, offers the nonresidency Master of Arts in Creative Writing in an online format to learners in the United States and around the world via the independent educational company, Connected Education. Connected Education has specialized in developing and delivering online educational programs since 1985. In 1993, Connected Education was nominated for the Smithsonian Computerworld Award for Pioneer in the Use of Technology in Education. Bath College was founded by an amalgam of three colleges in 1975; the oldest of these was founded in 1907. BCHE is a university-sector college, offering a range of undergraduate and graduate study on campus. Like other British universities, BCHE has been granted degree-awarding powers, up to and including the master's, by Her Majesty's Privy Council. The distance learning creative writing program operates as an extension of the on-campus degree program. Bath College online writing faculty are published writers, working in the imaginative literary forms, including fiction, poetry, playwriting, and script writing, as well as nonfiction. Learning modules include both theoretical study units and writing workshop assignments. Students may study special genres, including suspense and mystery. The program is delivered using asynchronous computer conferencing, in an ongoing dialogue and exchange that typifies in-person graduate seminars. A virtual campus environment provides learners with an online café for informal discussion, and a library and special readings room. A double module creative thesis of at least 20,000 words is due at degree culmination. Learners may opt out of the dissertation, completing only the theory context and workshop modules to earn the Postgraduate Diploma or Certificate in Creative Writing.

A conversion rate of 1 United States dollar to .60 British Pound Sterling is used. Conversion rates may vary.

▉ BELLEVUE UNIVERSITY

Bellevue University Online
1000 Galvin Road South
Bellevue, NE 68005
402-293-3702
800-756-7920, ext. 3702
E-mail: ssampson@scholars.bellevue.edu (Sue Sampson, Associate Director)
URL: http://bruins.bellevue.edu

Campus Visits

None

Admission

MBA applicants should hold a regionally accredited bachelor's degree with a GPA of 2.5 or better during the last 60 semester credits of earned undergraduate work or a GPA of 3.0 or better on prior graduate work. Results of the MAT, GMAT, or GRE must be submitted along with two letters of reference. Three years of relevant career experience is expected for most degree programs. A computer, modem, and Internet access are required to complete the online course work.

Programs

36–48 credits
Master of Business Administration/Accounting
Master of Business Administration/Business Administration
Master of Business Administration/International Business
Master of Business Administration/International Management
Master of Business Administration/Management Information Systems

36 credits
Master's in Leadership

Tuition & Fees

Basic Tuition:	$275 per credit
Master's Tuition:	$9,900–$13,200
Financial Aid:	Guaranteed student loans, Grants, State grants, veteran's benefits

Notes

Bellevue University is a private, independent, comprehensive university founded in 1965. All graduate programs focus on the adult student who brings significant personal and professional experience and expertise to the classroom. Distance learning programs operate as extensions of on-campus offerings that include both undergraduate and graduate degree options. The online MBA at Bellevue is an application-oriented academic curriculum based on the evolving realities of the world in which we live and work. The degree consists of 12 credits of foundation course work (applicants with undergraduate degrees in business may have already met these foundation requirements); 21 credits of core course work; a 3-credit capstone course; and 12 credits in a specialty emphasis. Instructional methods include case studies and group projects that require the successful application of textbook theory and readings. Students take the courses in an accelerated, 12-week format to facilitate rapid progression toward the MBA. Students who study part time for six consecutive semesters will earn their MBA in 18 months. The program is delivered primarily online via FirstClass, an Internet-based, server/client groupware application that supports online conferencing and communication between faculty and students.

BEREAN UNIVERSITY OF THE ASSEMBLIES OF GOD

Distance Master's Admission
1445 Boonville Avenue
Springfield, MO 65802
417-862-2781
800-443-1083
E-mail: Berean@ag.org
URL: http://www.berean.edu

Campus Visits

Three one-week supervised residencies are required at EMERGE Ministries in Akron, Ohio, for counseling majors only.

Admission

Applicants with bachelor's from accredited colleges should have GPAs of at least 2.5. Applicants with bachelor's from institutions not holding recognized academic accreditation should have at least a 3.0 GPA to be granted provisional admission. All applicants must complete at least twenty-four credits in Bible/theology at the undergraduate level prior to full admission to master's study. Counseling majors will need to complete at least fifteen credits of undergraduate level behavioral science courses prior to master's study. Applicants to the Biblical Studies program should have a language background in Greek or Hebrew. Applicants living outside the United States should apply to Berean's international affiliate, International Correspondence Institute (ICI) University, for worldwide mission study.

Programs

36 credit
Master of Arts/Biblical Studies
42 credit
Master of Arts/Christian Counseling
36 credit
Master of Arts/Ministerial Studies/Leadership
Master of Arts/Ministerial Studies/Missions
Master of Arts/Ministerial Studies/Education

Tuition & Fees

Basic Tuition: $129 per credit
Master's Tuition: $4,644–$5,418
Financial Aid: 10% Family discounts, veteran's benefits

Notes

Berean is an Assemblies of God, private, independent Christian Pentecostal college founded in 1948 specifically to offer correspondence training to lay and pastoral candidates. Applicants should uphold the doctrines of the Holy Spirit and Christianity as espoused by the church. The graduate distance degree programs are designed to serve those who wish to enhance their ministerial skills or enter pastoral counseling positions. Berean is accredited by the Distance Education and Training Council to award undergraduate and graduate degrees via distance learning. Berean is a member of the Association of Christian Schools International (ACSI) and chartered by the State of Missouri to operate higher education programs. More than 7,000 learners study through Berean's distance programs each year. Delivery methods include video and audio cassette modules. Christian counseling majors must secure and complete a supervised Christian counseling internship in their home community. Up to six credits earned at another accredited graduate program may be transferred toward a Berean master's degree.

BETHEL THEOLOGICAL SEMINARY

In-Service Master of Divinity
Admissions
3949 Bethel Drive
St. Paul, MN 55112
612-638-6288
1-800-255-8706 ext. 6288
E-mail: bethelsem@aol.com
URL: http://www.bethel.edu

Campus Visits

Studies require two intensive two-week sessions on campus each year, one in January, and one in July.

Admission

The Master's of Divinity program is for established Christian ministers who seek to advance their education. Applicants should hold a bachelor's degree and be prepared to sign the Seminary's affirmation of faith and lifestyles statement. Applicants must have a computer, a modem, and Internet access to participate via electronic conferencing between campus residencies.

Programs

36 courses
Master of Divinity

Tuition & Fees

Basic Tuition:	$655 per course
Master's Tuition:	$4,585 per year
Financial Aid:	Government loans, tuition grants, military benefits, congregational awards

Notes

Bethel Theological Seminary is a private, Christian institution founded in 1871, affiliated with the Baptist General Conference, offering graduate-level seminary studies. The seminary is regionally accredited and accredited by the Association of Theological Schools. Distance learning programs operate as extensions of on-campus offerings. The Master's of Divinity is an in-ministry, low-residency, nontraditional program intended for those who are already established in the ministry. Learners communicate with faculty and their colleagues using electronic mail and phone conferencing between campus residencies. Curriculum is computer-assisted, enhanced with audio and videotape modules. A one-year ministry practicum is a required part of the five-year degree program.

BOISE STATE UNIVERSITY

Instructional & Performance Technology Program
Continuing Education
1910 University Drive
Boise, ID 83725
208-385-4457
800-824-7017, ext. 4457
E-mail: bsu-ipt@micron.net
URL: http://www.idbsu.edu/conted

Campus Visits

No campus visits are required to earn a non-thesis master's. One semester is required on campus if an optional thesis is completed.

Admission

An accredited bachelor's is required but the degree need not be in a subject related to instructional technology. A score of at least 50 on the Miller Analogies Test (MAT) and a 2.7 undergraduate GPA overall or 3.0 for the last two years of bachelor's study are required for admission. Applicants must have a computer, modem, and Internet access as the program is offered in an online format. International learners are welcome. Applicants have been admitted from the United States, Canada, Japan, and Italy.

Programs

36 credits
Master of Science in Instructional & Performance Technology

Tuition & Fees

Basic Tuition: $315 per credit, part-time
Master's Tuition: $11,340
Financial Aid: Government loans, military aid

Notes

Boise State University is a government-supported college founded in 1932. The instructional technology program was launched on campus in 1987 and offered in distance format not long thereafter. The program graduates approximately twenty-four distance learners each year. The program focuses on the use of instructional technology, primarily in adult training programs. Studies prepare learners for careers in instructional design and human resources training and program design. Studies in course design, computer-assisted learning, and adult learning styles are included in the program. The program uses asynchronous computer conferencing via the Internet. An IBM-compatible PC with color graphics and a modem is required. It may sometimes be possible to complete the degree using a Macintosh platform. A maximum of nine transfer credits may be applied to the degree. Individual courses are open to non-degree learners.

BRUNEL UNIVERSITY

Distance Learning Department
Department of Electrical Engineering
Uxbridge, Middlesex
United Kingdom UB8 3PH
01895.203219
E-mail: Kathleen.McGuinness@brunel.ac.uk
URL: http://www.brunel.ac.uk/depts/elec/Postgraduate_Programme/WWW_MSc_Brochure/
DL.html

Campus Visits

No campus visits are necessary. Examinations are at the end of each semester (January and May) and may be arranged to be taken at convenient designated examination centers, such as offices of the British Council.

Admission

The program normally admits applicants from the computer science and electrical engineering realms. Applicants should have an accredited first degree in technology, engineering, or a related subject. Experienced applicants without traditional academic credentials will also be considered for admission. A computer and modem and access to the Internet will facilitate studies and communication with faculty and staff. International applicants are welcome with TOEFL.

Programs

8 course modules
Master of Science in Data Communications

Tuition & Fees

Basic Tuition:	1,000–2,500 British Pounds Sterling per stage ($1,600–$4,000 US)
Master's Tuition:	5,000 British Pounds Sterling ($8,000 US)
Financial Aid:	None

Notes

Brunel University, located in western London, was founded in 1966. On-campus programs include a variety of undergraduate and graduate offerings. The Data Communications program was launched in 1990 and is designed to allow practitioners to execute advanced study in the development, design, installation, trouble-shooting, management, and audit of data systems and networks in a business environment. The distance program is offered as an extension of on-campus offerings. The program normally takes three years to complete. However, an accelerated or "fast-track" option may be added in the near future. All learners complete an academic project or dissertation. Applicants typically carry out their final project at their place of employment. Learners communicate with each other and faculty through E-mail and the Internet. Course details may be found at http://www.brunel.ac.uk/admin/registry/module/prospect/course_detail/demmsys.htm.

A conversion rate of 1 United States Dollar to .60 British Pound Sterling is used. Conversion rates may vary.

CALIFORNIA COLLEGE FOR HEALTH SCIENCES

222 West 24th Street
National City, CA 91950
619-477-4800
800-221-7374
E-mail: cchsinfo@cchs.edu
URL: http://www.cchs.edu/

Campus Visits

None

Admission

Applicants should hold a bachelor's degree in any subject and have completed an undergraduate introductory psychology course. Otherwise, such a course will have to be completed through the California College—via distance learning—prior to working toward the master's degree. International applicants are welcome, but the college provides no special assistance in English as a second language. In addition, a current resume or curriculum vitae must accompany the application for admission.

Programs

36 credits

Master of Science in Community Health Administration & Wellness Promotion

Tuition & Fees

Basic Tuition:	$100 per credit
Master's Tuition:	$3,600
Financial Aid:	None

Notes

California College is an independent private institute, which has offered health training since 1978. It is nationally accredited by the Distance Education & Training Council to provide health training degree programs. The California College is licensed by the State of California, Council for Private Postsecondary and Vocational Education to provide vocational training. Applicants communicate with faculty and other learners via surface mail or electronic mail. Up to 6 credits of any master's may be earned through transfer credits. Up to 9 credits of the degree may be granted for combined documented experiential learning and transfer credits. A $200 fee is charged to review experiential learning for degree credit.

CALIFORNIA INSTITUTE OF INTEGRAL STUDIES

Online Doctoral Program
9 Peter Yorke Way
San Francisco, CA 94109
415-674-5500
E-mail:info@clis.edu
URL: http://www.ciis.edu

Campus Visits

A six-day residential seminar is required each August. A four-day residential seminar is required each March.

Admission

A master's in a field related to integral studies or education and learning is generally required or encouraged for admission. Candidates of unusual promise may sometimes be admitted to doctorate study without an earned master's degree but must complete the master's en route, with 130 graduate quarter units earned. A computer, modem, and access to the Internet are required for course work completed through asynchronous electronic conferencing.

Programs

90–130 quarter units
Doctor in Transformative Learning and Change

Tuition & Fees

Basic Tuition: $350 per quarter unit
Doctorate Tuition: $31,500–$45,500
Financial Aid: Government loans, payment plans, veteran's benefits

Notes

The California Institute is a private college founded in 1968 promoting alternative East-West paradigms for learning. A variety of professional degree programs are offered on campus. The integral studies program blends spirituality, social wholeness, and learning theory to promote holistic learning. The transformative learning program intends to produce graduates capable of facilitating the capacity for transformative learning within individuals, groups, and institutions. The program is being offered online with electronic conferencing and virtual classrooms. Instruction is supplemented with audio, video, and print materials.

CALIFORNIA STATE UNIVERSITY

Humanities External Degree Program
1000 East Victoria, SAC2-2126
Carson, CA   90747
310-243-3743
E-mail: HUXonline@dhvx20.csudh.edu
URL: http://orca.csudh.edu/~hux/index.html

Campus Visits

None

Admission

A bachelor's degree from a regionally accredited college is required for admission, but the degree need not be in the humanities. Applicants should have a minimum 3.0 undergraduate GPA from the last two years of undergraduate study. A computer, modem, and Internet access will facilitate learning online. No special exams are currently required for admission but the general GRE may be required for admission beginning in 1998. International applicants are welcome with TOEFL at 550 or above.

Programs

30 credits

Master of Arts in the Humanities/Interdisciplinary
Master of Arts in the Humanities/Art
Master of Arts in the Humanities/English
Master of Arts in the Humanities/History
Master of Arts in the Humanities/Music
Master of Arts in the Humanities/Philosophy

Tuition & Fees

Basic Tuition: $135 per credit
Master's Tuition: $4,050
Financial Aid: Government loans, veteran's benefits, DANTES military benefits

Notes

California State University, Dominguez Hills, is a government-supported college founded in the 1960s. The university supports a variety of undergraduate and graduate degree programs on campus. The external humanities degree is one of the oldest and least expensive distance graduate programs in the United States. The degree offers a broad interdisciplinary exposure to all areas of the humanities—history, literature, philosophy, music, and art—and the development of an integrative perspective among them. Learners can specialize in a particular discipline of the humanities, or in specific cultural theme areas that can be traced across all of the humanistic disciplines. While a creative project or thesis can be completed, the program emphasizes the critical rather than the performance aspects of the humanities. Electronic mail or surface mail may be used for course correspondence. Up to nine credits may be transferred toward the master's degree. Regardless of transfer status a minimum of twenty-one credits of the degree must be earned through the California State program.

CALIFORNIA STATE UNIVERSITY DOMINGUEZ HILLS—QA

Quality Assurance Distance Learning
Master's Degree
1000 East Victoria
Carson, CA 90747
310-516-3355
E-mail: smackay@dhvx20.csudh.edu (Scott Mackay)
URL: http://www.csudh.edu/msqa

Campus Visits

None

Admission

An accredited bachelor's degree is required for admission. Applicants without a bachelor's in a technical or mathematical field should inquire about meeting prerequisites prior to entry. Applicants are expected to have a foundation of study in mathematics and computers. Applicants should have a minimum 2.5 undergraduate GPA from the last two years of upper division work for the bachelor's degree. The program is offered worldwide via asynchronous computer conferencing. A computer, modem, and Internet access are required. International applicants with TOEFL scores of 550 or higher are welcome.

Programs

33 credits
Master of Science in Quality Assurance/Health Care
Master of Science in Quality Assurance/Manufacturing
Master of Science in Quality Assurance/Service

Tuition & Fees

Basic Tuition: $414 per course
Master's Tuition: $4,554
Financial Aid: Government loans, veteran's benefits

Notes

California State University at Dominguez Hills is a government-supported college founded in the 1960s. The quality assurance degree was first offered on campus in 1978. In 1989, California State began offering the quality assurance degree program via distance learning in an interactive, site-based television format. In 1996, the program was offered via the Internet to learners worldwide. The degree is designed to prepare engineers, technology managers, and quality specialists to design and implement industry-wide quality measures and assurance procedures. Applicants may major in health care, service industries, or manufacturing career areas. Electronic mail, listservs, asynchronous computer conferencing, and videos of classroom lectures are used for degree delivery. Courses are open to non-degree learners. Up to nine credits may be transferred toward the master's degree. Regardless of transfer status, a minimum of twenty-four semester credits of the degree must be earned through the California State program.

CITY UNIVERSITY

Distance Learning
919 S.W. Grady Way
Renton, WA   98055-2942
425-637-1010
800-422-4898
E-mail: admissions@cityu.edu
URL: http://www.cityu.edu/

Campus Visits

None

Admission

Applicants to City University's master's programs are expected to hold an accredited bachelor's. A bachelor is not required to earn a graduate-level business certificate, however. Applicants to the school psychology program should hold a bachelor's degree in education, psychology, or sociology. Applicants to teacher education and professional counseling programs should have a minimum undergraduate GPA of at least 2.75 and some experience in their chosen career fields. International learners are welcome with TOEFL. Access to a computer, a modem, the Internet, and a fax machine may be required for some programs.

Programs

45 quarter credits
Master of Arts in Human Behavior (Counseling)
Master of Arts in Marriage & Family Counseling

45–62 quarter credits
Master of Arts in Mental Health Counseling
Master of Arts in Vocational Rehabilitation Counseling

49–55 quarter credits
Master of Education in Curriculum & Instruction (K-12)
Master of Education in Educational Technology (K-12)
Master of Education in Special Education (K-12)
Master of Education in English as a Second Language

56 quarter credits
Master of Education in School Guidance & Counseling (K-12)

18–24 quarter credits
Certificate in Business Management
Certificate in Financial Management
Certificate in Information Systems
Certificate in Managerial Leadership
Certificate in Marketing
Certificate in Public Administration

45 quarter credits
Master of Public Administration

60 quarter credits
Master of Public Administration/Business Administration

45 quarter credits
Master of Business Administration/Business Management
Master of Business Administration/Financial Management
Master of Business Administration/Individualized
Master of Business Administration/Information Systems
Master of Business Administration/Managerial Leadership

Master of Business Administration/Marketing
Master of Business Administration/Public Administration

Tuition & Fees

Basic Tuition: $268 per quarter credit
Certificate Tuition: $4,824–$6,432
Master's Tuition: $12,060–$16,080
Financial Aid: City University scholarships, Canadian loans

Notes

City University is a private, independent college founded in 1973 to meet the educational needs of nontraditional adult learners. Distance learning programs operate as extensions of City's on-campus offerings at the undergraduate and graduate levels. Distance courses begin the first of each month and are accelerated, designed to be completed within ten weeks. Some courses and programs are available through City's Internet site. Other courses and programs rely primarily on surface mail or fax lesson submissions. Individual courses are generally open to non-degree learners. The education and counseling master's may require local mentors to complete required practicums. Additional "mentor fees" apply. The certificate and master's in financial planning prepare individuals for the national Certified Financial Planner (CFP) examination. The information systems program prepares individuals to sit for the national Certified Data Processor (CDP) examination. Counseling degrees have been designed to meet counselor licensing requirements in Washington and California State. Counseling degrees may also meet licensing requirements in other states. Up to twelve quarter credits may be transferred toward most master's degrees.

CLARKSON COLLEGE

Coordinator of Distance Education
101 South 42nd Street
Omaha, NE 68131-2715
402-552-3037
800-647-5500
E-mail: admiss@clrkcol.crhsnet.edu
URL: http://www.clarksoncollege.edu

Campus Visits

None

Admission

Applicants should hold accredited bachelor's degrees and have a computer and modem to access a bulletin board system, which is used to facilitate learning. Nursing applicants must be Registered Nurses who hold bachelor's degrees from NLN-accredited schools with a minimum 3.0 GPA. Health care administration applicants may have undergraduate degrees in any subject provided they satisfy undergraduate-level foundation studies in accounting, economics, statistics, and computer applications prior to beginning the master's program. Satisfactory scores on the College Level Exam Program (CLEP) may be accepted as meeting some undergraduate course prerequisites.

Programs

27 credits post-master
Certificate in Family Nurse Practitioner
36 credits
Master of Science in Health Care Administration
36–45 credits
Master of Science in Nursing/Nurse Administrator
Master of Science in Nursing/Nurse Educator
Master of Science in Nursing/Primary Care Family Nurse Practitioner

Tuition & Fees

Basic Tuition:	$302 per credit
Certificate Tuition:	$8,154
Master's Tuition:	$10,872–$13,590
Financial Aid:	Government loans, scholarships, Nebraska State aid, short-term loans

Note

Clarkson College, founded in 1888, is a private college specializing in health and medical studies. A variety of health-related undergraduate and master's degrees are offered on campus. Distance programs began in 1990 and operate as extensions of on-campus offerings with the goal of bringing quality health care training to professionals in rural and isolated areas. Course delivery occurs primarily through mailed audiotapes of lectures and the use of a computer bulletin board conferencing system and teleconferences. Health care learners must complete a final internship and a research project and pass a comprehensive degree exam. Nursing applicants must complete a thesis. Graduates of the nursing practitioner program will qualify to write the ANA certification exam. Nurses who already hold a master's degree may take the shorter post-master certification program to become a nurse practitioner. Up to nine credits of course work can be competed by nondegree learners. Up to nine credits may be accepted in transfer toward a master's degree.

COLLEGE FOR FINANCIAL PLANNING

National Endowment for Financial Education
Admissions Office
4695 South Monaco Street
Denver, CO 80237-3403
303-220-1200
E-mail: n/a
URL: http://www.nefe.org

Campus Visits

None

Admission

Admission to the Master's, Retirement Planning, and Accredited Tax Advisor programs requires both a bachelor's degree with a 2.5 GPA and adequate professional experience. Those new to financial services should consider the foundations in financial planning course with the internship. The foundations program results in the entry-level professional designation, Financial Paraplanner. A high school diploma or GED is required to enter the Certified Financial Planner (CFP) program or the Accredited Tax Preparer (ATP) program. The Accredited Tax Advisor (ATA) program requires an undergraduate degree, career experience, or a related industry license.

Programs

36 credits (12 courses)
Master of Science in Financial Planning/Estate Planning
Master of Science in Financial Planning/Retirement Planning
Master of Science in Financial Planning/Tax Planning
Master of Science in Financial Planning/Wealth Management

1 course
Accredited Asset Management Specialist (AAMS)

6 courses
Accredited Tax Advisor (ATA)

1 course
Accredited Tax Preparer (ATP)

5 courses
Certified Financial Planner (CFP)

1 course
Chartered Mutual Funds Counselor (CMFC)

1 course, plus internship
Foundations in Financial Planning/Financial Paraplanner

4 courses
Retirement Planning Program

Tuition & Fees

Basic Tuition:	$525 per course (master's); $450–$695 per course (others)
Certificate Tuition:	Varies
Master's Tuition:	$6,300
Financial Aid:	Payment plans

Notes

The National Endowment for Financial Education (NEFE), founded in 1972, is a professional training institute for financial services professionals. The College for Financial Planning (CFFP) is the accredited degree granting division of NEFE and offers the master's program, the Certified Financial Planner Education program, and the Foundation in Financial Planning program. Other NEFE divisions are the Institute for Tax Studies (offering the Accredited Tax Advisor and Preparer programs), and the Institute for Wealth Management (offering the Asset Management and Chartered Mutual Funds programs). The College for Financial Planning is regionally accredited and the master's degree program is also accredited by the Distance Education and Training Council (DETC). Some of the training courses offered by NEFE divisions outside the CFFP have also been approved by the American Council on Education's Program on Non-Collegiate Sponsored Instruction (ACE/PONSI) as being the equivalent of courses taught at regionally accredited colleges. The Certified Financial Planner (CFP) program prepares learners to write the national Certified Financial Planner exam. Similarly, other courses of study, like the Chartered Mutual Funds Counselor (CMFC) program, prepare learners for professional financial services designations such as the CMFC. Some courses also satisfy state and national continuing education requirements for financial services and IRS professionals. Courses are delivered in self-study module form via surface mail with objective and case study competency exams used to measure learning. Learners are given proctored exams in January, May, and September of each year at more than 200 examination centers located throughout the United States.

COLLEGE OF SAINT SCHOLASTICA

Intensive Summer Programs
Master's in Management
1200 Kenwood Avenue
Duluth, MN 55811
218-723-6415
800-447-5444

Campus Visits

Attendance is required at a two-week campus intensive each summer. Four summers are generally required to complete the program.

Admission

Applicants should hold a bachelor's degree from an accredited college but the bachelor's need not be in business. Applicants have been accepted from many fields, including banking, mining, retail, health care, international business, manufacturing, and public administration. Because the program requires the application and analysis of business principles in real world ways, all applicants should have career experience. It is recommended that applicants have knowledge of college-level math, statistics, economics, and computers prior to applying. International applicants are welcome. Since Duluth is near the Canadian border, applicants from Canada have routinely entered the program. No special exams are required for admission.

Programs

53 quarter credits

Master of Arts in Management

Tuition & Fees

Basic Tuition:	$310 per quarter credit
Master's Tuition:	$16,450
Financial Aid:	None

Notes

The College of Saint Scholastica is a private, comprehensive university established in 1912 and affiliated with the Roman Catholic Church. The college has been rated one of the top regional Midwestern liberal arts colleges in annual surveys by *U.S. New and World Report*. A variety of degrees are offered on campus. The distance master's with intensive summer visits was launched in the early 1990s. All learners complete the twenty-six quarter credit common core, then choose seven quarter credits in electives and projects to focus studies on areas that interest them. The program encourages creativity and the entrepreneurial spirit. The program focuses on the need for communication and leadership skills to foster more responsible management approaches. Up to nine graduate quarter credits may be accepted in transfer toward the fifty-three quarter credit master's degree. The final forty-four quarter credits of the degree must be completed as formal course work through Saint Scholastica.

COLLEGE OF SAINT SCHOLASTICA—DE

Master of Education Admissions
Department of Education
1200 Kenwood Avenue
Duluth, MN 55811
218-723-6169
800-888-8796
E-mail: ctrettel@fac1.css.edu
URL: http://www.css.edu/acad/grad/gradpage.html

Campus Visits

Degree-seekers attend overnight orientation seminars that are offered at special sites in the upper Midwest as well as on campus. A one-and-a-half-day capstone seminar must be attended on campus at the end of the program.

Admission

Applicants should hold bachelor's degrees from accredited institutions with a minimum 2.8 undergraduate GPA. A minimum of two years of teaching experience and employment in a school or access to a classroom for executing required assignments is also required.

Programs

48 quarter credits
Master of Education in Curriculum and Instruction (K-12)

Tuition & Fees

Basic Tuition: $150 per quarter credit
Master's Tuition: $7,200
Financial Aid: Budget payment plan, installment payment plan, Stafford loans, private loans

Notes

The College of Saint Scholastica is an independent, comprehensive, liberal arts college founded by the Benedictine order of the Roman Catholic Church in 1912. Distance learning programs operate as extensions of on-campus offerings. The distance education program uses a practice-based orientation to address curriculum issues in a K-12 environment, including special needs learners. The distance master's program uses video, current journal articles, and trade books. Toll-free faculty support lines and E-mail are used to facilitate interaction between faculty and students. Videotaped sessions include both lecture and practicum scenes of master teachers applying principles in real classrooms. In 1994, the college was ranked by *U.S. News and World Report* as one of the top ten regional liberal arts colleges in the Midwest. Degree-seekers receive a two-year tuition guarantee. In addition to tuition, applicants pay a $68 per course videotape and materials fee.

COLORADO STATE UNIVERSITY—MBA

College of Business
Distance Education Center
151 Rockwell Hall
Fort Collins, CO 80523-12705
970-491-2865
800-491-4622
E-mail: bizdist@lamar.colostate.edu
URL: http://cobweb.cobus.colostate.edu

Campus Visits

None

Admissions

Applicants should hold regionally accredited bachelor's degrees. Applicants to the MBA program need not hold a bachelor's in business but must meet specific undergraduate course prerequisites. Calculus, statistics, business law, microeconomics, marketing, finance, accounting, production, management, and several other foundation level undergraduate courses are required for admission. Acceptable scores on the College Level Examination Program (CLEP) in undergraduate business subjects may substitute for some of the required undergraduate courses. The Master of Science in Management, as distinct from the Master of Business Administration, has fewer prerequisites and a less quantitative emphasis. The Graduate Management Admissions Test (GMAT) may or may not be required for admission depending on applicant's GPA and professional work history. International learners who have taken the TOEFL are welcome. Computer, modem, and Internet access are required.

Programs

33 credits
Master of Business Administration
Master of Business Administration/Finance
Master of Business Administration/Management (Human Resources)
Master of Business Administration/Marketing
Master of Business Administration/Quality Improvement
32 credits
Master of Science in Management

Tuition & Fees

Basic Tuition:	$312 per credit (Colorado)
	$364 per credit (others)
Master's Tuition:	$9,984–$10,296 (Colorado)
	$11,648–$12,012 (others)
Financial Aid:	Government loans, DANTES military benefits, veteran's benefits

Notes

Colorado State University, established in 1862, is government-supported. Distance learning programs have been in operation for almost three decades and operate as extensions of on-campus offerings. The business administration program is accredited by the American Assembly of Collegiate Schools of Business (AACSB) and has been objectively ranked among the top 25 percent of graduate business schools in the nation. The Master of Science in Management is designed for learners interested in the management process, human resources, or organizational behavior. Learners receive mailed videotapes of on-campus lectures. Videotapes will be delivered to corporate or military sites or to sites such as public libraries as arranged by individual learners. At least twenty-four credits of any master's must be completed through Colorado State University. Internet and Web-based conferencing and videoconferencing are used in the instructional process.

COLORADO STATE UNIVERSITY—SURGE

Continuing Education—Spruce Hall
Fort Collins, CO 80523-1040
800-525-4950
E-mail: askdede@lamar.colostate.edu
URL: http://www.colostate.edu/Depts/CE

Campus Visits

No visits are required to complete the master's degree unless students opt to write a thesis. The thesis is optional and must be presented on campus. Doctoral residencies vary by program but generally the last two semesters must be spent on campus to complete thesis research.

Admissions

Applicants are expected to hold regionally accredited bachelor's degrees. Admission policies vary with the degree sought. Specific undergraduate course prerequisites are enforced. The GRE is generally required for admission. Learners living in the United States or Canada are welcome.

Programs

30–33 credits

Master of Education in Vocational Education (Human Resources/Adult Training)
Master of Science in Agricultural Engineering
Master of Science in Chemical Engineering
Master of Science in Civil Engineering
Master of Science in Electrical Engineering
Master of Science in Engineering Management
Master of Science in Environmental Engineering
Master of Science in Mechanical Engineering
Master of Science in Systems Engineering
Master of Business Administration
Master of Science in Computer Science
Master of Science in Statistics

72 credits

Doctor of Philosophy in Engineering/Agricultural Engineering
Doctor of Philosophy in Engineering/Chemical Engineering
Doctor of Philosophy in Engineering/Civil Engineering
Doctor of Philosophy in Engineering/Electrical Engineering
Doctor of Philosophy in Engineering/Environmental Engineering
Doctor of Philosophy in Engineering/Mechanical Engineering
Doctor of Philosophy in Engineering/Systems Engineering

Tuition & Fees

Basic Tuition:	$312 per credit (Colorado)
	$364 per credit (others)
Master's Tuition:	$9,360–$10,296 (Colorado)
	$10,920–$12,012 (others)
Doctorate Tuition:	$22,464 (Colorado); $26,208 (others)
Financial Aid:	Government loans, DANTES military benefits, veteran's benefits

Notes

Colorado State University is a government-supported institution established in 1862. Distance learning programs operate as extensions of on-campus offerings. Distance learning degree programs have been in operation for more than two decades. The Colorado SURGE program sponsored the first video-based distance degree completion program in the United States. Learners receive mailed videotapes of on-campus lectures. Videotapes can be delivered to the student's office, military base, public library, or home, on a weekly basis. All SURGE students are required to have Internet access. SURGE students use an electronic communications software product called "e.mbanet." Use of e.mbanet will allow greater communication capability with faculty, staff, and other students, posting of class materials, group work, and real-time chats. A minimum of twenty-four credits of any master's degree must be earned from Colorado State. A minimum of thirty-two credits of any doctorate must be earned after admission to Colorado State.

COLUMBIA INTERNATIONAL UNIVERSITY

Columbia Biblical Seminary & Graduate School of Missions
Independent Distance Learning (IDL)
7435 Monticello Road
P.O. Box 3122
Columbia, SC 29230-3122
803-754-4100
800-777-2227
E-mail: yesciu@ciu.edu
URL: http://www.ciu.edu

Campus Visits

None

Admissions

A bachelor's degree and evidence of Christian conversion are required. Students older than thirty-five with ministry experience who lack a bachelor's degree will be considered. Applicants should be members of an Evangelical church.

Programs

31 credits
Certificate of Biblical Studies

Tuition & Fees

Basic Tuition:	$150 per credit
Certificate Tuition:	$4,650
Financial Aid:	Christian worker discounts, spouse discounts, inmate discounts, veteran's benefits

Notes

Columbia International University is a comprehensive private Christian university, founded in 1923. CIU supports two resident schools, the Columbia Bible College, and the Columbia Biblical Seminary. A variety of undergraduate, graduate, and professional programs are offered on-campus. The Independent Distance Learning (IDL) program operates as an extension of on-campus offerings. The Certificate in Biblical Studies represents the first year of core courses for Columbia Biblical Seminary's Missions graduate degree programs. It is intended to provide basic mission training for lay ministry by providing the first year of the two-year master's, which can be completed on campus. The program strives to provide a practical bridge between secular education and vocational or lay ministry. The program requires a fourteen-week supervised evangelistic experience. Individual courses are open to non-certificate learners. Courses are delivered using videotape and audiotape technologies.

COLUMBIA UNIVERSITY—AEGIS

Teacher's College
AEGIS Doctoral Program
525 West 120th Street, Box 50
New York, NY 10027
212-678-3760
E-mail: n/a
URL: n/a

Campus Visits

A campus screening interview and on-site writing assignment are required of all finalists. A three-week summer session is required in June for three sessions over two years. Additional campus seminars are required one weekend each month in the fall and spring semesters over the same two-year period.

Admission

Applicants are required to submit a professional resume detailing their experience in adult education. A minimum of five years of professional experience is expected. Applicants must also submit a professional or academic paper in the area of adult education that demonstrates their ability to undertake doctorate-level studies. Applicants should have completed a minimum of forty graduate credits in an accredited graduate school with a grade of B or better, either in a master's program or through some post-master's professional study. International applicants are welcome if their TOEFL scores are at or above 600. Proof of access to a local university library is required.

Programs

7 semesters
Doctor of Education in Adult & Continuing Education

Tuition & Fees

Basic Tuition: $6,550 per semester
Doctorate Tuition: $45,850
Financial Aid: Government loans, Columbia scholarships, New York State aid

Notes

Columbia University is a private college founded in 1754. A variety of undergraduate, graduate, and professional degrees are offered on campus. The AEGIS program is designed for senior professionals in adult education and was first offered in independent study form in 1981. Specialties are available within the study of adult education but may vary with faculty and program capacity. Applicants are admitted in odd-numbered years only. The program takes from three to five years to complete, including the required dissertation. Individual courses are not open to non-degree learners. Some courses use E-mail conferencing and lesson submission.

COLUMBIA UNIVERSITY TEACHER'S COLLEGE

Computing in Education
525 West 120th Street, Box 8
New York, NY 10027
212-678-3773
E-mail: HB50@columbia.edu (Howard Budin, Director)
URL: http://www.tc.columbia.edu/~academic/ccte

Campus Visits

Intensive four-week sessions must be attended on campus each July. At least two summer sessions must be completed to earn the degree.

Admission

All applicants must have access to a computer and a modem. The computing and education program is designed for school teachers or school media center specialists or librarians who want to learn to better use computers and instructional technology for grades K-12. International applicants are welcome with TOEFL.

Programs

32 credits
Master of Arts in Computing & Education (K-12)

Tuition & Fees

Basic Tuition: $490 per credit
Master's Tuition: $15,680
Financial Aid: Government loans, Columbia scholarships

Notes

Columbia University is a private college founded in 1754. Campus offerings include a variety of undergraduate, graduate, and professional degrees. Distance learning programs operate as extensions of on-campus offerings. The computing and education program was first offered in 1975 and offered in distance format with intensive summer visits beginning in 1983. The computing and education program is designed for school teachers or media center specialists to learn to use computers and instructional technology for grades K-12. Much of the course work may be completed via E-mail or electronic conferencing.

COLUMBIA UNIVERSITY—COLUMBIA VIDEO NETWORK (CVN)

Columbia School of Engineering & Applied Science
540 Mudd Building
500 West 120th Street, Mailcode 4719
New York, NY 10027
212-854-6447
E-mail: cvn@columbia.edu
URL: http://www.cvn.columbia.edu

Campus Visits

None

Admission

Master's degree applicants should hold a bachelor's degree in engineering or a closely related field, or an allied science (nonengineering majors may have to complete undergraduate or preparatory course work in engineering or advanced mathematics to adequately prepare for any one graduate degree program). Columbia requires a minimum undergraduate GPA of 3.0, a personal-professional statement, and supporting letters of reference. The GRE is required for master's degree applicants, with some programs requiring both the general GRE and the engineering GRE. Applicants to the Professional Degree (PD) program should hold master's degrees. The PD generally requires a master's degree in the intended area of study, but applicants with a master's degree in a related field will be considered on a case-by-case basis. The GRE general test and computer science subject test are required for PD Computer Science applicants. The GRE is not required for PD Engineering applicants. Applicants should have access to a VCR for videotape playback, and the Internet and World Wide Web to access the home pages of selected courses and instructors. International applicants are welcome, and the TOEFL is required for them.

Programs

30 credits

Master of Science/Computer Science
Master of Science/Electrical Engineering
Master of Science/Electrical Engineering–Lightwave (Photonics Engineering)
Master of Science/Electrical Engineering–Microelectronic Circuits
Master of Science/Electrical Engineering–Microelectronic Devices
Master of Science/Electrical Engineering–Telecommunications Engineering
Master of Science/Electrical Engineering–Wireless and Mobile Communications
Master of Science/Metallurgy and Materials Science
Master of Science/Mechanical Engineering
Master of Science/Operations Research

30 credits post-master's

Professional Degree/Computer Science
Professional Degree/Electrical Engineering
Professional Degree/Mechanical Engineering

Tuition & Fees

Basic Tuition:	$890.57 per credit; $350 per course videotape fee (United States); $700 per course videotape fee (International)
Master's Tuition:	$26,717.10 plus videotape fees
Doctorate Tuition:	$26,717.10 plus videotape fees
Financial Aid:	None

Notes

Columbia University is a private, comprehensive university founded in 1754. On-campus degree offerings include an array of undergraduate, graduate, and professional programs. The Columbia Video Network (CVN) allows students to participate in the same lectures, take the same exams, and receive the same degrees as on-campus students. A key component of CVN is flexibility without compromising the high caliber of teaching, resources, and standards inherent in the Columbia School of Engineering and Applied Science. Candidates can earn their distance master's degrees with a non-thesis option. The Professional Degree (PD) is a postgraduate degree for engineers desiring an advanced degree beyond the master's level, but not wishing to emphasize research. The PD is a practitioner's degree that allows engineers to integrate cutting edge theoretical concepts with practical skills acquired in the workplace. The substance of the PD is identical to that of the doctoral degree, but without a dissertation or thesis requirement. Students may access the program from a distance in one of two ways. Independent learners may register to receive mailed videotapes of course lectures. Company-sponsored students may watch lectures at corporate reception sites that are equipped to receive live lectures through a desktop videoconferencing system or through mailed videotapes. Students may also access course materials and assignments via the World Wide Web pages of instructors. Corporations may become reception sites by agreeing to provide basic degree support services such as: employee tuition assistance, drop-off and pick-up services for videotapes and course materials, site administrative duties, access to the World Wide Web and Internet for students, and access to desktop videoconferencing facilities or a VCR to play course videotapes. Companies throughout the United States, Europe, and Asia have chosen CVN to provide courses for their employees working towards degrees. The University charges no fees to corporations wishing to participate in courses or degree programs. All learners pay the per-credit tuition plus any applicable videotape fees. CVN accepts up to six semester credits in transfer toward any master's degree. Courses may be audited for lower fees and most courses are open to non-degree learners meeting the necessary prerequisites.

CONCORDIA UNIVERSITY WISCONSIN

Independent Master's Department
Graduate Office
12800 North Lakeshore Drive
Mequon, WI 53097
800-665-6564
414-243-4442
E-mail: lbecker@bach.cuw.edu (Lucy Becker, Program Assistant)
URL: http://www.cuw.edu

Campus Visits

Most degree programs require from one day to two weeks on campus each year. Nursing and educational licensing degrees may require longer program attendance.

Admission

Applicants should hold accredited bachelor's with appropriate GPAs and preparatory study for advanced study in their chosen area. Nursing applicants should be registered nurses who hold bachelor's degrees in nursing from NLN-accredited college programs. Some educational (K-12) programs may be restricted to entry by licensed teachers only. Applicants living within southeast Wisconsin (within a fifty-mile radius of the campus) are required to take the on-campus program if available; distance programs are available to local students only if an on-campus program is not offered in the desired field of study. A computer, modem, and Internet access may be required for some programs.

Programs

36–39 credits
Master of Business Administration/Chinese Language MBA
Master of Business Administration/Church Administration
Master of Business Administration/Finance
Master of Business Administration/Health Care Administration
Master of Business Administration/Human Resource Management
Master of Business Administration/Global Business
Master of Business Administration/Management
Master of Business Administration/Marketing

36 credits
Master of Education
Master of Education/Educational Administration
Master of Education/Reading
Master of Arts Biology
Master of Arts History
Master of Arts Religious Life
Master of International Business
Master of Literary Studies
Master of Managerial Communication
Master of Science Computer Science

54 credits
Master of Science/Clinical Psychology

57 credits
Master of Science/Counseling Psychology

48 credits
Master of Science in Education/Counseling

43–46 credits

Master of Science Nursing/Family Nurse Practitioner
Master of Science Nursing/Nurse Educator
Master of Science Nursing/Geriatric Nurse Practitioner

36 credits

Master of Public Administration/Criminal Justice Administration
Master of Public Administration/Government Administration

Tuition & Fees

Basic Tuition:	$300 per credit
Master's Tuition:	$10,800–$17,100
Financial Aid:	Government loans, discounts for certified teachers with the Lutheran Church—Missouri Synod

Notes

Concordia University Wisconsin is a private, comprehensive liberal arts college, founded in 1881 by the Lutheran Church—Missouri Synod. Bachelor's and master's degrees are offered on campus in more than forty-seven majors. Distance programs operate as extensions of on-campus offerings. In addition to holding regional accreditation, departments hold accreditation or approval from the National League of Nursing (NLN), the Wisconsin Department of Instruction (DIP) (for K-12 public teacher certification), and the Association of Collegiate Business Schools and Programs. Counseling programs are either approved or under review for approval by the National Board for Certified Counselors (NBCC), the American Counseling Association (ACA), and the Wisconsin Department of Regulation and Licensing. Distance programs are delivered using multiple platforms including surface mail, fax, phone, video, E-mail, and Internet-assisted means. Delivery methods vary by program of study.

COVENANT THEOLOGICAL SEMINARY

Extension Office
Individually Mentored External Training Program (IMET)
12330 Conway Road
St. Louis, MO 63141
314-434-4044
800-254-8064
E-mail: 75442.2757@compuserve.com
URL: http://www.inlink.com/~covenant

Campus Visits

None

Admissions

A bachelor's degree is required to begin the Certificate in Biblical & Theological Studies but is not required to study toward the Continuing Education Certificates. A pastor's reference form is also required.

Programs

30 credits
Certificate in Biblical & Theological Studies
12 credits
Continuing Education Certificate/Christianity & Contemporary Culture
Continuing Education Certificate/Church History
Continuing Education Certificate/Theological Studies

Tuition & Fees

Basic Tuition: $135 per credit
Certificate Tuition: $1,620–$4,050
Financial Aid: None

Notes

The Covenant Theological Seminary is a private Christian (Presbyterian) graduate seminary, first accredited in 1973. The Individually Mentored External Training (IMET) program allows learners to complete courses and certificates with no campus or site visits. It is designed to allow learners to "test" the waters before committing to the on-campus or site-based extension ministry degree program. Up to eighteen credits earned in the nonresidency program may later be accepted for transfer as core studies toward an on-campus Master of Arts or Divinity. A pilot Master of Arts in General Theological Studies (MAGTS) can be completed through combined independent study and course attendance at special extension sites maintained across the United States. Courses are delivered primarily through mailed audio and videotapes of on-campus sessions. Additional fees ($75 per course) may apply to the rental of video course materials. Faculty mentors are available through toll-free phone lines and E-mail. Lecture materials, textbooks, and examinations are identical to those used on campus. IMET courses are also available for noncredit rental or Continuing Education Unit (CEU) designations ($35 per CEU) and may be used for Sunday School, Bible-study programs, or personal enrichment.

DUKE UNIVERSITY

Fuqua School of Business Global Executive MBA
P.O. Box 90116
Durham, NC 27708-0116
919-660-8011
E-mail: fuqua-gemba@mail.duke.edu
URL: http://www.fuqua.duke.edu/

Campus Visits

The Global Executive MBA (GEMBA) program combines attendance at multiple international program sites with study through advanced interactive distance learning technologies. During the nineteen-month program learners must attend four two-week site sessions and one three-week site session. Site sessions are held around the globe in Europe (Salzburg, Austria), Asia (Shanghai, China), and the Americas (Durham, North Carolina and Sao Paulo, Brazil).

Admission

An undergraduate degree from a U.S. college or its international equivalent is required. GEMBA applicants should have a minimum of eight years' experience in a managerial capacity, and should have (or expect to shortly assume) cross-country managerial responsibility within their companies. Achievement in quantitative areas and a working familiarity with information technologies are considered. Applicants should have letters of sponsorship and backing from their companies prior to entering the program. Classes are admitted each May. International applicants are welcome with English proficiency as demonstrated by their TOEFL scores. A computer and modem and access to the Internet are required.

Programs

15 courses
Master of Business Administration/Global Executive

Tuition & Fees

Basic Tuiion:	$82,500
Master's Tuition:	$82,500, includes residency fees
Financial Aid:	None

Notes

Duke University is a private, comprehensive institution affiliated with the Methodist Church and founded in 1838. On-campus programs include a variety of undergraduate, graduate, and professional programs. The distance Master's of Business Administration (GEMBA) combines normal residential business education with advanced distance learning technologies, thereby allowing executives from around the globe to engage in MBA studies while they continue to contribute to their firms' bottom lines. Program emphasis is on global and multinational management issues. The GEMBA curriculum contains the fundamental business curriculum found in Fuqua's other MBA programs. A rigorous academic program, GEMBA fully integrates three essential components for effective management: a firm grasp of core business skills, expertise in global management, and proficiency in the latest interactive communications technologies. Interactive learning technologies used during the degree may include application-sharing software, CD-ROM multimedia courseware, E-mail, electronic bulletin boards, streaming audio, synchronous group discussions or chats, computer-based videoconferencing, and Internet access through a Web browser. A team-oriented learning environment is maintained.

DURHAM UNIVERSITY

Business School
MBA Distance Learning Programme Office
Mill Hill Lane
Durham City
United Kingdom DHI 3LB
0191-374-2219
E-mail: MBA.DL@durham.ac.uk
URL: http://www.dur.ac.uk/~dbr0www2/

Campus Visits

A short orientation is held in Durham and in cities worldwide each September. Annual one-week seminars are held at the start of each of the second and third stages of the program. Though learners are encouraged to attend these seminars, exemption to seminar attendance may be granted in cases of hardship.

Admission

All applicants should have at least two years of career experience and mathematical literacy at a level sufficient to undertake advanced quantitative study. The GMAT may be required at the discretion of the admission committee. Applicants may be admitted if they hold an honors or accredited bachelor's degree or other advanced professional credentials, such as qualifying membership in the Institute of Chartered Accountants or a related certifying board. Applicants without academic or professional credentials but with adequate management experience may be provisionally admitted to study for the advanced diploma. If advanced diploma applicants perform well on their exams for the first four courses (stage one) they may continue for the master's degree. Applicants are encouraged worldwide provided they have fluency in English. All instruction occurs in English.

Programs

8 courses (2 stages)
Advanced Diploma in Business Administration
12 courses (3 stages) plus dissertation
Master of Business Administration

Tuition & Fees

Basic Tuition:	2,200 British Pounds Sterling per stage, plus 1,100 project supervision fee ($3,520 per stage US)
Diploma Tuition:	4,400 British Pounds Sterling ($7,040 US)
Master's Tuition:	7,700 British Pounds Sterling ($12,320 US)
Financial Aid:	MBA and Career Development Loans

Notes

The University of Durham was founded in 1832 and is the third oldest university in England, following Oxford and Cambridge in its founding. The Durham Business School was founded in 1965 to focus on research-based studies in business administration. The distance learning MBA was first offered in 1988. It employs the same faculty, standards, and procedures as the on-campus MBA. It is one of the few European distance MBAs that is fully accredited by the Association of MBAs (AMBA). The program requires the completion of twelve courses in three stages with a final dissertation of 15,000–20,000 words. Learners submit two to four assignments to their tutors for each course. The assignments are used to provide extensive feedback to the learners on their progress. The program is competency based. To pass each course learners must pass the course final and stage exams, which are taken at proctored settings worldwide. Tuition given includes all texts and study materials. Communication with faculty and tutors may occur via phone or E-mail.

A conversion rate of 1 United States dollar to .60 British Pound Sterling is used. Conversion rates may vary.

EAST CAROLINA UNIVERSITY

School of Industry & Technology
Internet-Based Distance Learning Master's Program
Flanagan 105
Greenville, NC 27858-4353
919-328-4861
800-398-9275
E-mail: itduvall@homer.sit.ecu.edu (J.B. Duvall, Director)
URL: http://www.sit.ecu.edu/trp/home.htm

Campus Visits

None

Admission

Applicants must possess a bachelor's degree from a regionally accredited institution in technology, industrial technology, engineering, manufacturing, communications, or a related discipline. Applicants must have access to the Internet and will be required to send and receive E-mail, conduct Web searches, and use a variety of Internet tools. Students with a minimum of three years of career experience in technology may choose to pursue the Portfolio Option. This option requires successful completion of twelve courses, and a portfolio of experiences. Students without three years of work experience may pursue the Thesis or Practicum Options. An undergraduate GPA of at least 2.5 is required in addition to satisfactory performance on the GRE.

Programs

30–36 credits

Master of Science in Industrial Technology/Concentration in Manufacturing
Master of Science in Industrial Technology/Concentration in Digital Communication
   Technology

Tuition & Fees

Basic Tuition: $120 per credit
Master's Tuition: $3,600–$4,320
Financial Aid: Veteran's benefits, DANTES military benefits

Notes

East Carolina University, a part of the University of North Carolina, is a government-funded university supporting eight professional schools and a student body of more than 17,000. Distance programs are provided through the Division of Continuing Studies. The online M.S. degree program in Industrial Technology provides twelve-week classes in the Fall, Spring, and Summer semesters. Each of these courses uses Internet tools such as E-mail, E-mail listservs, Internet Relay Chat, Internet Audio and Video, and Net Meeting for problem-solving and learning. Assignments are distributed and returned weekly, with periodic virtual class meetings online throughout the semester. Most students in the online program pursue the Portfolio (non-thesis) Option. Nine credits of course work may be completed while the student is on non-degree status.

EMBRY-RIDDLE AERONAUTICAL UNIVERSITY

Graduate Program Manager
Department of Independent Studies
600 South Clyde Morris Boulevard
Daytona, FL   32114-3900
904-226-6910
800-866-6271
E-mail: indstudy@cts.db.erau.edu
URL: http://www.ec.db.erau.edu

Campus Visits

None

Admission

Applicants should be aviation professionals who hold accredited bachelor degrees. All applicants must have a computer and modem for electronic course completion. Courses are delivered using asynchronous computer conferencing and E-mail lesson submissions. International and military-based learners are welcome. No special exams are required for admission.

Programs

36 credits

Master of Aeronautical Science/Aviation Aerospace Management Specialty
Master of Aeronautical Science/Operations Specialty

Tuition & Fees

Basic Tuition: $285 per credit
Master's Tuition: $10,300
Financial Aid: Military aid, veteran's aid, government loans

Note

Embry-Riddle is a private university established in 1926 to serve aviation professionals. Campuses are maintained in Daytona Beach, Florida, and Prescott, Arizona, as well as in Germany. Distance learning programs operate as extensions of on-campus offerings and were first offered in 1980. The distance program awards bachelor's and associate's degrees in aviation specialties and has been in operation for several years. The master's program is intended for professionals seeking to gain an advanced understanding of aviation management techniques. The graduate program requires the use of electronic conferencing and electronic mail through a forum on the commercial online service CompuServe. Tuition rates for independent study are significantly lower than those charged for on-campus learning. Videotapes of on-campus lectures are mailed to learners worldwide.

EMPIRE STATE COLLEGE—SUNY

State University of New York
External Master's
28 Union Avenue
Saratoga Springs, NY 12866-4390
518-587-2100, ext. 429
E-mail: mtozzi@sescva.esc.edu (Maria Tozzi)
URL: http://www.esc.edu/

Campus Visits

Four days are required on campus at the beginning and end of each semester, three times each year. Most learners reside in New York State or close to state boundaries.

Admission

Applicants should hold an accredited bachelor's degree.

Programs

36 credits
Master of Arts in Policy Studies/Business
Master of Arts in Policy Studies/Labor
Master of Arts in Policy Studies/Social Policy

36 credits
Master of Arts in Liberal Studies

Tuition & Fees

Basic Tuition: $213 per credit (New York); $351 per credit (others)
Master's Tuition: $7,668 (New York); $12,636 (others)
Financial Aid: Government loans, New York State aid

Notes

Empire State is the government-supported, adult, distance education division of the State of New York (SUNY) educational system. Empire has been offering master's and bachelor's degrees through distance means since the 1970s. Policy master's degrees are structured for learners who want to study how business and governmental policy intersect in corporations, government agencies, and nonprofits. The labor and policy major supports the study of unions, union issues, workers rights, management rights, labor arbitration, and related issues. The social policy major supports the sociological study of where and how policy intersects with the concerns of social and cultural groups such as women and other minorities. The Master of Liberal Studies degree supports the individualized, interdisciplinary design and study of any combination of subjects in the liberal arts or sciences. Popular primary study areas include, but are not limited to, art, economics, education, environmental issues, history, international relations, journalism, literature, media studies, political science, psychology, social science, sociology, women's studies, and writing. Learners should inquire directly about designing an interdisciplinary degree that meets their individual and career needs.

FIELDING INSTITUTE

Sylvia Williams, Director of Admissions
2112 Santa Barbara Street
Santa Barbara, CA   93105-3538
805-687-1099
800-340-1099
E-mail: admissions@fielding.edu
URL: http://www.fielding.edu

Campus Visits

An admissions workshop is required for degree seekers. A one-week session is held each winter in Santa Barbara and each summer at an East Coast location. Four-day research sessions are held at regional sites nationwide as learners progress through the degree.

Admission

Applicants must hold regionally accredited bachelor's. Doctoral applicants who enter without a master's must complete their master's en route. Clinical psychology majors are not admitted for master's study only. Programs are open to mid-career or career-changing professionals who have Internet access. Psychology applicants should have experience in clinical psychology and the ability to locate and complete local practicums and internships, and to attend local monthly meetings, which will be held on weekends. Applicants are judged primarily on academic research and career achievements.

Programs

10 courses
Certificate in Group Psychotherapy
Certificate in Neuropsychology
48 credits
Master of Arts in Organizational Design & Effectiveness
96 credits
Doctor of Educational Leadership & Change
Doctor of Philosophy in Clinical Psychology
Doctor of Philosophy in Human & Organization Development

Tuition & Fees

Basic Tuition:	$11,000 per year
Certificate Tuition:	Varies
Financial Aid:	Government loans, minority scholarships, veteran's benefits, Canadian loans

Notes

Fielding is a private graduate school founded in 1974 that specializes in distance-based studies in psychology and the applied human services for mid-career professionals. Human and organization degrees may be individualized to focus on many career areas, including, but not limited to, human resources, instructional technology, career change, women's issues, multiculturalism, public and social policy administration, health care administration, conflict resolution in corporations, higher education administration, social psychology, adult learning, and social welfare management. Learners must have a computer and modem to communicate over the Fielding Electronic Network (FEN). Clinical psychology graduates have been admitted to licensing exams in most states. The clinical program has been granted accreditation by the American Psychological Association (APA). Clinical psychology students take longer to complete degrees as a one-year supervised internship is required.

FLORIDA STATE UNIVERSITY

Master of Science/Information Studies
Master of Science /Library Science
School of Information Studies
Tallahassee, FL 32306-2100
850-644-8121
E-mail: grad@slis-two.lis.fsu.edu
URL http://www.fsu.edu/~lis

Campus Visits

FSU requires students to attend a three-day orientation prior to the fall semester. During this program students will take part in intensive instruction for accessing World Wide Web sites, submitting assignments, and corresponding with faculty. Distance education courses will be delivered via password-protected Internet web sites.

Admission

All applicants must meet the university's and the school's standards for admission and acceptance for the master's degree program. Applicants must possess a bachelor's degree from an accredited college/university, must provide evidence of a grade point average of 3.0 or above (A=4.0) for the last two years of the bachelor's degree (or a 3.0 for a master's degree from an accredited university), or a minimum score of 1000 on the combined verbal/quantitative portions of the GRE. A minimum TOEFL score of 550 is required for international students. The School of Information Studies has a "Fall Only" admission policy. Students must have a computer and Internet access in order to complete course work.

Programs

42 semester hours
Master of Science/Information Studies
42 semester hours
Master of Science/Library Studies

Tuition & Fees

Basic Tuition:	$590.00 per course (Florida); $1,506.17 per course (others)
Master's Tuition:	$8,260 (Florida); $21,086.38 (others)
Financial Aid:	Federal Stafford loans, Florida State aid/loans, Program scholarships, Professional association scholarships

Notes

Florida State University is a government-supported university, founded in 1857, and located in the state capital, Tallahassee. On-campus programs include a full array of undergraduate, graduate, and professional degree programs. The School of Information Studies is among the top ranked schools of library and information studies in the nation. It is accredited by the American Library Association. The Master of Science in Information Studies and in Library Science requires the completion of 15 credit hours of core course work plus 30 hours of elective courses. No thesis or comprehensive examination is required. Off-campus instruction is Web-based via the Internet. Students can access assignments and participate in online course discussions with their professors and classmates. FSU will accept a maximum of 6 semester hours transferred from other programs, upon approval of the student's academic advisor and the Dean of Information Studies.

FROSTBURG STATE UNIVERSITY

The Modern Humanities Institute
Summer Master's in Modern Humanities
Frostburg, MD 21532
301-687-4428
E-mail: n/a
URL: n/a

Campus Visits

Applicants attend month-long intensive study sessions during July and work to complete independent studies and readings at home the rest of the academic year.

Admission

A bachelor's degree is required for admission but the degree need not be in the humanities. An academic liberal arts background is desirable but not essential. For non-provisional admission a minimum GPA of 3.0 is required. International students who have taken the TOEFL are welcome.

Programs

30 credits
Master of Arts in Modern Humanities

Tuition & Fees

Basic Tuition: $168 per credit (Maryland); $195 per credit (others)
Master's Tuition: $5,040 (Maryland); $5,850 (others)
Financial Aid: Government loans, scholarships, Maryland State aid for residents

Notes

Frostburg State University, founded in 1898, is government supported. On-campus programs include an array of bachelor's and master's degrees. The modern humanities program offers a broad interdisciplinary exposure to all areas of the humanities including history, literature, and philosophy. The program focuses on the response of the major thinkers of the twentieth century to the ethical and moral problems of the twentieth century. Surface mail and phone contact are used to deliver course content. Degree seekers complete twenty-seven credits of courses and a final, three-credit research project. All learners complete nine credits in each of the three humanities—history, literature, and philosophy—then complete a final research project in one of the three areas. Transfer credits are not accepted in the distance learning program.

GARRETT-EVANGELICAL THEOLOGICAL SEMINARY

MCE Admissions
2121 Sheridan Avenue
Evanston, IL 60201
847-866-3945
800-736-4627
E-mail: seminary@nwu.edu
URL: n/a

Campus Visits

Two-week intensives must be attended on campus in June, July, and January each year.

Admission

The program is open to Christian Educators who have at least two years of experience in the ministry. Ministry service is required to complete the final master's internship.

Programs

84 quarter credits
Master in Christian Education in Ministry (MCE/M)

Tuition & Fees

Basic Tuition: $106 per quarter credit (average)
Master's Tuition: $8,835
Financial Aid: Grants and scholarships

Notes

Garrett-Evangelical is a private theological seminary founded in 1974 and affiliated with the United Methodist denomination. Its roots go back to the mid-1850s with the founding of the Garrett Biblical Institute. The seminary is both regionally accredited and accredited by the Association of Theological Schools of the United States and Canada. The seminary is located on the campus of Northwestern University. Interested applicants may visit the campus each spring or fall for Ministry Exploration Events.

GEORGE WASHINGTON UNIVERSITY—ELP

Graduate School of Education and Human Development
Executive Leadership Program
2134 G Street, NW, Suite 219
Washington, DC 20052
202-994-1607
800-4GW-SEHD
E-mail: seewhy@gwis2.circ.gwu.edu
URL: http://www.va.gwu.edu/wwwelp/

Campus Visits

Learners attend cohort study groups on campus one weekend each month for two and one-half years.

Admission

The program is open to professionals with at least five years of full-time, professional experience in human resources, education, and training or a closely related field. A regionally accredited master's degree is required for admission with a GPA of at least 3.3. Either the GRE or the MAT is required with scores in the 50th percentile. Computer networking capabilities and Internet access will facilitate cohort-based learning and communication between learners. A personal interview is required. The application deadline is February 1 each year.

Programs

69 credits post-master's
Doctor of Education in Executive Leadership

Tuition & Fees

Basic Tuition:	$575 per credit
Doctorate Tuition:	$39,675
Financial Aid:	Government loans, half-tuition fellowships, payment plans

Notes

George Washington University is a private college founded in 1821. On-campus programs include an array of bachelor's, master's, and doctorate degrees. Extension sites are maintained in Alexandria and Richmond/Hampton, Virginia, and Singapore (Asia-Pacific campus). George Washington University has been recognized by *U.S. News and World Report* as one of the top graduate schools in human development and education in the United States and awarded a Program Excellence Award by the American Society of Training and Development. The program promotes active learning by using a research/practice balance in the curriculum along with a team learning orientation. The human resources program sponsors faculty from seven disciplines: organizational development, total quality management, adult learning, group and organizational theory, organizational learning, and global/multicultural HRD. The Executive Leadership Doctoral program, leading to the Doctor or Education (Ed. D) focuses on six themes: leadership, the learning organization, research, the changing work environment, integration and application, and specialization. A different theme is studied each semester, culminating in a research dissertation dedicated to the specialization. Cohorts begin study each February and proceed through the program as study teams.

GEORGE WASHINGTON UNIVERSITY—JEC

c/o JEC College Connection
9697 East Mineral Avenue
P.O. Box 6612
Englewood, CO 80155-6612
800-777-MIND
E-mail: edcenter@jec.edu
URL: http://gwis.circ.gwu.edu/~etl

Campus Visits

None

Admission

The GRE or the Miller Analogy Test (MAT) and an accredited bachelor's degree with an undergraduate GPA of at least 2.75 are required for admission. All learners need access to a computer and modem and the Internet to complete electronic course work via E-mail and conferencing.

Programs

36 credits
Master of Arts in Educational Technology Leadership

Tuition & Fees

Basic Tuition: $725 per course
Master's Tuition: $8,700
Financial Aid: Government loans, payment plans

Notes

George Washington University is a private college, located in Washington, D.C., founded in 1821. JEC College Connection is a nonprofit cable broadcast and distance learning company. The master's degree is offered by George Washington, via College Connection's educational platforms, which include cable broadcasts, two-way voice mail, and electronic conferencing via the Internet. Learners without access to College Connection or Jones Knowledge TV Cable learning channel may rent videotapes of lecture broadcasts. The degree program focuses on the use of instructional technology in all environments and hold the distinction of being the first educational technology degree offered via distance means in the United States. Courses integrate new curricular experiences involving cooperative learning, project-based assesments, field-based inquiry, and product demonstrations, with traditional listen and read methods. A maximum of twelve semester credits may be transferred toward the master's degree if these credits were earned less than five years prior to degree candidacy. Individual courses are open to non-degree learners.

GEORGE WASHINGTON UNIVERSITY–PM

George Washington University
Distance Learning Program in Project Management
2101 F Street, NW
Building AL
Washington, D.C. 20052
202-994-6122
E-mail: pmprog@gwis2.circ.gwu.edu
URL: http://www.sbpm.gwu.edu/programs/mspm

Campus Visits

Students are required to attend a one-day Saturday orientation on the main campus at the beginning of the program. It is also likely that students will be required to attend an intensive one-week workshop in Washington, D.C., prior to the completion of the degree.

Admission

Applicants should possess a bachelor's degree from an accredited institution, with an undergraduate GPA of 3.0 or higher. Professional work experience, a statement of purpose, letters of reference, and a personal interview (via phone or in person) are required. The GMAT and GRE are not required, although good scores on these exams (560 or better for the GMAT, for example) could be helpful to the applicant. Applicants should be computer literate and have Internet access and a VCR. International applicants with TOEFL scores of 600 or above are welcome to apply.

Programs

36 credits
Master of Science Project Management

Tuition & Fees

Basic Tuition:	$655 per credit
Master's Tuition:	$23,400
Financial Aid:	Guaranteed student loans, veteran's benefits

Notes

George Washington University is a private, comprehensive university founded in 1821. The university launched its Master of Science in Project Management program on campus in 1996 and its distance learning option in January 1998. The project management track focuses on issues and techniques in areas as diverse as new product development, marketing, research and development, information systems, banking, and real estate development. The program is ideal for managers who want to enhance their ability to get a job done on time, within budget, and with high customer satisfaction. The program focuses on achieving a balance of project management practice and theory. The program provides applicants with excellent preparation for the Project Management Professional (PMP) certification exam. The program is flexible enough to allow students the opportunity to shape their courses to fit their career needs. Course materials are delivered via mailed videotapes of lectures and collaborative online learning.

GEORGIA INSTITUTE OF TECHNOLOGY

Center for Distance Learning
Atlanta, GA 30332-0385
404-894-8572
800-323-5973
E-mail: vbis@conted.gatech.edu
URL: http://www.conted.gatech.edu/distance

Campus Visits

None

Admission

Applicants must hold an accredited bachelor's degree but the bachelor's degree does not have to be in engineering or from an ABET-accredited engineering program. Certain undergraduate course prerequisites, such as calculus, may be necessary prior to program entry. Applicants with nonengineering academic backgrounds generally complete the Master of Science (MS) rather than the ABET-accredited Master of Science in Engineering (MSE) through Georgia. The GRE is recommended for applicants with a less-than-strong undergraduate record of achievement and may be required for some engineering programs.

Programs

24 quarter credits
Certificate in Computer Integrated Manufacturing Systems
Certificate in Test & Evaluation (Electrical Engineering)

50 quarter credits
Master of Science in Electrical & Computer Engineering/Computer Engineering
Master of Science in Electrical & Computer Engineering/Digital Signal Processing
Master of Science in Electrical & Computer Engineering/Power & Telecommunications
Master of Science in Environmental Engineering

45 quarter credits
Master of Science in Health Physics/Radiological Engineering

48 quarter credits
Master of Science in Industrial Engineering

45 quarter credits
Master of Science in Mechanical Engineering

Tuition & Fees

Basic Tuition:	$297 per quarter credit
Master's Tuition:	$13,365–$14,850
Certificate Tuition:	$7,128
Financial Aid:	Short-term loans, veteran's benefits

Notes

The Georgia Institute of Technology is a government-supported college founded in 1885. A variety of bachelor's, master's, and doctorate degrees are offered on campus. Distance learning programs, first offered in 1977, operate as extensions of on-campus offerings. Engineering distance learning courses are delivered nationwide via mailed videotapes of on-campus lectures. Thesis and non-thesis options exist. Individual courses are open to non-degree learners. Up to nine quarter credits of graded graduate work completed elsewhere may be transferred toward a Georgia master's degree based on departmental approval. While videotapes are usually sent to work sites and exams proctored by human resources officials, unemployed applicants can have videotapes sent to public libraries or other college sites. Asynchronous computer communications enhances learning and course communications. Limited video-based doctorate work may be completed by independent study.

◼ GODDARD COLLEGE

Off-Campus Programs
Graduate Admissions
Plainfield, VT 05667
802-454-8311
800-468-4888
E-mail: ellenc@earth.goddard.edu
URL: http://www.goddard.edu/

Campus Visits

Two week-long intensives are required on-campus each year to complete the degree. Additional short residencies may be required for teaching and counseling majors.

Admission

Goddard uses an open admissions policy and does not rely on the results of any traditional test or exam to determine a learner's eligibility for advanced study. A computer, modem, and Internet access will facilitate learning.

Programs

36 credits

Master of Arts/Business, Leadership & Community Organization
Master of Arts/Natural, Physical & Ecological Studies
Master of Arts/Psychology & Counseling
Master of Arts/Feminist Studies
Master of Arts/History & Social Inquiry
Master of Arts/Individualized
Master of Arts/Writing & Literature
Master of Arts/Visual Arts
Master of Arts/Media Studies & Communications
Master of Arts/Social Ecology (Environmental Studies)
Master of Arts/Teaching & Education

36–60 credits

Master of Arts in Psychology & Counseling

48 credits

Master of Fine Arts in Writing (Fiction or Nonfiction)

36–48 credits

Master of Arts in Teacher Education
Master of Arts in Teacher Education/School Guidance

Tuition & Fees

Basic Tuition:	$4,639 per semester
Master's Tuition:	$13,917–$23,195
Financial Aid:	Government loans, veteran's aid, Goddard grants, payment plans

Notes

Goddard is a private college founded in 1938 on the principles of alternative and transformative learning. Adult degree programs were launched on campus in 1963, and offered in distance mode shortly thereafter. Within the individualized master's degree option, Goddard encourages applicants to design degrees in any non-technical area of interest to them. (Goddard cannot support purely technical studies in areas such as engineering.) Recent graduates have self-designed programs that focus on the following: entrepreneurship, software design, the political uses of advertising, computer systems in small business, adult learning, nonprofit leadership and training, building a cooperative market community, peace studies, environmental policy and pollution, video and film making, mental health and the immune system, socially responsible journalism, rural health education, and the history of Victorian social novels. The Master's in Social Ecology allows learners to study the relationship of human beings to the planet they inhabit and how governmental and corporate policy affects the biosphere. Education degrees can be designed to qualify applicants for K-12 public school teacher certification in Vermont and other states. Teacher certification areas may include but not be limited to art education, early childhood, elementary, expressive arts in education, secondary English, secondary social studies, secondary math, secondary science, and school guidance counseling. Teaching practicums, completed at a school near one's residence, are commonly required for educational certification. Counseling degrees may meet professional licensing requirements in several states. Counseling majors seeking to meet certification needs may plan to complete the longer five semester or sixty-credit master's course of study, which may include a supervised counseling internship. The Master of Fine Arts programs supports majors in poetry, prose, essay, plays, and nonfiction. MFA learners are required to do a one-semester, supervised teaching practicum in writing. No letter grades are awarded. Goddard records all learning on a pass/fail basis only. A maximum of one semester or twelve credits may be considered to transfer toward a master's degree. Distance learners may occasionally use E-mail, the Internet, and a computer messaging system to correspond with classmates and faculty.

GOUCHER COLLEGE

Center for Graduate and Continuing Studies
Master of Arts in Historic Preservation
Limited Residency Program
1021 Dulaney Valley Road
Baltimore, MD 21204-2794
410-337-6200
800-607-4646
E-mail: center@goucher.edu
URL: http://www.goucher.edu/announce/mahp.html

Campus Visits

A two-week summer residency is required to begin studies. Students are required to attend a one- to two-week summer residency each year thereafter. The final residency will include a defense of the required thesis.

Admission

The program is open to learners with accredited bachelor's degrees who have at least two years post-baccalaureate work experience. The GRE is optional. Students must be able to secure and complete preservation field work in their local communities as the degree progresses and should have access to the Internet or electronic mail. Most courses will be offered with some online components.

Programs

36 semester credits
Master of Arts in Historic Preservation

Tuition & Fees

Basic Tuition:	$1,350 per course; $500 exam fee; $2,000 thesis fee
Master's Tuition:	$14,650
Financial Aid:	Government loans, veteran's benefits

Notes

Goucher College is a private liberal arts college founded in 1885. The Master of Arts in Historic Preservation program enrolled its first distance learning class in 1995. The program meets the guidelines of the National Council of Preservation Education for instruction in historic preservation. The program is designed for those interested in preservation studies. Courses will be delivered using surface mail, teleconferencing, and the Internet. After completion of required core courses, students may tailor their studies and thesis to meet individual preservation goals. Up to seven credits of graduate course work completed in an accredited institution in the last five years may be reviewed for transfer. A $100 fee is assessed for each transfer course.

GOUCHER COLLEGE—MFA

Center for Graduate and Continuing Studies
Master of Fine Arts in Creative Nonfiction
Limited Residency Program
1021 Dulaney Valley Road
Baltimore, MD 21204-2794
410-337-6200
800-697-4646
E-mail: center@goucher.edu
URL: http://www.goucher.edu/~mfa/program/

Campus Visits

A two-week summer residency is required to begin studies. Students are required to attend two-week summer residencies each year thereafter.

Admission

The program is open to those with accredited bachelor's degrees. The GRE is optional. Creative nonfiction students must be able to secure and complete a literary internship as the degree progresses. All students need Internet access.

Programs

4 semesters
Master of Fine Arts in Creative Nonfiction
40 credits
Master of Arts, Arts Administration

Tuition & Fees

Basic Tuition:	$4,650 per semester; $485 per credit
Master's Tuition:	$18,600–$19,400
Financial Aid:	Government loans, veteran's benefits

Notes

Goucher College is a private liberal arts college founded in 1885. The Master of Fine Arts in Creative Nonfiction enrolled its first student in August 1997. The program is designed for those interested in creative nonfiction subgenres such as the personal essay, memoir, magazine writing, and literary journalism. The arts administration program is designed for those in all areas of arts management and requires a final major paper that evolves from a required internship. Students and faculty communicate using surface mail, teleconferencing, and the Internet. $650 is charged for room and board for the required summer residencies.

GRACELAND COLLEGE

Outreach MSN Program
Division of Nursing
221 West Lexington, Suite 110
Independence, MO 64050
904-226-6910
800-537-6276
E-mail: MSN@GC-Outreach.com
URL: http://www.GC-Outreach.com

Campus Visits

Two to three nursing practicum residencies of two to three weeks each must be attended on campus in Independence, Missouri, to earn the MSN degree.

Admission

Degree-seeking applicants must hold bachelor's from NLN-accredited schools of nursing, be licensed as Registered Nurses (RNs), and have had at least two years of career nursing experience in the last five years. The GRE is required if the applicant's undergraduate GPA is under 3.0. The expected GRE minimum score is 800 or higher on the combined verbal and quantitative sections.

Programs

41–47 credits
Master of Science in Nursing/Clinical Nurse Specialist/Family Nursing
Master of Science in Nursing/Family Nurse Practitioner
Master of Science in Nursing/Nurse Administrator

24–27 credits
Post-master's Certificate/Family Nurse Practitioner

Tuition & Fees

Basic Tuition:	$320–$398 per credit
Certificate Tuition:	$7,680–$8,640
Master's Tuition:	$13,120–$15,040
Financial Aid:	Government loans

Note

Graceland College is a private institution founded in 1895 and affiliated with the Reorganized Church of Jesus Christ of Latter Day Saints (RLDS), headquartered in Independence, Missouri. Graceland's Division of Nursing was organized in 1969 and has offered a low-residency distance Bachelor of Science in Nursing (BSN) since 1987. The Nursing program is accredited by the National League of Nursing (NLN). Applicants from all fifty states have enrolled in Graceland's low-residency nursing programs. Courses are delivered via directed independent study including a videotape and toll-free faculty consultation as academic support. Learners pair with college-approved preceptors in their home communities to complete field-based nursing practicums. Non-degree learners may register for and complete an independent study course in pharmacotherapeutics without holding RN licenses or submitting other documents. Up to ten credits earned at another accredited graduate school may be considered for transfer toward the nursing master's degree.

GRADUATE SCHOOL OF AMERICA

Admissions
330 2nd Avenue South, Suite 550
Minneapolis, MN 55401
612-339-8650
800-987-1133
E-mail: tgsainfo@tgasa.edu
URL: http://www.tgsa.com

Campus Visits

All applicants attend a summer orientation residency. Master's candidates attend at least one additional weekend seminar per year. Doctoral candidates attend at least three additional weekend seminars during their first two years of study, and one seminar during each additional year of study.

Admission

Master's applicants must hold accredited bachelor's. Doctoral applicants must hold master's degrees. Because learners design much of their own study plan, applicants should have professional experience in the area they wish to study. Applicants should have access to a computer and modem. Electronic conferencing methods are used to communicate with faculty and other learners. The orientation includes an introduction to using the Internet and E-mail.

Programs

48 quarter credits
Master of Science in Education
Master of Science in Education/Adult Learning
Master of Science in Education/Distance Education
Master of Science in Education/Instructional Design
Master of Education/Educational Administration
Master of Science in Human Services
Master of Science in Interdisciplinary Studies
Master of Science in Organization & Management
72 quarter credits post-master's
120 quarter credits
Doctor of Philosophy in Education
Doctor of Philosophy in Human Services
Doctor of Philosophy in Interdisciplinary Studies
Doctor of Philosophy in Organization & Management

Tuition & Fees

Basic Tuition:	$795 per course (online)
	$1,995 per quarter (Master's); $2,445 per quarter (Doctorate)
Master's Tuition:	$7,980 (4-quarter minimum)
Doctorate Tuition:	$19,560 (8-quarter minimum)
Financial Aid:	Payment plans, veteran's benefits, institutional grants/student loans available to all learners through Minnesota Higher Education Service Office (SELF loans)

Notes

The Graduate School of America is a private proprietary university founded in the early 1990s specifically to serve as a low-residency, field-based study program for self-directed adults seeking to integrate advanced study with their professional lives. In 1997, the Graduate School achieved regional accreditation status with the North Central

Association of Colleges and Schools. This initial accreditation is valid for five years. After completing the required core foundation courses in any one of four broad theory areas—Education, Human Services, Interdisciplinary Studies, or Organization & Management—learners design their studies to concentrate on a specific sub-area of interest to them. For example, an education major might study instructional systems design, or wilderness education, or health education. A human services major might study counseling, criminal justice, sociology, or gerontology in more depth. An organization and management major might study entrepreneurship, technology management, marketing, or training in more depth. The interdisciplinary studies program allows learners to combine any two subjects to create highly personal study plans. Interdisciplinary degrees may focus on, but are not limited to, communication, creative arts, future studies, gender studies, health ethics and care, literary criticism, multicultural studies, political science and policy change, peace studies, philosophical paradigms, spirituality and religion, technology and change, urban studies, women's studies, or men's studies. Learners are invited to inquire directly about areas of study that interest them. While technology and change, or technology management, or the philosophy of science may be studied, the Graduate School cannot support pure technical (e.g., engineering science) or lab science degrees. The master's program supports a non-thesis option. Applicants with a master's degree may transfer up to forty-eight quarter credits toward the doctorate. Up to twelve quarter credits may be transferred toward the forty-eight quarter credit master's degree. Regardless of transfer credit standing, master's candidates must complete a minimum of four quarters (one year) of study. Doctoral candidates must complete a minimum of eight quarters (two years) of study.

GRAMBLING STATE UNIVERSITY

College of Graduate Education
GSU Program
P.O. Box 4302
Grambling, LA 71245
318-274-6134
E-mail: wilsonct@vax0.gram.edu
URL: n/a

Campus Visits

Two consecutive summer sessions of six weeks each must be attended on campus in Grambling.

Admission

Applicants must be able to access a satellite downlink facility (KU Band) in their local community to receive the live broadcast lecture sections of each course. The Graduate Record Examination (GRE) is required for admission. For regular admission, a minimum GRE of 1000 (or 800 for provisional admission) is expected with a GPA of 3.0 on the last earned degree. A master's degree is generally required. Others may be admitted provisionally. International applicants are welcome with the TOEFL.

Programs

66 credits post-master's

Doctor of Education in Developmental Education/Curriculum and Instruction-Reading
Doctor of Education in Developmental Education/Higher Education Management
Doctor of Education in Developmental Education/Instructional Systems & Technology
Doctor of Education in Developmental Education/Student Development & Personnel Services

Tuition & Fees

Basic Tuition:	$282 per 3-credit hours (Louisiana); $1,218 per 6-credit hours (others)
Doctorate Tuition:	$6,204 (Louisiana); $13,398 (others)
Financial Aid:	Government loans, limited scholarships, graduate assistantships

Notes

Grambling State University is a government-supported college established in 1901. A variety of on-campus degree programs are offered. Distance courses are offered as an extension of on-campus programs. Grambling began broadcasting graduate-level education courses in 1990. All distance learning courses are delivered through satellite downlink with limited surface-mail interaction. Each course features nine videotaped lecture sessions, which are mailed to learners, and three live interactive satellite broadcasts. E-mail options exist for communication with some faculty. Individual courses are open to non-degree learners who can arrange for a satellite downlink site locally. A minimum of thirty-six semester credits of the sixty-six post-bachelor's doctoral minimum must be earned through formal courses with Grambling. At least eighteen of these thirty-six credits must be earned on campus, typically by attending two nine-credit summer sessions.

GRAND CANYON UNIVERSITY

Office of Distance Learning
3300 West Camelback Road
Phoenix, AZ 85017-1097
800-600-5019
E-mail: rgraham@grand-canyon.edu (Ron Graham, Director for Distance Learning)
URL: http://www.grand-canyon.edu

Campus Visits

None

Admission

The Commission on Institutions of Higher Education, North Central Association of Colleges and Schools (NCA), has approved the Grand Canyon Master of Arts in Teaching distance degree program for students in Arizona, California, Colorado, Nevada, New Mexico, and Utah. Students organize themselves into study teams of two to four members that meet weekly to review course videotapes and classroom assignments and to speak with faculty via a telephone conference. Applicants should hold a bachelor's degree from a regionally accredited college or university, with a minimum GPA of 2.8 in previous college work, and possess a valid teaching certificate. The university will accept qualified applicants with at least one year of verifiable teaching experience. Teachers with substitute or emergency credentials are not eligible for this degree program.

Programs

30 credits
Master of Arts in Teaching

Tuition & Fees

Basic Tuition:	$190 per credit
Degree Tuition:	$5,700
Financial Aid:	Federal Stafford loans, interest-free payment plans

Notes

Grand Canyon University is a private university founded in 1949. It serves a traditional on-campus population of almost 2,200 undergraduate and graduate students each year. The School of Education supports a state-approved teacher education program and offers both the bachelor's and master's degrees on campus. During the past fifteen years, the university has placed 92 percent of its education graduates in schools across the country. For the past five years, the university has been recognized by *U.S. News & World Report* in its annual rankings of best colleges. The Master of Arts in Teaching (MAT) distance learning program is conducted via videotape. In each videotaped course, nationally recognized educational experts present education-based theory. This theory is then translated into practical teaching strategies and demonstrated on video by teachers in actual classroom situations. In lieu of a research thesis, students complete a comprehensive portfolio called the "Capstone Project", which showcases their achievements in the program. Faculty facilitation and support is provided mainly through phone, fax, and E-mail.

GRAND RAPIDS BAPTIST SEMINARY

Graduate Seminary Admissions
1001 East Beltline Avenue, NE
Grand Rapids, MI 49505-5897
616-222-1422
800-697-1133
E-mail: semadm@cornerstone.edu
URL: http://www.cornerstone.edu/grbs

Campus Visits

Degree-seekers must attend two, two-week sessions on campus in January and June of each year.

Admission

The In-Service Master of Religious Education is intended for individuals currently engaged in ministry service wishing to earn their degrees while remaining in service to their congregations. Applicants should hold their bachelor's degree with a minimum GPA of 2.5, and at least three years of ministry service. The Doctor of Ministry degree requires earning the Master of Divinity or its equivalent, with a minimum 3.0 GPA in the course work, the completion of three years of full-time ministry experience while holding the master's degree, and current involvement as a professional in the ministry.

Programs

32 credits
Master of Religious Education/Christian Education
Master of Religious Education/Christian School Administration
Master of Religious Education/Missions
Master of Religious Education/Pastoral Studies

30 credits
Doctor of Ministry/Biblical Counseling
Doctor of Ministry/Cross-Cultural
Doctor of Ministry/Education Management
Doctor of Ministry/Pastoral Studies

Tuition & Fees

Basic Tuition: $243 per credit (Master's); $250 per credit (Doctorate)
Master's Tuition: $7,776
Doctorate Tuition: $7,500
Financial Aid: Baptist Seminary grants, Baptist seminary matching tuition grants, scholarships, Federal Stafford loans, emergency revolving loans, Bol armed forces chaplain loans, veteran's benefits

Notes

Grand Rapids Baptist Seminary is the graduate division of Cornerstone Baptist Educational Ministries, a private educational institute. Its degree-granting status was awarded by the state of Michigan in 1949. In addition to holding regional accreditation, Grand Rapids Seminary is a charter member of the Association of Approved Schools of the General Association of Regular Baptist Churches, as well as an Associate Member of the Association of Theological Schools. The In-Service Master's in Religious Education consists of six credits of English Bible, six credits of theology/doctrine, a twelve-credit ministry concentration, and eight hours of electives. A three-credit research project is built into the ministry concentration and is to be completed near the end of the degree program. The Doctor of Ministry is a professional continuing education degree program. Its purpose is to enable those actively involved in the church and para-church vocations to more carefully formulate a theology of ministry, and to further develop competence in the enactment of ministry. The program is also intended to enhance the cultural sensitivity and global awareness of those involved in professional ministry. The 30-credit degree consists of fifteen credits of core studies, a nine-credit concentration, and six hours of electives. Core studies include a two-credit integrative essay and a four-credit dissertation/research project that are to be competed near the end of the degree program. The school delivers the distance learning/extension programs primarily via mailed textbooks and audiocassettes of lectures. E-mail is also used to facilitate communication in certain cases.

HENLEY MANAGEMENT COLLEGE

Greenlands
Henley-on-Thames, Oxfordshire
United Kingdom RG9 3AU
01-49-157-1454
E-mail: mba@henleymc.ac.uk
URL: http://www.henleymc.ac.uk

Campus Visits

Attendance at the first three-day residential workshop is highly recommended.

Admission

Normal admission is based on the possession of a bachelor's degree or its equivalent. Because of the applied nature of the program, applicants should be employed or have access to an agency they can use to complete work-based learning projects. A minimum of three years of career experience is required, with five years preferred. Those not holding traditional academic credentials may enter the Diploma in Management program provided they are at least twenty-four years of age and have at least three years of management experience. Those who successfully complete the diploma, which are parts one and two of the MBA, may continue to complete the MBA proper. Senior managers without academic degrees are asked to submit scores on the GMAT in support of their application. Access to a computer, modem, and the Internet will facilitate learning through an interactive electronic classroom environment.

Programs

2 course modules
Diploma in Management
3 course modules
Master of Business Administration
Master of Business Administration/Project Management

Tuition & Fees

Basic Tuition:	2,000–3,750 British Pounds Sterling per module ($3,200–$6,000 US)
Diploma Tuition:	4,450 British Pounds Sterling ($7,120 US)
Master's Tuition:	8,500 British Pounds Sterling ($13,600 US)
Financial Aid:	None

Notes

The Henley Management College operates under Royal Charter, the equivalent of American regional accreditation. The distance learning MBA serves learners in over twenty countries worldwide and is offered as an extension of on-campus offerings. Learners move through three study stages, taking case study exams at the end of each stage, and completing a final dissertation to earn the Henley MBA. Learners have access to tutors as they self-study toward competency in each course module. A final dissertation of 15,000 words is required for the degree. Henley sponsors an interactive electronic classroom environment on the Internet. Lotus Notes is used to facilitate asynchronous electronic conferencing. The electronic classroom links learners and tutors, connects learners to the Henley libraries, and provides twenty-four-hour student support. Transfer credit requests will be considered. Course exemptions may be granted for those holding professional credentials gained through independent examination.

A conversion rate of 1 United States dollar to .60 British Pound Sterling is used. Conversion rates may vary.

HERIOT-WATT UNIVERSITY—EUN

c/o Electronic University Network
1977 Colestin Road
Hornbrook, CA 96044
541-482-5871
800-22-LEARN
E-mail: EUNLearn@aol.com
URL: http://www.wcc-eun.com

Campus Visits

None

Admission

Individuals eighteen years of age or older who believe they have adequate preparation to enter the program may do so. A bachelor's degree is not required to enter the program. Though a bachelor's is not required, the program assumes undergraduate-level knowledge in key business areas such as accounting, finance, and statistics.

Programs

36 credits
Master of Business Administration

Tuition & Fees

Basic Tuition: $820 per course (Self-study); $985 per course (Instructor-guided); $1,185 per course (Instructor-guided with software)

Master's Tuition: $7,380 (Self-study); $8,865 (Instructor-guided)

Financial Aid: Educational credit loans

Note

Heriot-Watt, a Scottish university, traces its origins to 1821, and has operated under British Royal Charter, the equivalent of American regional accreditation, since 1966. The MBA program is accredited by the British Association of MBAs (AMBA) and has been offered through distance means for several years. It is a self-paced program, consisting of nine courses. Like many European programs, the Heriot-Watt program is competency-based. Applicants study course modules, then take a proctored final comprehensive exam when ready. Exams are offered twice a year, in June and December. Applicants may purchase course modules and self-study for final exams on their own through a lower cost self-study option or register for instructor-guided courses, which give learners access to instructors who reside in the United States who will assist them in their studies. All applicants complete seven core courses, then complete two elective courses. The program is offered online in the United States via the Electronic University Network (EUN) on the Internet. Applicants wanting to take undergraduate-level preparatory study may do so online through the Electronic University Network. Applicants can choose to take courses with instructor guidance or enroll in a complete self-study option. Under the self-study option, learners study course modules on their own and take final comprehensive exams to earn the degree. Under the instructor-guided option, applicants may access electronic forums and receive tutoring from instructors who are based in the United States. A maximum of two courses may be challenged by exam or requested to be waived through petition. An exam fee of 55 British Pounds Sterling (approximately $88 U.S.) is charged for each course that is challenged. Individual courses are open to nondegree learners.

ICI University

International Graduate Study Centers
6300 North Belt Line Road
Irving, TX 75063
214-751-1111
800-444-0424
E-mail: alice@ici.edu
URL:http://www.ici.edu

Campus Visits

None

Admission

The program is open to those who hold accredited bachelor's degrees with a minimum 3.0 GPA. Undergraduate course prerequisites include at least twenty-four credits of Bible and theology work. Access to a computer and modem will facilitate learning but is not required. International learners are welcome if English fluency is demonstrated. Fluency may be demonstrated by submitting a written essay to the program committee. Study centers and mentors are located worldwide to facilitate mission teaching.

Programs

36 credits
Master of Arts in Biblical Studies/New Testament & Old Testement
Master of Arts in Minsterial Studies/ Education
Master of Arts in Minsterial Studies/Missions
Master of Arts in Ministerial/Leadership

Tuition & Fees

Basic Tuition: $126 per credit
Master's Tuition: $4,500
Financial Aid: Dantes military aid

Notes

ICI University is a private Christian college accredited by the Distance Education and Training Council to award degrees. ICI is owned and operated by the Division of Foreign Missions of the General Council of the Assemblies of God. ICI serves learners worldwide through a network of graduate learning centers dedicated to mission and teaching work. Course delivery occurs through surface mail and the Internet, using web-based and electronic outreach. All courses are mentor-directed. All degree candidates must complete a six-credit final thesis project. The university charges $5.00 to receive program catalog.

IDAHO STATE UNIVERSITY

College of Pharmacy—Nontraditional Doctorate
Campus Box 8356
Pocatello, ID 83209-8356
208-236-2935
E-mail: NTPD@pharmacy.isu.edu
URL: http://pharmacy.isu.edu

Campus Visits

An on-campus admissions interview is required. An on-campus comprehensive assessment practicum is required prior to beginning the final twenty-eight week clerkship.

Admission

Applicants must hold an accredited bachelor's degree in pharmacy and a valid U.S. pharmacy license. Twenty-eight weeks of supervised clerkship are required to complete the doctorate. A maximum of fifty students is admitted each year. Admissions preference is given to Idaho residents. Applicants should consider having access to a computer and modem to connect electronically with faculty and other learners. Currently it is not mandatory to have computer capabilities, but it may prove to be beneficial for some students.

Programs

58 credits
Doctor of Pharmacy

Tuition & Fees

Basic Tuition: $166 per credit (Idaho); $373 per credit (others)
Doctorate Tuition: $9,628 (Idaho); $21,634 (others)
Financial Aid: Select military employee benefits, Indian Health Service Employee benefits, Government loans.

Notes

Idaho State University, founded in 1901, is government supported. A variety of undergraduate, graduate, and professional study programs are offered on campus. The College of Pharmacy has offered studies on campus since 1918. The field-based, nontraditional Doctor of Pharmacy program is designed to let pharmacy practitioners continue their education while remaining in practice. The program has the full approval of the American Council on Pharmaceutical Education (ACPE). Courses may be used to satisfy continuing education requirements. All degree seekers complete thirty credits of didactic work and twenty-eight credits of clerkships. Course delivery occurs through mailed videotapes of on-campus lectures and the use of interactive computer conferencing.

INDIANA UNIVERSITY

Smith Research Center
2805 East Tenth Street, Suite 150
Bloomington, IN 47408-2698
800-759-4723
E-mail: disted@indiana.edu
URL: http://www.indiana.edu/~eric_rec/disted/menu.html

Campus Visits

None

Admission

The distance learning certificates are intended primarily for school teachers who hold accredited bachelor's degrees and want to undertake specialized, advanced study in educational research. A computer and modem may be required for electronic conferencing for some courses. International learners are welcome.

Programs

12 credits

Teacher/Researcher Certificate in Elementary Reading/Language Arts
Teacher/Researcher Certificate in Secondary Reading/English
Teacher/Researcher Certificate in Administration of Language Arts

Tuition & Fees

Basic Tuition:	$125.80 per credit
Certificate Tuition:	$1,509.60
Financial Aid:	None

Notes

Indiana University, founded in 1820, is government supported. A variety of undergraduate, graduate, and professional degrees are available on campus. Indiana University supports one of the oldest and largest distance learning programs in the United States. Associate and bachelor's degrees are also available through distance means. Some graduate education certificate courses will be available via E-mail and Internet access.

INDIANA UNIVERSITY—IUPUI

Indiana University—IUPUI
Adult Education Graduate Programs
620 Union Drive
Union Building, Room 503
Indianapolis, IN 46202
317-274-3472
E-mail: rjenniso@iupui.edu (Rosemary Jennison)
URL: http://www.indiana.edu/~scs/programs/adulted.html http://www.indiana.edu/~scs/programs/adulted.html

Campus Visits

The program is migrating to web-based, Internet delivery during the 1998–99 academic year. The school anticipates that students seeking master's degrees will be required to spend an intensive week of residential study each year at established regional sites. The doctoral program is still being developed, and the necessity of campus visits has yet to be determined.

Admission

Applicants should hold bachelor's or master's degrees with a minimum undergraduate GPA of 3.5, and a minimum GRE score of 1250. Applicants should also have experience in the field of adult education or training.

Programs

36 credits
Master of Education
60 credits post-master's (Approximate)
Doctorate of Adult Education

Tuition & Fees

Tuition Basic:	$150 per credit (Estimate)
Master's Tuition:	$5,400
Doctorate Tuition:	$9,000
Financial Aid:	Inquire directly

Notes

Indiana University is a government-supported university founded in 1820. Indiana University has offered the Master of Science in Adult Education on campus since 1946. Residential classes and site-based, regional broadcast classes are available on campus in Bloomington, Indiana, at IU East, at IU Fort Wayne, and in Indianapolis at the Indiana University—Purdue University Indianapolis (IUPUI) program site. In the 1998–99 academic year, the program will migrate towards an Internet and web-based platform, making it accessible to students worldwide. Classes will be delivered through printed media, videotapes, Internet chat and bulletin boards, E-mail, and electronic mailing lists. The program is theory-based and practice-oriented, and is appropriate to anyone who works with adults in a teaching/learning relationship. The master's degree requires the completion of 36 credits: 15–21 credits in major core courses; 3–6 credits in electives; 9–12 credits in a specific concentration (i.e., distance learning, organizational leadership, etc.); with 3–6 additional bridge credits. Inquire directly for information on the doctorate degree whose distance learning format is still under development.

INDIANA UNIVERSITY OF PENNSYLVANIA

Graduate Studies in Literature
111 Leonard Hall
Indiana, PA 15705-1094
412-357-2264
E-mail: mhayward@grove.iup.edu
URL: http://www.iup.edu/en/

Campus Visits

Summer sessions must be attended on campus, with independent study work completed the rest of the academic year. Some specialties at the master's level may not be completed entirely through summer sessions. Inquire directly about specific majors. The doctorate requires a minimum of two consecutive summer sessions spent on-campus with independent study completed the rest of the academic year.

Admission

Applicants to the doctorate program must hold a master's, with bachelor's in English or a related field, with an undergraduate GPA of at least 2.6. Applicants to master's study should hold a regionally accredited bachelor's degree with a GPA of at least 2.6. The teaching program does not encourage applications from learners not already employed as teachers of English or from learners who do not have past teaching experience. International applicants are welcome, with TOEFL scores at or above 500-530. Those pursuing teaching English as a second language should have higher TOEFL scores.

Programs

36–42 credits
Master of Arts in English/Generalist
Master of Arts in English/Literature
Master of Arts in English/Teaching English
Master of Arts in English/Teaching English to Speakers of Other Languages

30 credits post-master's
Doctorate in English Literature & Criticism

Tuition & Fees

Basic Tuition:	$164 per credit (Pennsylvania); $289 per credit (others)
Master's Tuition:	$5,900–$6,900 (Pennsylvania); $10,400–$12,100 (others)
Doctorate Tuition:	$5,000 (Pennsylvania); $8,700 (others)
Financial Aid:	Government loans, fellowships, minority graduate scholarships

Notes

Indiana University of Pennsylvania, founded in 1857, is government supported. The university has consistently been recognized by outside authorities as a low-cost, high-quality provider of education at the undergraduate and graduate level. The low-residency English programs operate as an extension of on-campus offerings. The English generalist specialty is recommended for those considering teaching in community college environments, future doctoral study, or a career in publishing or translation. The literature specialty accommodates intensive study in American or British literature. The teaching specialty is for school teachers who can complete in-service supervised teaching as a part of their degree. A teaching internship is required for those attempting teaching majors. A Master's in Literature or a related field is required to enter the doctorate program. While the Internet is not yet actively used for instruction, the English department is in the process of preparing hypertext information on the World Wide Web for their low-residency programs.

INDIANA WESLEYAN UNIVERSITY

Adult and Professional Studies Program
MBA Online Program
4406 South Harmon Street
Marion, IN 46953
800-621-8667
E-mail: graduate@indwes.edu
URL: http://www.indwes.edu/MBAOnline

Campus Visits

Degree seekers must attend two intensive course sessions on campus during the twenty-eight-month degree program. Each intensive course session lasts three days, from Thursday through Saturday to accommodate long-distance travelers.

Admission

Applicants should hold a bachelor's degree from a regionally accredited college, with a minimum GPA of 2.5 in previous college work. A minimum of three years of significant career experience is expected of all applicants. Applicants should have completed the appropriate undergraduate prerequisite courses in math, economics, finance, and accounting. Indiana Wesleyan offers undergraduate-level prerequisite course work online in math, accounting, finance, and economics for students needing it. All applicants must have a computer with a modem and Internet access, and a Windows '95 PC system with at least 16 megs of RAM and a 28.8 modem to access the electronic campus.

Programs

46 credits
Master of Business Administration

Tuition & Fees

Basic Tuition:	$345 per credit
Degree Tuition:	$15,870
Financial Aid:	Federal Stafford loans, payment plans

Notes

Indiana Wesleyan University is a private university that was founded in 1920. It serves a traditional on-campus population of more than 1,800 students each year and supports the largest MBA program enrollment of any college in the state of Indiana. The university launched adult and nontraditional programs in 1985, and currently serves more than 3,500 students. The MBA program is delivered online, using asynchronous conferencing, E-mail, live chat forums, and collaborative whiteboard software. All students receive an orientation on the use of the World Wide Web to access Indiana Wesleyan's online campus. In lieu of a research thesis, all students must complete a final applied management project.

INSTITUTE OF TRANSPERSONAL PSYCHOLOGY

Global Programs
Admissions
744 San Antonio Road
Palo Alto, CA 94303
415-493-4430
E-mail: itpinfo@netcom.com
URL: http://www.tmn.com/itp/index.html

Campus Visits

Applicants attend two brief residencies held at locations on the East and West Coasts of the United States.

Admission

There are no specific requirements for admission to certificate programs or individual certificate courses. Applicants to master's programs should hold a bachelor's with at least eight semester credits or twelve quarter credits in psychology or the social sciences with a GPA of 2.0 (C) or better for all upper-level work. International applicants are welcome.

Programs

27 quarter units
Certificate in Transpersonal Studies
Certificate in Creative Expression
Certificate in Spiritual Psychology
Certificate in Wellness Counseling
Certificate in Women's Spiritual Development

48–54 quarter units
Master of Arts in Transpersonal Studies
Master of Transpersonal Psychology

Tuition & Fees

Basic Tuition:	$774 (per course)
Certificate Tuition:	$6,966
Master's Tuition:	$12,630–$14,472
Financial Aid:	Government loans

Notes

The Institute of Transpersonal Psychology, founded in 1975, is a candidate for regional accreditation with the Western Association of Schools and Colleges (WASC). The Institute provides graduate programs in psychology and counseling. On-campus programs include certificates, master's programs, and a doctoral program. Curriculum originates from a transpersonal perspective, integrating the intellectual, emotional, spiritual, physical, community, and creative expression aspects of being human in one approach. The global or low-residency correspondence programs are not designed to meet clinical/counseling licensing requirements in any state. Curriculum is delivered via surface mail, phone, and an online computer network using faculty mentors to assist learners in their studies. Applicants with Internet access may participate through the Learning In Networked Knowing (LINK) electronic community on the World Wide Web.

INTERNATIONAL UNIVERSITY

9137 East Mineral Circle, Suite 140
P.O. Box 6512
Englewood, CO 80155-6512
800-777-MIND
E-mail: info@international.edu
URL: http://www.international.edu

Campus Visits

None

Admission

Applicants should possess a bachelor's degree earned from an accredited college or university, or the equivalent of the bachelor's degree. In addition, knowledge and skills in basic public speaking and writing must be demonstrated.

Programs

35 credits
Master of Arts in Business Communication
6–9 credits
Certificate in New Business Solutions Through Communicating Technology
Certificate in Leadership and Influence
Certificate in Management Skills with a Human Directive
Certificate in Cyber Marketing Using the Internet
Certificate in Team Strategies for the Effective Manager
Certificate in Advanced Public Relations for the Wired World

Tuition & Fees

Basic Tuition: $700 per 3-credit course; $465 per 2 credit course
Master's Tuition: $5,500 plus fees
Certificate Tuition: $1,395–$2,100
Financial Aid: Payment plans

Notes

International University is a new college, founded by Mind Extension University in the early 1990s, to provide direct educational programs to adult learners. International University has been accepted into candidacy for accreditation by the North Central Association of Colleges and Schools. IU uses the latest instructional technologies, including the Internet and E-mail, to deliver courses via the computer. Because IU has no geographical restrictions, instructors who are experts in their fields are recruited from institutions across the United States and throughout the world. Faculty members called "Content Experts" design the courses and set rigorous evaluation standards for students' performance. An additional group of experts, the Teaching Faculty, facilitate the courses and interact directly with students. Technical and instructional support services are provided throughout each course. A computer, modem, and Internet access are required. Courses are divided into eight-week terms. Each week a new module, with clearly defined learning outcomes, is to be completed. The curriculum is competency-based and includes an integration of real-life work issues.

IOWA STATE UNIVERSITY

Off-Campus Programs
Professional Agriculture
4 Curtiss Hall
Ames, IA 50011-1050
515-294-9666
800-747-4478
E-mail: agedsinfo@iastate.edu
URL: http://www.grad-college.iastate.edu

Campus Visits

Three-to-five short summer lab workshops are required. Selected courses may require attendance at site-based interactive broadcasts in Iowa.

Admission

Applicants should hold a regionally accredited bachelor's in agriculture or a closely related field. The program is for farm management or animal science professionals. International applicants are not generally admitted due to the lab and workshop residency requirements.

Programs

32 credits

Master of Agriculture in Professional Agriculture

Tuition & Fees

Basic Tuition:	$163 per credit
Master's Tuition:	$5,216
Financial Aid:	Iowa State aid for residents, Federal government aid

Notes

Iowa State is a government-supported college founded in 1858. A variety of undergraduate, graduate, and professional degrees are offered on campus. The university offers more than a hundred graduate programs and majors. Distance learning programs operate as extensions of on-campus offerings. The Professional Agriculture program requires completion of thirty-two semester credits with twenty-four credits in at least three of the five agricultural science departments. Four credits of workshops, including short labs and applied statistics, are required. Four credits of creative work replace the traditional theory thesis. Courses are delivered via videotape, surface mail, and interactively, via the Iowa Communications Network (ICN). Applicants residing outside Iowa should inquire about course availability if they are unable to attend site-based broadcasts. This is a professional program with no thesis option, not intended for Ph.D. preparation. Iowa also offers an off-campus bachelor's in agriculture with a low-residency requirement.

IOWA STATE UNIVERSITY—ENGINEERING

Engineering Distance Education
240 Engineering Annex,
Ames, IA 50011
515-294-7470
E-mail: n2ecj@iastate.edu (Edwin C. Jones)
URL: http://www.eng.iastate.edu/ede/homepage.html

Campus Visits

At least one campus visit will be required to present and defend the thesis. Additional visits may be required for some areas of study.

Admission

Applicants should hold the appropriate bachelor's degree in engineering or its equivalent from an accredited engineering program. Overseas learners are not generally admitted.

Programs

30 credits

Master of Engineering/Aerospace Engineering
Master of Engineering/Agricultural Engineering
Master of Engineering/Chemical Engineering
Master of Engineering/Engineering Mechanics
Master of Engineering/Systems Engineering
Master of Science in Engineering/Aerospace Engineering
Master of Science in Engineering/Agricultural Engineering
Master of Science in Engineering/Biomedical Engineering
Master of Science in Engineering/Ceramic Engineering
Master of Science in Engineering/Chemical Engineering
Master of Science in Engineering/Civil Engineering
Master of Science in Engineering/Computer Engineering
Master of Science in Engineering/Electrical Engineering
Master of Science in Engineering/Industrial Engineering
Master of Science in Engineering/Mechanical Engineering
Master of Science in Engineering/Metallurgy
Master of Science in Engineering/Operations Research

Tuition & Fees

Basic Tuition: $270 per credit (1997–98)
Master's Tuition: $8,100
Financial Aid: Veterans' benefits, payment plans, government loans

Notes

Iowa State University is a government-supported institution, chartered in 1858. It is a comprehensive public university, offering an array of undergraduate, graduate, and professional programs on-campus. Engineering faculty began offering professional engineering studies off-campus in 1913. The engineering distance learning program operates as an extension of on-campus offerings. Iowa State is a member of the National Technological University (NTU) and offers engineering courses and degrees through real-time delivery via fiber optic networks to sites in Iowa as well as site-free studies through mailed videotapes of broadcast programs. Distance learners receive regularly mailed videotapes of classroom lectures with accompanying classroom handouts. Corporations may arrange for site delivery of selected programs through Iowa State. A maximum of eight credits of any thirty-credit master's degree may be transferred in from another accredited college with the approval of the learner's program committee.

ISIM University

501 South Cherry Street
Admissions Office, Room 350
Denver, CO 80222
303-333-4224
800-441-ISIM
E-mail: admissions@isimu.edu
URL: http://www.isimu.edu

Campus Visits

None

Admission

An accredited bachelor's degree in any area is a normal prerequisite for admission, but the bachelor's requirement will be waived if the applicant has at least twenty years of career business experience. No special exams are required for admission.

Programs

36 credits
Master of Science in Information Management/Management
Master of Science in Information Management/Telecommunication Technologies
36 credits
Master of Business Administration

Tuition & Fees

Basic Tuition: $375 per credit; $1,125 per class
Master Tuition: $13,500
Financial Aid: Payment plans, private educational loans

Notes

ISIM University is a private graduate school, founded in 1987, and accredited by the Distance Education and Training Council as a degree-granting institute. Programs are offered in a computer-based, interactive, online format via an electronic classroom, as well as in a traditional print-based, self-study format. The school is a four-time winner of the "Best Higher Education Distance Learning Program" designation awarded by the U.S. Distance Learning Association in open review. Up to 9 credits may be earned based on challenge exams or career experience that is documented in a portfolio format. Up to 15 credits may be accepted in transfer toward the degree. Applicants can choose between a print-based, surface mail format or an Internet-based, asynchronous computer conferencing option. The online format utilizes an accelerated learning format. Courses may be completed in eight-week cycles. Degree seekers complete work-based final projects in lieu of a research thesis. The school also designs and delivers distance learning-based corporate training courses in information systems management, computers, and business and technology areas. Individual courses are open to non-degree learners.

JOHN F. KENNEDY UNIVERSITY

School of Management
1250 Arroyo Way
Walnut Creek, CA 94596
510-295-0600
E-mail: saiken@jfku.edu
URL: n/a

Campus Visits

A two-week campus session is required each summer.

Admission

Applicants to the certificate program must hold an accredited master's degree. Applicants to the master's program are required to complete undergraduate prerequisites in macroeconomics, personality and psychotherapy, and adulthood or aging studies. Incoming students are required to demonstrate the ability to write a coherent essay and must demonstrate this ability by passing the Kennedy English Proficiency Test (KEPET) or by completing an undergraduate business communications course. A supervised internship in career counseling is required for both programs. Applicants must secure internships at appropriate sites near their home communities.

Programs

26–32 quarter credits
Post-Master's Certificate in Career Development
60 quarter credits
Master of Arts in Career Development

Tuition & Fees

Basic Tuition:	$264 per quarter unit
Master's Tuition:	$15,840
Certificate Tuition:	$6,864–$8,448
Financial Aid:	Government loans, limited scholarships

Notes

John F. Kennedy is a private college founded in 1964. On-campus offerings include bachelor's, master's, and first professional degrees. The Career Development field-based, distance learning program is intended for anyone involved in career planning and counseling at the professional level, whether in corporations or through private practice. The curriculum is appropriate for counselors, therapists, human resource practitioners, and organizational experts seeking to advance or enhance their understanding of career counseling and development. Courses are delivered primarily through surface mail, with E-mail and Internet-assisted delivery under development. John F. Kennedy also sponsors an annual summer institute for career counseling professionals nationwide.

JOHNS HOPKINS UNIVERSITY

School of Hygiene & Public Health
Distance Learning Program
2013 East Monument Street
Baltimore, MD 21205
888-JHU-MPH1
E-mail: alentz@sph.jhu.edu (Andrew Lentz, Program Administrator)
URL: http://www.sph.jhu.edu/~distance/certificate/

Campus Visits

On-campus sessions are held for one- to two-week periods at least three times during the fifteen-month program.

Admission

The program is open to accomplished health practitioners who hold bachelor's degrees and can complete community-based practicums.

Programs

35 quarter credits

Certificate in Public Health/Health Systems Management & Evaluation
Certificate in Public Health/Health Policy Analysis & Planning
Certificate in Public Health/Community Health Promotion & Education
Certificate in Public Health/Health Information Management

Tuition & Fees

Basic Tuition: $453 per quarter credit
Certificate Tuition: $15,855
Financial Aid: Payment plans

Notes

Johns Hopkins is a private, comprehensive institution founded in 1876. On-campus programs include a variety of undergraduate, graduate, and professional programs. The Johns Hopkins School of Public Health is the oldest, largest, and most acclaimed School of Public Health in the United States. The distance certificate program, launched in the spring of 1997, uses full-time faculty and curriculum from the on-campus School of Public Health. Students complete the program with a practicum at a local workplace. Practicums allow participants to integrate theory with practice in data analysis, problem assessment, and policy analysis. Courses are delivered using a variety of distance learning technologies, including video and audiotapes, printed materials, E-mail, chat-boards, asynchronous online bulletin boards, and phone conferencing. Credits earned in the distance learning certificate program are fully transferable to the on-campus eighty quarter credit Master of Public Health degree.

JOHNSON BIBLE COLLEGE

Distance Learning Department—Graduate Studies
Box 777090
Knoxville, TN   37998
423-579-2290
800-669-7889
E-mail: jketchen@jbc.edu (John Ketchen)
URL: n/a

Campus Visits

Three required visits; some of the visits can be combined. First visit is for a three-day orientation in August. The second visit (after most credits are completed) is for project or thesis defense. A final one-day visit is required to take a comprehensive exam.

Admission

Learners without bachelor's from regionally accredited colleges may petition for admission. The Graduate Record Examination (GRE) is required for admission. International learners are welcome.

Programs

30–33 credits
Master of Arts in New Testament/Preaching
Master of Arts in New Testament/Research
Master of Arts in New Testament/Contract

Tuition & Fees

Basic Tuition:	$125 per credit
Master's Tuition:	$3,750–$4,125
Financial Aid:	Veteran's benefits

Notes

Johnson College is a private Christian institution founded in 1893, affiliated with the Christian Churches/Churches of Christ (Christian religion). Distance learning programs were first offered in 1988. Resident students may also take undergraduate programs offered on campus. Courses are delivered via mailed videotapes. Access to a computer, modem, and the Internet will facilitate studies. Students communicate with graduate faculty by E-mail, fax, and/or toll-free telephone. Degree studies focus on New Testament.

KANSAS STATE UNIVERSITY

Division of Continuing Education
Engineering Programs
131 College Court Building
Manhattan, KS 66506-6001
913-532-2562
800-432-8222
E-mail: estauff@dce.ksu.edu (Ellen Stauffer, Engineering Program Coordinator)
URL: http://www.dce.ksu.edu/dce

Campus Visits

None

Admission

Engineering science applicants should hold a bachelor's in engineering from an ABET-accredited school, or a bachelor's in a mathematical science, or a closely related discipline with a minimum 3.0 GPA in the last two years of undergraduate study. The GRE is required for candidates to engineering science programs who do not hold ABET-accredited engineering bachelor's. GRE quantitative scores should be at or above the 80th percentile. Candidates without ABET-accredited degrees may need to take qualifying undergraduate courses or demonstrate knowledge proficiency through work and career achievements. Software engineering applicants should have completed undergraduate courses in programming, data structures, algorithms, and software engineering or have the equivalent practical software engineering knowledge. A computer, modem, and Internet access are required for most programs.

Programs

30–36 credits
Master of Science in Chemical Engineering
Master of Science in Civil Engineering
Master of Science in Electrical Engineering
Master of Science in Manufacturing Systems Engineering
33 credits
Master of Software Engineering

Tuition & Fees

Basic Tuition:	$287 per credit
Master's Tuition:	$8,610–$10,332
Financial Aid:	Scholarships

Notes

Kansas State University is a government-supported college founded in 1863. On-campus offerings include a variety of undergraduate, graduate, and professional programs. Distance learning programs, launched in 1983, operate as extensions of on-campus offerings. Programs are delivered using multiple platforms. Delivery methods include mailed videotapes of on-campus lectures, weekly online web page assignments, weekly chat sessions on the Internet, and the use of phone and fax communications. Applicants in Kansas will also be able to access some courses through attendance at live, interactive video reception sites located throughout the state.

LAKEHEAD UNIVERSITY

Master of Forestry—Distance Education
Faculty of Forestry
Thunder Bay, Ontario
Canada P7B 5E1
807-343-8507
E-mail: pduinker@lakeheadu.ca (Peter Duinker, Chair, Forestry Grad. Studies Committee)
URL: http://www.lakeheadu.ca/~forwww/forestry.html

Campus Visits

Applicants must attend a campus residency of one term. Applicants may choose to attend one six-week term in May/June or July/August, or one longer twelve-week term in the fall or winter.

Admission

Applicants should hold a four-year, honors bachelor in forestry, with a minimum 3.0 (B) undergraduate GPA. Applicants with undergraduate degrees in disciplines allied to forestry, such as agriculture, biology, environmental studies, and geography, may be admitted, but asked first to take additional courses in forestry to deepen their background prior to taking graduate-level courses.

Programs

5 credits (4 full-course equivalents; 1 report)
Master of Forestry

Tuition & Fees

Basic Tuition:	$3,536 per full-course equivalent (International); $1,768 per full-course equivalent (Canadian)
Master's Tuition:	$8,840/yr. (International); $4,420/yr. (Canadian)
Financial Aid:	Scholarships, assistantships

Notes

Lakehead University is a provincially chartered university, and a member of the Association of Universities and Colleges of Canada (AUCC). The distance master's operates as an extension of on-campus offerings and is offered through the combined efforts of Lakehead and the University of Guelph, also a provincially chartered university. The Master of Forestry via Distance Education (MF-DE) focuses on land use and natural resources planning. The degree requires the completion of structured courses, a professional report that represents original scholarly work with a public, oral defense, and the completion of a graduate seminar where learners present a seminar dealing with their area of research and work. The graduate seminar is completed on campus in the residency phase. Courses are delivered using print, electronic, and audio/videotape means. Access to the Internet will facilitate communications.

LEICESTER UNIVERSITY

C/O International Business Education, Inc.
6921 Stockton Avenue
El Cerrito, CA 94530
510-528-3555
888-534-2378
E-mail: leicester@degree.net
URL: n/a

Campus Visits

No campus or site visits are required. An optional residential weekend is held each year in one or more North American cities.

Admission

Entry is open to applicants who hold an accredited American bachelor's degree or the international equivalent who have undergraduate GPAs of approximately 3.0 (B average) or higher on a 4.0 scale. Applicants with at least three years of relevant experience and credentials earned by exam will also be considered.

Programs

4 course modules, plus a dissertation
Master of Science/Training
Master of Science/Training & Human Resources

Tuition & Fees

Basic Tuition:	$4,800 per year
Master's Tuition:	$9,600
Financial Aid:	Federal Stafford loans, payment plans

Notes

Leicester University is a government-supported British Commonwealth university founded in 1918, located in the city of Leicester, England. It has awarded degrees under Royal Charter since 1957. It is accredited to award degrees in the United States by the Distance Education & Training Council (DETC). More than 12,000 students attend Leicester degree programs on campus, which include undergraduate, graduate, and doctoral programs, while several thousand more study through distance learning in Europe, Asia, and North America. International Business Education, Inc., is the private North American distributor and registration agent for the Leicester degree program. The Leicester (pronounced "Lester") program provides an international perspective on training and human resources. The Centre for Labour Studies at Leicester emphasizes an interdisciplinary perspective that draws from the social sciences, economics, management studies, and adult education. Annual tuition and fees include the cost of course binders, which contain self-study reading materials drawn from texts, academic journals, and other sources; and may include videos, audiocassettes, and other instructional support materials. The master's degree program consists of four modules: the Individual; the Organizational; the National Context; and the International Context. A final dissertation research paper ranging from forty to seventy pages is required. Academic study support is provided via phone, fax, and e-mail. Students may attend optional annual two-day meetings in selected cities in North America to gain additional support and meet with faculty, tutors, and fellow students. North American students may begin the degree program in either late April or October.

LESLEY COLLEGE

Graduate School of Arts & Social Sciences
Independent Study Degree Program
29 Everett Street
Cambridge, MA 02138-2790
617-349-8454
800-999-1959, ext. 8325
E-mail: jsapaugh@mail.lesley.edu
URL: http://www.lesley.edu

Campus Visits

An admissions interview is required but may be completed via telephone for learners who reside at a distance. A one-day colloquium is suggested to begin each fall semester. Degree-seekers meet four times on campus with their faculty teams over a three-year period.

Admission

Applicants must hold a bachelor's degree from a regionally accredited college but no special exams are required for admission. Learners should be self-directed and in charge of planning their own educational experience. International learners are welcome with TOEFL scores at or above 550.

Programs

36–39 credits
Post-Master's Certificate of Advanced Graduate Study in Independent Study (Individualized)
36 credits
Master of Arts in Independent Study (Individualized)
36 credits
Master of Education in Independent Study (Individualized)

Tuition & Fees

Basic Tuition:	$395 per credit; $14,220 per academic year
Certificate Tuition:	$14,220–$21,330
Master's Tuition:	$14,220–$21,330
Financial Aid:	Government loans

Notes

Lesley is a private, independent college founded in 1909. The Independent Study Degree Program (INDS) is the oldest graduate program offered at Lesley. The INDS program is designed for learners whose fields of study are nontraditional or interdisciplinary, or for those whose unique professional or personal situations make systematic independent degree design and study their preferred mode of education. Individualized study areas have included, but are not limited to, counseling/psychology, creative arts in learning, expressive therapies, education and training, health studies, history, management, multicultural issues, software engineering, and women's studies. Faculty teams, which include local mentors, evaluate individual undertakings. Practicums, readings, internships, and courses taken at local colleges may all be included in an individualized Lesley degree plan. Most programs of study are interdisciplinary or cut across traditional subject areas. Regardless of transfer credit standing, all degree-seekers must complete at least three semesters of full-time study or six semesters of half-time study. Lesley is experimenting with learning over computer networks. Some courses and tutorials may occur in an online team format in the future.

LIBERTY UNIVERSITY

School of Lifelong Learning
External Degree Program
P. O. Box 11803
Lynchburg, VA 24506-1803
804-582-2000
800-228-7354
E-mail: webmaster@liberty.edu
URL: http://www.liberty.edu

Campus Visits

A one-week summer residency is required each year. Additional short residencies may be required of counseling majors. International applicants are welcome with TOEFL scores at or above 500–600.

Admission

Applicants are expected to hold accredited bachelor's degrees. For a master's in counseling, the applicant's undergraduate GPA should be 3.0 or higher. For the master's in religion, the applicant's undergraduate GPA should be 2.0 or higher. Applicants without bachelor's degrees from regionally accredited colleges may petition for admission. Applicants to the counseling programs should have taken or be prepared to take—through Liberty's distance program—undergraduate prerequisites in statistics and basic psychology. Computer competency is expected of all learners.

Programs

36 credits
Master of Arts in Counseling
45 credits
Master of Arts in Religion
48 credits
Master of Arts in Professional Counseling
90 credits
Master of Divinity

Tuition & Fees

Basic Tuition:	$195 per credit
Master's Tuition:	$7,020–$17,550
Financial Aid:	Government loans, early payment discounts, spouse discounts, Virginia State aid for residents, payment plan, scholarships, DANTES military aid, veteran's benefits

Notes

Liberty University is a private Christian college founded in 1971 by the Reverend Jerry Falwell and affiliated with the Thomas Road Baptist Church. On-campus offerings include bachelor's, master's, and doctorate degrees. The external degree program operates as an extension of on-campus offerings and is primarily VHS video-based. The religion master's covers Christian religion following the tenets of the Baptist faith. Courses are delivered via mailed videotapes. Counseling majors must locate and complete supervised counseling internships in pastoral or community counseling clinical settings. Counseling degrees may not meet state-specific counselor licensing requirements in all states that require licensing for mental health practice. The Professional Counselor program is designed to meet state-specific counselor licensing regulations in some states.

LOMA LINDA UNIVERSITY

School of Public Health
Office of Extended Programs
Loma Linda, CA 92350
909-824-4595
800-854-5661
E-mail: mNewbold@sph.llu.edu
URL: http://www.llu.edu

Campus Visits

Learners complete five weeks of independent study, attend an intensive session of lecture and laboratory work at a given site for three-to-five days, then complete five more weeks of independent study each quarter of enrollment. Sites are maintained in Anchorage, Alaska; Phoenix, Arizona; Hinsdale, Illinois; Sacramento, California; Portland, Oregon; and Washington, D.C. Sites may vary over time. All majors may not be supported at all sites. International health majors are required to attend additional concentrated summer sessions in Loma Linda, California. A Summers Only program in Health Administration is designed to meet the needs of international applicants. The MPH degree may be completed over four years, during the month of August, on the Loma Linda, California campus.

Admission

The program is open to health professionals who hold accredited bachelor's degrees with a 3.0 or better GPA. A limited number of students whose background and experience show potential for success but whose GPA is less than 3.0 may be accepted on a provisional basis; they are required to submit GRE scores with their application. Applicants are expected to have relevant career experience or professional licenses. Field practicums may be required. Specific course prerequisites may apply. International learners are welcome with TOEFL scores of 550 or better.

Programs

51 quarter credits
Master of Public Health in Health Promotion and Education

49 quarter credits
Master of Public Health in Health Administration

55 quarter credits
Master of Public Health in International Health

Tuition & Fees

Basic Tuition:	$350 per quarter credit
Master's Tuition:	$17,150–$20,475
Financial Aid:	Government loans, public health traineeships, California State aid, Loma Linda scholarships, veteran's benefits, western states student aid, WHO international aid

Notes

The School of Public Health is one of six schools in Loma Linda University, a private health sciences university affiliated with the Seventh-Day Adventist Church. The School of Public Health is accredited by the Council on Education for Public Health. The MPH degree has been offered off-campus since 1973. Up to nine quarter units may be reviewed for transfer toward a Loma Linda master's degree. Pre-session assignments, textbooks, and syllabi are sent to students at least five weeks prior to the intensive session. Students complete assignments and take examinations during the five weeks following the intensive session. The courses are taught by regular full-time faculty members who go to the site for the intensive session. Faculty are also available via phone, fax, and E-mail.

LOYOLA INSTITUTE FOR MINISTRY EXTENSION

Loyola University New Orleans
6363 St. Charles Avenue, Box 67
New Orleans, LA 70118
504-865-3728
800-777-LIMX
E-mail: lim@beta.loyno.edu
URL: http://www.loyno.edu

Campus Visits

Applicants must study with one of forty-five local diocese study groups in the U.S., Canada, Scotland, England, and Geneva, Switzerland. Inquire directly for study group locations in your geographic area.

Admission

Laypersons and professionals interested in the Catholic religious order are invited to apply. Application for graduate study requires a bachelor's degree from an accredited college or university, official transcripts, minimum of 2.5 GPA, two letters of recommendation, and a statement of educational purpose.

Programs

36 credits
Master in Religious Education
Master in Pastoral Studies

Tuition & Fees

Basic Tuition: $500 per 3 credit course, $315 per 3 CEU course
Master's Tuition: $6,000
Financial Aid: None

Notes

Loyola University New Orleans is an independent Roman Catholic (Jesuit) college founded in 1870. On-campus programs include a variety of undergraduate, graduate, and professional degrees. The graduate distance learning program is open to laypersons as well as ministers.

MANKATO STATE UNIVERSITY

Department of Educational Leadership
MSU 52—Experiential Master's Program
P.O. Box 8400
Mankato, MN 56002-8400
507-389-1116
E-mail: n/a
URL: n/a

Campus Visits

One full quarter of study is required on campus to begin the degree. Applicants can attend their orientation quarter in Mankato, Minnesota.

Admission

Applicants should hold regionally accredited bachelor's degrees with minimum GPAs of 3.0 in the last two years of study. A GRE or MAT score is required if GPA is lower than 3.0.

Programs

51 quarter credits
Master of Science in Experiential Education

Tuition & Fees

Basic Tuition: $90.67 per quarter credit (Minnesota); $137.47 per quarter credit (others)
Master's Tuition: $4,624 (Minnesota); $7,011 (others)
Financial Aid: Government loans, assistantships

Notes

Mankato State University is a government-supported college founded in 1867. The experiential education program developed out of the Outward Bound program in 1971 and is the oldest such academic program in the United States. The program covers adventure education and is open to applicants who are strongly motivated to experiment with new ideas about education. Applicants study the use of outdoor and wilderness challenges such as rope and obstacle courses and survival training on the self-esteem issues of selected groups. Areas other than outdoor or wilderness education may be integrated into an individualized degree plan. Applicants usually work in some area that uses outdoor education or counseling techniques. Probation officers, counselors, substance abuse counselors, recreational and physical educational experts, school teachers, women's studies experts, vocational rehabilitation counselors, and health educators may find the program useful. Up to half the degree may be individualized so that applicants can study the effects of adventure education on any selected target group. Up to fifteen quarter credits may be transferred in toward the degree. Applicants from North Dakota, South Dakota, Wisconsin, and Manitoba, Canada, may pay the lower tuition rates.

MARYGROVE COLLEGE

Master of Arts in Teaching
Distance Learning Program
8425 West McNichols Road
Detroit, MI 48221-2599
313-862-8000, ext. 450
800-604-6088
E-mail: n/a
URL: n/a

Campus Visits

Applicants must attend an orientation session with the collegial study team located closest to them. The distance program is approved for delivery and teacher certification in Ohio, Pennsylvania, Michigan, and New Jersey. Applicants from other states should inquire directly about program availability.

Admission

The program is open to certified teachers (K-12) with access to a classroom to complete teaching practicums. Applicants must hold regionally accredited bachelor's degrees with minimum 3.0 undergraduate GPAs. Applicants with lower GPAs may qualify for probationary admission. Accepted applicants must be willing to study as a part of a local collegial study team. Study teams consist of from three to eight learners. The program is not open to learners residing abroad or to those who cannot access a study team. Results of the MAT must be submitted within the first semester of study. Applicants must have access to a VCR to play study tapes and a camcorder to tape required in-class assignments.

Programs

30 credits
Master in the Art of Teaching

Tuition & Fees

Basic Tuition:	$585 per 3-credit course
Master's Tuition:	$5,850
Financial Aid:	Federal Stafford loans

Notes

Marygrove is an independent, comprehensive institution affiliated with the Roman Catholic Church, founded in 1910. Distance programs operate as extensions of on-campus offerings. Distance learning courses are delivered via multiple means. Videotapes of lectures and teaching practicums form the main delivery mode. Each course consists of approximately fifteen video-based lessons. Each course also includes a printed text and study guide with lesson assignments. Many assignments require learners to undertake classroom applications. Assignments include videotape segments, audiotape responses, and written evaluations. All learners build a professional portfolio as they move through the program. The portfolio provides a cumulative record of the professional achievements of each learner as the program progresses. Learners work weekly in local study teams of from three to eight learners to enhance their understanding. Faculty mentors are accessible via phone conferencing to provide guidance and assessment for individuals and study teams. A maximum of six credits may be accepted in transfer toward the master's degree.

MARYWOOD COLLEGE

Get Your Master's With the Masters
Art Department
2300 Adams Avenue
Scranton, PA 18509
717-348-6278
800-338-4207
E-mail: n/a
URL: http://www.marywood.edu

Campus Visits

Depending on the degree program chosen, two-week summer sessions are required each summer for three to five summers. The Summer Sessions occur on Marywood's campus, where well-equipped studios, computer labs, research facilities, and the Learning Resources and Media Centers are available for student use. The fall and spring sessions are held in New York where students take advantage of the multiple visual, historical, and professional resources beneficial to the ad designer and illustrator.

Admission

The Marywood program admits professional art directors, designers, illustrators, and art teachers. Applicants should hold accredited bachelor's degrees in art, art education, or a qualifying related area. Teaching or other professional experience is an asset. A portfolio of professional work consisting of at least twenty slides is required for admission. The Miller Analogies Test may be required.

Programs

36 credits
Master of Arts in Studio Art/Illustration
Master of Arts in Studio Art/Advertising Design
60 credits
Master of Fine Arts/Visual Arts–Illustration, Ad Design

Tuition & Fees

Basic Tuition:	$400 per credit (MA), $410 per credit (MFA)
Master's Tuition:	$14,400 (MA), $24,600 (MFA)
Financial Aid:	Government loans, limited scholarships

Notes

Marywood is an independent, comprehensive Catholic college founded by the Servants of the Immaculate Heart of Mary in 1915. A variety of bachelor's, master's, and professional degrees are offered on-campus. On-campus design programs include many specialty art concentrations, including art therapy, art education, and other areas of studio art. Distance learning programs operate as extensions of on-campus offerings. The art faculty at Marywood include graduates and professionals from Parsons School of Design, the Pratt Institute, the Rhode Island School of Design, University of Southern Illinois, and Syracuse University. All degree seekers submit a final creative research project.

McGill University

Distance Education
Department of Occupational Health
Faculty of Medicine
1140 Pine Avenue West
Montreal, Quebec
Canada H3A 1A3
514-398-6989
E-mail: CZGT@MusicA.McGill.ca
URL: http://www.mcgill.ca/occh

Campus Visits

Once every term all learners meet on campus for a three-day practicum. These are a required part of the program. There are six practicals in all.

Admission

This program is open to medical doctors, nurses, and industrial hygienists. Applicants must hold a doctorate in medicine, a bachelor's degree in nursing or another discipline relevant to the field of study, such as chemistry, engineering, environmental sciences, physics, medicine, or other health science. They must have maintained a minimum 2.8 grade average on a 4.0 scale. Priority is given to candidates who have at least two years of experience in occupational health.

Programs

45 credits
Master of Science in Occupational Health Science

Tuition & Fees

Basic Tuition: $166.83 per course (Canadian); $745.83 per course (others)
$200 per course materials fee, $300 per practicum (all)
Master's Tuition: $6,302.45 (Canadian); $14,987.45 (others)
Financial Aid: Loans and bursaries are available for Canadian citizens

Notes

To earn a master's, learners must complete ten courses and an extended project report in occupational health. The program covers the study of industrial hygiene, occupational disease, toxicology, work physiology and ergonomics, epidemiology and biostatistics, chemical hazards, and the social and behavioral aspects of occupational health. Course waivers or equivalencies may be granted upon examination by the faculty. Learners may write their papers and exams in either English or French. The required on-campus practicals expose learners to clinical situations and laboratory exercises. Courses are delivered using print, videotapes, fax, and E-mail.

Tuition and fees are stated in Canadian dollars.

MICHIGAN TECHNOLOGICAL UNIVERSITY

Off-Campus Courses
Extended University Programs
1400 Townsend Drive
Houghton, MI 49931 1295
906-487-3170
800-405-4678
E-mail: disted@mtu.edu
URL: http://www.admin.mtu.edu/eup

Campus Visits

Master's degree candidates are required to spend one week of induction and one study week on campus per year, for a total of three weeks. Doctoral students spend an average of two weeks on campus each year for qualifying, comprehensive, and final doctoral dissertation defense examinations.

Admission

Master's degree candidates are required to have a bachelor of science degree (or its equivalent) in engineering or a related scientific discipline from an accredited university, have three years of engineering experience, submit letters of reference and a personal essay, and have the sponsoring approval of their work supervisor/manager. To be considered for the doctoral program, candidates must have a Master of Science in engineering or a closely allied field, and submit letters of reference and an application essay. Applicants must have a cumulative GPA of at least 3.5 in prior graduate-level course work. All candidates must receive approval for program participation from their supervisor at their place of employment.

Programs

52 quarter credits
Master of Engineering

30 quarter credits post-master's
Doctor of Philosophy in Mechanical Engineering/Engineering Mechanics

Tuition & Fees

Basic Tuition:	$250 per quarter credit
Master's Tuition:	Varies with individual corporate contract
Doctoral Tuition:	Varies with individual corporate contract
Financial Aid:	None

Notes

Michigan Technological University (MTU) is a government-supported university founded in 1885. MTU is among the nation's premier universities specializing in engineering and science education. Students from throughout the United States and the world pursue degrees in the sciences, engineering, forestry, business, liberal arts, social sciences, and two-year or four-year technology studies. On-campus programs serve more than 6,300 students each year, and 10 percent of these are graduate students. The off-campus programs focus on creating technical experts in areas of interest for their employers. The university suggests corporate or consortium sponsorship to maximize the cost effectiveness of the program. Students admitted into the master's program will be assigned an MTU graduate faculty advisor with expertise in their proposed project areas. The recommended course work will be tailored to individual student and project needs. Some course work required for the completion of the master's degree can be, and in many cases will be, taken at other universities, with the approval of the student's advisor. Another essential element of the MTU degree program is that students may complete a major portion of their degree requirements through an industry-sponsored, job-related project. Students may receive course credit for formal corporate/industrial education upon review and approval of the graduate faculty at MTU. To facilitate student-faculty interaction, the university anticipates that the MTU faculty advisor will spend from three to six months in residence at the student's company to advise and direct the doctoral student's research. The company will cover expenses associated with the advisor's travel, living accommodations, compensation, etc., with specific arrangements negotiated on a case-by-case basis. All doctoral students must maintain a continuing enrollment of at least six credits per quarter (course and/or research), three credits of which must be taken from MTU.

Montana State University—Bozeman

Distance Learning
Burns Telecommunications Center
EPS 120
P.O. Box 173860
Bozeman, MT 59717-3860
406-994-3580 (Science)
406-994-6768 (Mathematics)
E-mail: smrc@montana.edu (Science Education); burke@math.montana.edu (Mathematics)
URL: http://www.montana.edu/btc/sciedmasters.html (Science Education);
http://www.math.montana.edu/~dave/msme (Mathematics)

Campus Visits

Degree programs begin with on-campus summer sessions ranging from three to six weeks in length, which must be attended every year until the degree is earned. Distance learning course work is available online between these intensive summer sessions.

Admission

Applicants should hold a bachelor's degree in an area of science, science education, or mathematics with an undergraduate GPA of 3.0 or higher. The program requires the GRE general test with most successful applicants having combined minimum verbal and quantitative scores of 1000 or higher. The Mathematics Education degree requires a minimum GRE verbal score of 420. Science degree applicants should hold teacher certification to teach science in grades 6–8 or 9–12 with two years of successful science teaching experience in middle school, high school, or other appropriate educational settings, such as a museum or community college. The Mathematics Education degree is designed for middle school, high school, or junior college teachers of mathematics, and requires teacher certification and two years of successful classroom experience. Applicants who do not hold teacher certification will be considered on a case-by-case basis. A computer and Internet access is required to complete online course work.

Programs

30 credits

Master of Science in Science Education
Master of Science in Mathematics/Mathematics Education

Tuition & Fees

Basic Tuition:	$117.75 per credit (Montana); $286.30 (others)
Master's Tuition:	$3,532.50 (Montana); $8,489.00 (others)
Financial Aid:	Government loans, other aid may also apply

Notes

Montana State University—Bozeman is a government-supported university founded in 1893. A variety of undergraduate and graduate degree programs are offered on campus, and distance learning programs operate as extensions of on-campus offerings. The Science Education degree was developed by Montana State University faculty active in science, science education, and mathematics. The program is a unique interdisciplinary degree, approved by the Montana Board of Regents of Higher Education in May 1996, with offerings from the biology, chemistry and biochemistry, education, earth sciences, microbiology, plant sciences, and physics departments. Instructors have doctorate degrees in the subjects they teach. Science education majors complete fifteen credits in core math and science courses, and an additional fifteen credits in other science courses. Courses are delivered primarily via asynchronous, computer-mediated communication. Online courses may use printed manuals, textbooks, case studies, problems, computer databases, website visitations, and online evaluation activities, but there are no lectures.

Students communicate with each other and faculty via E-mail and group electronic message boards. Distance learning courses have an additional fee of approximately $30 per course. In addition to distance degree programs, Montana State University—Bozeman offers online courses for teachers through its National Science Foundation-funded National Teachers Enhancement Network (NTEN) project. NTEN is a national model network of residency-free, graduate-level, distance learning courses in the sciences offered via the Internet to secondary science teachers nationwide. Some of these courses are tuition-subsidized (offered for full graduate credit for low fees of approximately $50 per course) for school teachers. Further information on NTEN courses is available online at http://www.montana.edu/wwwxs, via E-mail from kboyce@montana.edu, or by contacting NTEN, Montana State University, 204 Culbertson Hall, P.O. Box 172200, Bozeman, MT 59717-2200, 406-994-6683.

NATIONAL-LOUIS UNIVERSITY

Adult Education Doctoral Program
Graduate Student Office
2840 Sheridan Road
Evanston, IL 60201
800-443-5522, ext. 5151
E-mail: thea@chicago1.nl.edu
URL: http://www.nl.edu/ace/

Campus Visits

A weekend on-campus assessment is required for admission and program planning. Two-week summer intensive sessions must be attended for three consecutive years. All degree seekers must attend on-campus seminars one weekend a month for eight months until the degree is completed.

Admission

Applicants should hold a master's degree in adult education or a closely related area and have at least three years of professional practice in adult education or training. Applicants must submit a professional or academic paper that demonstrates their ability to undertake advanced studies. An additional critical writing piece will be required prior to admission screening and attending the on-campus assessment interview. A computer, modem, and Internet access are required. No special exams are required for admission.

Programs

66 credits post-master's
Doctor of Education in Adult Education

Tuition & Fees

Basic Tuition: $333 per credit
Doctorate Tuition: $21,978
Financial Aid: Government loans

Notes

National-Louis is a private college founded in 1886. The university has offered extension and adult education programs nationwide for the last two decades. The low-residency Doctorate in Adult Education program accepted its first class the summer of 1996. The program is designed for practicing professionals in adult education. The degree process strives to integrate theory with practice to provide for investigations that are more relevant to practitioners. The program requires the use of the Internet and electronic mail conferencing with faculty and study cohorts.

NEW HAMPSHIRE COLLEGE

Community Economic Development Program
Graduate School of Business
2500 North River Road
Manchester, NH 03106-1045
603-644-3103
E-mail: woulett@minerva.nhc.edu (Woullard Lett, Administrator)
URL: http://merlin.nhc.edu/home.html

Campus Visits

Classes meet one three-day weekend per month. Two additional days are also required in January and September to complete mandatory workshops.

Admission

For non-provisional admission, applicants should hold an accredited bachelor's degree and have at least two years of experience in community economic development or a closely related field, such as urban or rural planning or renewal. Applicants who do not hold a bachelor's, but have at least five years of experience in community economic development, and current involvement in a community project, may petition for admission. Applicants should have access to a computer and modem to access CEDNET, the New Hampshire College electronic computer network.

Programs

36 credits
Master of Science in Community Economic Development

Tuition & Fees

Basic Tuition:	$2,000 per term
Master's Tuition:	$8,000
Financial Aid:	Government loans

Notes

New Hampshire College is a private college founded in 1932. The graduate school of business offers a variety of degrees on campus and is accredited by the Association of Collegiate Business Schools and Programs. The community economic development program, founded in 1982, operates as a low-residency degree program. All applicants complete twelve credits of common core courses and sixteen credits of applied work project. The program attracts practitioners in all areas of community and economic development, including cooperative managers, micro-enterprise financial and loan developers, public housing and land use officials, labor and community developers, housing advocates, public administration officials, social and community development workers, and those working in urban renewal. Individual courses are not generally open to non-degree learners. A maximum of six transfer credits or two courses are accepted. Learning occurs via classroom instruction and via asynchronous computer communications via the Internet.

New Jersey Institute of Technology

Continuing Professional Education
Guttenberg Information Technologies Center, Suite 5600
University Heights
Newark, NJ 17102-1982
201-596-3060
800-624-9850
E-mail: cpe@njit.edu
URL: http://www.njit.edu

Campus Visits

None

Admission

Applicants should possess bachelor's degrees from regionally accredited colleges with a minimum undergraduate GPA of 2.8. Applicants should own a computer and modem, have Internet access, and be comfortable with using electronic mail and conferencing for communications and learning.

Programs

4 courses (16 credits)
Certificate in Construction Management
Certificate in Continuous Process Improvement (Quality Control)
Certificate in Health Care Information Systems
Certificate in Object-Oriented Design (C++)
Certificate in Practice of Technical Communications
Certificate in Project Management
Certificate in Programming Environment Tools
Certificate in Telecommunications Networking

30 credits
Master of Science in Engineering Management
Master of Science in Information Systems

Tuition & Fees

Basic Tuition:	$346 per credit (NJ, active duty military)
	$479 per credit (others)
Certificate Tuition:	$5,536
Master's Tuition:	$10,380 (New Jersey, active duty military); $14,370 (others)
Financial Aid:	Full-time matriculated students only

Notes

The New Jersey Institute of Technology is a government-supported research college established in 1881. The college specializes in technological research and education. Distance programs are offered as extensions of on-campus offerings and were first offered in 1985. The construction and project management, and continuous process (quality control) certificates are designed primarily for engineers or those in technical management. The Health Care Information Systems program is for MIS managers in the health care industry. The technical communications program focuses on technical writing and editing. Computer scientists are the audience for the programming environment tools, object-oriented design, and telecommunications networking certificates. The master's degree is offered for engineers who are employed in or moving up toward managerial positions. Courses are delivered through mailed videotapes of on-campus lectures (tele-lectures) and asynchronous online electronic conferencing.

NEW YORK INSTITUTE OF TECHNOLOGY

Online MBA
Graduate Admissions
P. O. Box 9029
Central Islip, NY 11722-9029
516-348-3059
800-222-NYIT
E-mail: wlawrence@admin.nyit.edu (William Lawrence, MBA Director)
URL: http://sunp.nyit.edu/olc

Campus Visits

None

Admission

Applicants should hold a bachelor's degree in any area with an adequate GPA and a minimum score of 400 on the GMAT. Access to a computer, modem, and the Internet are required. The program is delivered online.

Programs

36–42 credits

Master of Business Administration/General Management
Master of Business Administration/Accounting
Master of Business Administration/Finance
Master of Business Administration/Marketing
Master of Business Administration/Management of Information Systems
Master of Business Administration/International Business
Master of Business Administration/Health Care Administrations

Tuition & Fees

Basic Tuition: $390 per credit
Master's Tuition: $14,040–$16,380
Financial Aid: Government loans; other aid may also apply

Notes

The New York Institute of Technology is a private, comprehensive university founded in 1955. A variety of undergraduate, graduate, and professional programs are offered on campus. The NYIT online campus, one of America's first Internet-based distance degree programs, began offering undergraduate degrees and certificates through distance learning in 1985. For more than two decades, the NYIT School of Management has prepared on-campus graduate business students for successful careers. The MBA online program launched in 1997 is designed to be a fully-integrated web-based program of study. The MBA requires completion of a minimum of thirty-six credits and a maximum of forty-two. An MBA with a specialized area of concentration will require completion of a longer program of study.

NEW YORK UNIVERSITY

The Virtual College
Office of Public Affairs and Student Services
School of Continuing Education
7 East 12th Street, 11th Floor
New York, NY 10003-4475
212-998-9112
E-mail: sce.virtual@nyu.edu
URL: http://www.sce.nyu.edu/virtual

Campus Visits

None

Admission

While an accredited bachelor's is required for admission it need not be a bachelor's degree in computers or information technologies. The program accommodates non-technical professionals. A computer, modem, and Internet access are required. Applicants must have access to an ISDN phone line to access the Virtual College and participate in asynchronous online digital classroom and lab exercises. The GMAT is required for master's degree applicants. International students are accepted with a minimum TOEFL score of 600.

Programs

16 credits
Advanced Professional Certificate in Information Technology
36 credits
Master of Science Management in Control and Systems

Tuition & Fees

Basic Tuition:	$525 per credit
Certificate Tuition:	$8,400
Master's Tuition	$18,900
Financial Aid:	New York and New Jersey student loans, payment plans

Notes

New York University is a private college founded in 1831. Distance programs operate as extensions of on-campus offerings, which include undergraduate, graduate, and professional degree programs. The Virtual College teleprogram was launched in 1992 through funding by the Alfred B. Sloan Foundation and operates via asynchronous computer conferencing and electronic text transmission. Lotus Notes groupware is used to support the Internet-based instructional delivery system. Lotus ScreenCam is used to deliver online audiographic tutorials. Computers and modems are required for access. The information technology program focuses on systems analysis and design, systems auditing, and advanced database management. No transfer credits are accepted. The program is intended for non-technical managers seeking to understand and implement better information systems throughout their work environment. New York University is a recognized provider of continuing education for accountants.

NORTH CAROLINA STATE UNIVERSITY—ENGINEERING

College of Engineering—Graduate Extension
University Box 7547
246 Page Hall
Raleigh, NC 27695-7547
919-515-5440
E-mail: jim_fikry@ncsu.edu (Dr. Jim Firky)
URL: http://www2.acs.ncsu.edu/grad/catalog.prg-egr.htm

Campus Visits

None

Admission

Applicants should hold an accredited engineering or science bachelor's with a GPA of at least 3.0 on a 4.0 scale. Applicants residing outside North Carolina may be eligible for admission but should inquire directly.

Programs

30 credits

Master of Engineering with a Concentration in Chemical Engineering
Master of Engineering with a Concentration in Civil Engineering
Master of Engineering with a Concentration in Computer Science
Master of Engineering with a Concentration in Electrical & Computer Engineering
Master of Engineering with a Concentration in Industrial Engineering
Master of Engineering with a Concentration in Materials Science & Engineering
Master of Engineering with a Concentration in Mechanical Engineering

Tuition & Fees

Basic Tuition:	$580 per course (multiple students at a single site)
	$700 per course (single student)
Master's Tuition:	$5,800 (multiple students at a single site)
	$7,000 (single student)
Financial Aid:	None

Notes

North Carolina State University is a land-grant university and a constituent of the University of North Carolina. This thirty-credit-hour Master of Engineering degree, completed by distance learners, is offered by the graduate school and similar to the ones offered on-campus. Distance learners receive weekly videotapes of campus lectures and go through the same process of homework and final examination, which must be administered by a recognized proctor. Interaction with faculty is by electronic mail or telephone. Some courses may require access to the Internet or the university computing facilities. The degree is non-thesis, and learners may take up to six credit hours from approved project work or independent studies under the supervision of a member of the graduate faculty. Up to six credit hours may be transferred in toward the degree. Courses are open to non-degree learners for professional development.

NORTH CAROLINA STATE UNIVERSITY—IT

Office of Instructional Telecommunications
Certificates in Training & Development
Campus Box 7401
Raleigh, NC 27695-7401
919-515-7730
E-mail: oit@ncsu.edu
URL: http://www2.ncsu.edu/oit

Campus Visits

None

Admission

A bachelor's from an accredited college is required for admission to certificate study but the bachelor's need not be in training or human resources. Some courses require completion of on-the-job projects or papers. Most applicants are employed in a human resources or a community college setting where they can complete applied projects and assignments. International applicants are admitted.

Programs

15 credits

Certificate in Training & Development/Community College Program Development
Certificate in Training & Development/Human Resources/Business Organizational Design

Tuition & Fees

Basic Tuition: $525 per course (North Carolina); $625 per course (others); $725 per course (international)
Certificate Tuition: $2,625 (North Carolina); $3,125 (others); $3,625 (international)
Financial Aid: None

Notes

North Carolina State University is a government-supported college founded in 1887. Campus programs include undergraduate, graduate, and professional studies in many areas. The Certificate in Training & Development is offered by the department of Adult and Community College Education. Certificate courses are available via cable broadcast for those residing in the North Carolina viewing area. Videotapes of on-campus lectures are mailed to others. Lessons may be submitted via E-mail or surface mail for most courses. Up to nine credits of the graduate distance certificate can later be applied to a North Carolina master's or doctorate in training. Learners can specialize studies by taking up to three courses in the areas of community college development or business organizational design.

NORTH CAROLINA STATE UNIVERSITY—TOTE

Textile Off-Campus Televised Education
College of Textiles
Box 8301
Raleigh, North Carolina 27695-8301
919-515-1532
E-mail: teresa_langley@ncsu.edu
URL: n/a

Campus Visits

None

Admission

A bachelor's degree from an accredited college is required for admission with a preferred undergraduate GPA of 3.0 or better. Applicants must have completed appropriate undergraduate work in math, physics, and chemistry. The general GRE is required for all degree seekers.

Programs

33 credits
Master of Textiles/Specialization in Textile Management & Technology
Master of Textiles/Specialization in Textile Chemistry
Master of Textiles/Specialization in Textile Engineering & Science

15 credits
Certificate in Textiles/Advanced Textile Chemistry
Certificate in Textiles/Apparel Production
Certificate in Textiles/Dyeing & Finishing
Certificate in Textiles/Fiber Science
Certificate in Textiles/Textile Administration
Certificate in Textiles/Textile Fibers & Polymers
Certificate in Textiles/Textile Fundamentals
Certificate in Textiles/Yarn Manufacturing

Tuition & Fees

Basic Tuition:	$500 per course (North Carolina); $600 per course (others)
Certificate Tuition:	$2,500 (North Carolina); $3,000 (others)
Master's Tuition:	$5,500 (North Carolina); $6,600 (others)
Financial Aid:	Government loans

Notes

North Carolina State is a government-supported college founded in 1887. Campus programs include undergraduate, graduate, and professional studies in many areas. The textiles program is delivered via mailed videotapes of on-campus lectures. Instructors may be contacted via E-mail and telephone to discuss course matters. Some courses may require access to lab or special textile or chemical facilities. Learners are responsible for making lab arrangements in their communities or at work if labs are needed. The distance program awards a non-thesis degree. All degree seekers must pass a final comprehensive oral exam. Individual courses are open to non-degree learners.

NOVA SOUTHEASTERN UNIVERSITY—FCAE

Fischler Center for the Advancement of Education
3301 College Avenue
Fort Lauderdale, FL 33314
954-262-8500
800-986-3223
E-mail: fcaeinfo@fcae.nova.edu
URL: http://www.fcae.nova.edu

Campus Visits

Applicants studying with established regional clusters (groups of twenty to thirty learners) typically attend Saturday classes once each month with their geographic clusters. Clusters are located in California, Arizona, Delaware, Florida, Texas, Illinois, Indiana, Missouri, Pennsylvania, Massachusetts, Virginia, Vermont, South Carolina, Wisconsin, and Calgary (Canada). Other clusters may be added. International learners, or those unable to attend regional clusters, may meet residency requirements through the National Cluster format. Those studying through the National Cluster meet on campus for three to five days each February and October and also attend eight-day summer study institutes on campus in either Florida or Arizona. Master's learners must attend at least one summer institute. Doctorate learners must attend two summer institutes.

Admission

A computer, modem, and access to the Internet are required of all learners. Applicants must have career experience and access to community work sites, as hands-on practicums are central to the degree process. All doctoral applicants must hold an appropriate master's degree with a preferred 3.0 GPA. Master's applicants must hold a regionally accredited bachelor's with a 2.5 GPA. GRE scores are required only for those entering doctorate study through the Greenwood, South Carolina, study cluster. No special exams are required for admission to the other clusters but foreign learners must have TOEFL scores of at least 550. A professional portfolio is generally required for admission.

Programs

36 credits
Master of Science in Instructional Technology and Distance Education

60–66 credits post-master's
Doctor of Education in Adult Education
Doctor of Education in Child & Youth Studies
Doctor of Education in Computing & Information Technology
Doctor of Education in Health Care Education
Doctor of Education in Higher Education
Doctor of Education in Instructional Technology and Distance Education
Doctor of Education in Vocational, Technical, Occupational Education

Tuition & Fees

Basic Tuition:	$7,100 per year; $473 per credit
Master's Tuition:	$12,384
Doctorate Tuition:	$21,300
Financial Aid:	Government loans, educational credit loans, veteran's benefits, limited fellowships

Notes

Nova Southeastern University is a private college founded in 1964 with significant expansion into field-based graduate and professional studies since the 1980s. On-campus degree programs are offered at the undergraduate, graduate, and professional levels. Field-based distance learning programs operate as extensions of on-campus offerings. Nova has pioneered online graduate and professional degree and credential programs since the 1980s. The Fischler Center for the Advancement of Education is dedicated to the continuing training and support of teachers, educators, corporate trainers, and educational administrators. Programs meet teacher certification and endorsement needs in Florida and may meet certification needs in other states. Learners communicate with faculty and each other through extensive use of electronic mail and asynchronous computer conferencing. A maximum of six doctoral-level credits earned in the last three years may be applied in transfer toward some, but not all, Nova graduate degrees. All Nova Doctor of Education (Ed.D.) programs require at least three years of post-master's study through Nova.

NOVA SOUTHEASTERN UNIVERSITY—MA

Fischler Center for the Advancement of Education
Master's Program in Life Span Care & Administration
3301 College Avenue
Fort Lauderdale, FL 33314
954-476-8955
800-986-3223, ext. 8955
E-mail: powelln@fcae.acast.nova.edu (Norman Powell, Program Dean)
URL: http://www.nova.edu/lsca

Campus Visits

Applicants must attend one eight-day (two weeks for those enrolled in the Applied Addiction Studies specialization) summer institute on campus to graduate.

Admission

Applicants must hold an appropriate regionally or provincially accredited bachelor's degree with a 2.5 minimum GPA and be practitioners or administrators with at least two years of career experience in their field of study. All degree specializations require the completion of a work-based practicum in which principles are put into practice. Access to a computer, modem, and the Internet is essential, as all degree specializations use electronic communications. International learners are welcome with TOEFL scores at 550.

Programs

40 credits
Masters in Life Span Care & Administration/Child & Youth Care Administration
Masters in Life Span Care & Administration/Early Childhood Education Administration
Masters in Life Span Care & Administration/Elder Care Administration
Masters in Life Span Care & Administration/Family Support Studies

53 credits
Masters in Life Span Care & Administration/Applied Addiction Studies

Tuition & Fees

Basic Tuition:	$240 per credit
Master's Tuition:	$9,600–$12,720
Financial Aid:	Government loans, private educational loans, veteran's benefits

Notes

Nova Southeastern University is a private college, founded in 1964, with significant expansion into field-based graduate studies since the 1980s. Field-based, distance learning programs operate as extensions of Nova's on-campus offerings. Learners communicate with faculty and each other through extensive use of E-mail and conferencing networks. A maximum of six credits (A or B grade) earned at a regionally accredited college in the last ten years may be applied in transfer toward a Nova master's degree.

NOVA SOUTHEASTERN UNIVERSITY—SBE

School of Business & Entrepreneurship
3100 SW Ninth Avenue
Ft. Lauderdale, FL 33315
954-475-7681
800-672-7223, ext. 7681
E-mail: sbeinfo@sbe.nova.edu
URL: http://www.sbe.nova.edu

Campus Visits

For the MBA, attendance is required at regular weekend classes at established sites. Twenty Florida sites exist. One site exists in each of the states of Alabama, Georgia, Iowa, Louisiana, South Carolina, Washington State, and Calgary, Canada, and Vancouver, B.C. Doctoral applicants attend a regional field-based class site one weekend each month, then attend week-long intensive institutes each year in Fort Lauderdale, Florida. International learners, or those who do not live near a regional study site, may attend nine week-long intensive seminars on campus in Florida, coupled with at least two short weekend seminars, to complete the four-year doctoral degree.

Admission

All MBA applicants should hold regionally accredited bachelor's degrees and have a computer with a modem. Qualifying bachelor's degrees may be in any area but applicants will need to complete the following undergraduate classes or their CLEP equivalents prior to entering MBA study: statistics, accounting, finance, economics, and marketing. The GMAT is required. For doctoral study, applicants must hold a regionally accredited master's degree, have five years of career management experience, and submit GMAT scores. Doctoral learners must submit proof that they have satisfied graduate-level (master's) foundation studies in quantitative methods, economics, accounting, and management. International applicants are welcome with TOEFL scores at 550.

Programs

Credits vary

Certificate in Accounting
Certificate in Finance
Certificate in Human Resources Management
Certificate in Health Services Administration
Certificate in International Business
Certificate in Management Information Systems
Certificate in Marketing
Certificate in Public Administration

41 credits

Master of Business Administration/Accounting
Master of Business Administration/Finance
Master of Business Administration/Human Resources Management
Master of Business Administration/Health Services Administration
Master of Business Administration/International Business
Master of Business Administration/Management Information Systems
Master of Business Administration/Marketing
Master of Business Administration/Public Administration

60 credits post-master's

Doctor of Business Administration/Accounting
Doctor of Business Administration/Finance
Doctor of Business Administration/Health Services
Doctor of Business Administration/Human Resources Management
Doctor of Business Administration/Information Technology Management
Doctor of Business Administration/International Business
Doctor of Business Administration/Marketing

60 credits post-master's

Doctor of Public Administration
Doctor of International Business Administration

Tuition & Fees

Basic Tuition:	$395 per credit (master's); $480 per credit (doctorate)
Master's Tuition:	$16,195
Doctorate Tuition:	$28,800
Financial Aid:	Government loans, veteran's benefits

Notes

Nova Southeastern is the largest private university in the state of Florida, founded in 1964, dedicated to adult study using field-based sites and extension campuses. Distance learning programs operate as extensions of on-campus offerings. Unlike many NSU programs, the Master's in Business Administration requires regular attendance at weekend classes. Learners must attend an established site to complete the accelerated weekend MBA or certificate programs. Individual master's courses are not available by independent study through distance learning. Up to six credits not used toward a graduate degree may be transferred toward the NSU MBA. Doctoral learners will use an online system to teleconference with faculty and other NSU learners. Up to two courses (eight credits) earned in another doctoral program may be transferred toward the NSU business doctorate.

NOVA SOUTHEASTERN UNIVERSITY—SCIS

School of Computer and Information Sciences
3100 SW Ninth Avenue
Fort Lauderdale, FL 33315
954-262-2000
800-986-2247, ext. 2000
E-mail: scisinfo@scis.nova.edu
URL: http://www.scis.nova.edu

Campus Visits

All applicants attend an on-campus orientation session to learn how to use the university's online systems. Applicants then study with regional clusters, typically attending Saturday classes once each month with their clusters. Clusters are located in California, Arizona, Florida, Texas, Illinois, Missouri, Pennsylvania, Massachusetts, Virginia, South Carolina, and Calgary (Canada). New clusters will be developed over time. International learners, or those unable to attend regional clusters, may meet residency requirements with week-long summer institute study in Florida. All applicants must attend at least two week-long summer institutes to graduate. Non-cluster-based or international learners will attend three- to six-week-long institutes on campus.

Admission

Applicants to these programs must have career experience as well as access to local work environments where practicums and hands-on field research may be completed. All master's applicants must hold a regionally accredited bachelor's with a minimum 2.5 GPA. All doctoral applicants must hold a regionally accredited master's in an appropriate field with a minimum 3.25 GPA. A computer, modem, and online access are required. Scores on the GRE or a professional portfolio that demonstrates competency in the intended area of study is required of all learners. International learners are welcome with TOEFL at or above 550.

Programs

36 credit (average)
Master of Science in Computing Technology in Education
Master of Science in Computer Science
Master of Science in Computer Information Systems
Master of Science in Management of Information Systems

60–68 credits post-master's
Doctor of Education in Computing Technology in Education
Doctor of Philosophy in Computer Information Systems
Doctor of Philosophy in Computer Science
Doctor of Philosophy in Computing Technology in Education
Doctor of Philosophy in Information Science (Library Information Systems)
Doctor of Philosophy in Information Systems

Tuition & Fees

Basic Tuition:	$7,450 per year (doctorate); $330 per credit (master's)
Master's Tuition:	$11,880
Doctorate Tuition:	$22,350
Financial Aid:	Government loans, veteran's benefits, payment plans, Florida teachers and residents may qualify for special tuition rates and plans

Notes

Nova Southeastern University is a private college, founded in 1964, with significant expansion into field-based graduate studies since the 1980s. On-campus programs include a variety of undergraduate, graduate, and professional degrees. Distance field-based programs operate as extensions of on-campus offerings. Nova has pioneered online graduate and professional education since 1985. Learners communicate with faculty and each area through extensive use of electronic mail and conferencing networks. Delivery technologies include real-time electronic classrooms, asynchronous electronic discussion boards, and electronic mail submission of assignments and papers for marking by cluster and distance advisors and faculty. Nova's courses in computing technology have been approved for teacher certification in computer science (K–12) by Florida's Bureau of Teacher Certification, and may be accepted by other teacher certification boards nationwide.

OHIO UNIVERSITY

College of Business
MBA Without Boundaries
Copeland Hall
Athens, OH 45701-2979
614-593-2073
E-mail: stinson@oak.cats.ohiou.edu (John Stinson)
URL: http://oumba.cob.ohiou.edu/~oumba/
http://oumba.cob.ohiou.edu/~oumba/

Campus Visits

There are three one-week residencies required at the beginning, middle, and end of the program. There are three weekend residencies between each of the week-long residencies. The program takes two years to complete.

Admission

Participants are expected to have a minimum of two to four years of professional experience. The program admits individuals who have outstanding potential for long-term success in the program and the business world. In selecting candidates, the program considers prior academic performance, past accomplishments as demonstrated through work experience, letters of recommendation, and responses to questions on the MBA Admission Questionnaire. Personal interviews, conducted face-to-face, by phone, or by teleconference, are required. Applicants must have Internet access.

Tuition & Fees

Basic Tuition:	$29,000 all-inclusive fee
Master's Tuition:	$29,000 all-inclusive fee
Financial Aid:	Student loans, veteran's benefits

Notes

Ohio University is a comprehensive, government-supported institution founded in 1804. Ohio University breaks down the boundaries that characterize traditional MBA programs by offering a program designed specifically for high-potential working individuals who aspire to be leaders in the corporate world. The program combines project-based action learning with the power of electronic, online collaboration. It combines the personal touch of residential experiences with the convenience of online education. The program allows individuals to continue working while integrating their work experience into their learning experience. The program consists of nine active learning units. Each unit, with the exception of the first (which is completed during the first week of residency), begins and ends during a residency. Between residencies, participants do research, collaborate with other members of their learning team, and receive faculty tutoring, all via the OUMBA Intranet. The nine learning unit projects are Orientation: Basic Business Concepts; Making, Selling, and Financing Activities; Developing Strategy; Global Competition and International Trade; The Individual Project; Entrepreneurial Activity–Commercializing an Invention; Improving Operations; Business and Public Policy; and The Individual Problem. Ohio University received a first place award for innovation and educational leadership from the American Assembly of Collegiate Schools of Business for the development of the project-based, action learning methodology used in the MBA Without Boundaries. The $29,000 fee includes tuition, room and board for campus residencies, and a laptop computer with all relevant software.

THE OPEN UNIVERSITY OF THE UNITED KINGDOM

Central Enquiry Service (ODE6A)
P.O. Box 200
Milton Keynes   MK7 6YZ
United Kingdom
44-19-0-865-3231
E-mail: general-enquiries@open.ac.uk (please quote ODE6A in your message)
URL: http://www-iet.open.ac.uk/iet/MA/MA-IN-ODE.html

Campus Visits

None, but attendance at an examination center in the applicant's own country is required at the end of each year.

Admission

Applicants should hold a bachelor's degree and have access to the web via a PC with a CD-ROM drive. The program is delivered world wide (except in Australia), in English, through the media of print, video and audio, supported by web-based resources, CD-ROMs, and electronic tutoring and conferencing.

Programs

1 year part-time
Postgraduate Certificate in Open and Distance Education
2 years part-time
Postgraduate Diploma in Open and Distance Education
3 years
Master of Arts in Open and Distance Education

Tuition & Fees

Basic Tuition: 2,300 British Pounds Sterling per year ($3,700 US)
Certificate Tuition: 4,500 British Pounds Sterling per year ($7,400 US), plus 100 British Pounds Sterling examination fee if outside UK; Diploma Tuition: plus 100 British Pounds Sterling examination fee if outside UK
Master's Tuition: 6,750 British Pounds Sterling ($11,000 US), plus 100 British Pounds Sterling examination fee if outside UK
Financial Aid: None, but most students can pay fees in installments

Notes

Over 200,000 people study each year with the Open University, which has produced 150,000 graduates since it started in 1969. The Open University is one of the most respected practitioners of distance learning worldwide, and through its Institute of Educational Technology offers postgraduate qualifications for those working in institutions using or developing open and distance education systems. The courses draw on the Institute's long experience of developing distance teaching and its top-rated research, and include a balance of knowledge and skills. A grounding in theory and practice is followed by study of information technology applications. Year 1: Theory and Practice; Teaching and Learning; Searching the Literature; Research Methods in Open and Distance Education. Year 2: Media in Open and Distance Education; Teaching and Learning with the Web; Teaching and Learning Online; Multimedia Teaching and Learning. Year 3: Student Learning and Support; Management; Guided Reading; a Project or Dissertation. Parts of Years 1 and 2 were produced with Deakin University and the University of South Australia.

A conversion rate of 1 United States dollar to .60 British Pound Sterling is used. Conversion rates may vary.

OTTAWA UNIVERSITY

Master of Arts in Human Resources
Electronic Classroom
10865 Grandview Drive, Suite 2000
Overland Park, KS 66210-1503
913-451-1431
E-mail: OttawaINFO@aol.com
URL: http://www.ott.edu/~oukc/main.html

Campus Visits

Learners visit the Kansas City center a maximum of three times each year, during the weekend that begins each new semester of study. Other course assignments are completed over the Internet.

Admission

While a regionally accredited bachelor's degree is required for admission it need not be a bachelor's in human resources or business. A minimum 3.0 GPA is expected. Applicants may be admitted provisionally with GPAs in the 2.5–2.9 range. A computer, modem, and Internet access are required for distance learners to participate in the electronic classroom.

Programs

36 credits
Master of Arts in Human Resources

Tuition & Fees

Basic Tuition: $258 per credit
Master's Tuition: $9,288
Financial Aid: Government loans, veteran's benefits, Kansas state aid for residents

Notes

Ottawa University is a private college affiliated with the American Baptist church, founded in 1865. Distance programs operate as extensions of adult center offerings, which include undergraduate and master's programs. Ottawa has been offering nonresidential studies for adult learners since 1974. The Electronic Classroom option includes a computer conferencing and electronic text transmission system. Graduate students concentrate their studies on a research project or an applied case study that is carried out in their place of employment. A maximum of nine credits may be transferred in toward an Ottawa master's degree.

▪ Pepperdine University

Master of Science in Organization Development
School of Business & Management
400 Corporate Pointe
Culver City, CA 90230
310-568-5598
E-mail: n/a
URL: n/a

Campus Visits

A personal interview is required to determine final admission to the program. Interviews may sometimes be completed via phone but international applicants (other than Canadians) are expected to come to Los Angeles to complete the interview. Eight eight-day study sessions and one five-day session must be completed on campus over a two-year period. Campus intensives may be completed in either Northern California (Monterey) or Southern California (Palm Springs).

Admission

The program is open to learners who hold regionally accredited bachelor's degrees, preferably in business or the social sciences. Applicants should have three to five years of career experience and be employed in a setting where they can complete the hands-on projects that are key to degree completion. Applicants should have completed at least one course in organizational diagnosis and have completed a laboratory style human interaction course. Applicants must complete and submit a personality profile and self-evaluation inventory. Scores are required on any one of three entrance exams, the GRE, GMAT, or MAT. International learners are welcome provided they have fluency in English.

Programs

40 quarter credits
Master of Science in Organization Development

Tuition & Fees

Basic Tuition:	$742 per quarter credit
Master's Tuition:	$29,680
Financial Aid:	Government loans

Notes

Pepperdine University is a private liberal arts college affiliated with the Church of Christ, founded in 1937. In the 1970s, the university expanded to offer on-campus graduate and professional study programs. Educational outreach and study centers are maintained in Los Angeles, the San Francisco Bay Area, and Europe. The master's in organization development program is appropriate for human resource officials, corporate consultants, company executives, or entrepreneurs. The required on-campus intensives focus on exercises designed to help build skills at corporate diagnosis and intervention. A capacity for team and group work is essential to program success. Class size is usually limited to thirty-two learners. Learners typically continue through the two-year program together. The final applied project focuses on workplace issues rather than theoretical concerns.

PEPPERDINE UNIVERSITY—EDTECH

Graduate School of Education & Psychology
Educational Technology Doctorate
400 Corporate Pointe
Culver City, CA 90230
310-568-2370
E-mail: edtech@pepperdine.edu
URL: http://gsep.pepperdine.edu/gsep/home.html

Campus Visits

The Educational Technology (EdTech) program combines face-to-face seminars with distance learning online formats. Face-to-face seminars are held primarily on the weekends, with all learners attending additional one-week face-to-face sessions at least three times per trimester. Seminars are held close to the Los Angeles airport to accommodate commuters. A personal interview is required in Culver City, California, to determine admission to the program.

Admission

The program is open to accomplished individuals in education and business who hold a regionally accredited master's degree. Applicants should have five years of career experience, preferably at the managerial level, and have extensive hands-on instructional technology experience. Scores are required on the GRE, the MAT, or GMAT. International students are welcome provided they can meet the intensive face-to-face seminar requirements through attendance at the Pepperdine Center in Culver City, near the Los Angeles airport.

Programs

43 quarter credits post-master's
Doctor of Education in Educational Technology

Tuition & Fees

Basic Tuition:	$630 per quarter credit
Doctoral Tuition:	$27,090
Financial Aid:	Government loans, payment plans, limited merit scholarships

Notes

Pepperdine University is a private liberal arts college affiliated with the Church of Christ, founded in 1937. In the 1970s, the university expanded to offer on-campus graduate and professional study programs. In the fall of 1996, Pepperdine launched a limited residency Doctor of Education in Educational Technology. The program uses E-mail, E-conferencing, newsgroups, MOOs, and web technology as a part of the off-campus learning experience. Up to seven units from recent doctoral study may be presented for transfer consideration. The program has a strong team learning and hands-on project orientation. Tuition includes a laptop computer, modem, and communications software. New cohorts are admitted each September. A dissertation is required.

▉ PRESCOTT COLLEGE

Master of Arts Program
220 Grove Avenue
Prescott, AZ 86301
520-445-8048
520-776-5137 (fax)
E-mail: mapmail@aztec.acu.edu
URL: http://aztec.asu.edu/prescott.col/

Campus Visits

All MAP students attend two weekend colloquia each semester in Prescott, Arizona. These weekends are intended to bring together students from diverse cultures and different areas of study to share their work and build a community of spirited and caring co-learners. Weekends include extended conferences between students and their graduate advisors, presentations by students of their work-in-progress, discipline-specific workshops by faculty, brainstorming and networking sessions, panel discussions, and interdisciplinary seminars that supplement and cross the lines of individual learning programs.

Admission

Because students individually design their own curricula, applicants must have sound knowledge of the areas they wish to study, and a clear and specific plan for the actual studies. No special exams are required for admission.

Programs

45–60 semester credits

Master of Arts/Counseling & Psychology
Master of Arts/Cultural & Regional Studies
Master of Arts/Education
Master of Arts/Environmental Studies
Master of Arts/Humanities (Creative Arts)
Master of Arts/Outdoor Education/Wilderness Leadership

Tuition & Fees

Basic Tuition:	$3,864 per semester
Master's Tuition:	$11,592–$15,456
Financial Aid:	Federal family educational loans

Notes

Prescott is a small, private liberal arts college founded in 1966. Undergraduate programs are offered on campus. The master's low-residency program began in 1992 and is designed for creative adult learners and mid-career professionals. Individualized interdisciplinary studies are designed by the students in the above main study areas. Former learners have designed degrees in specialized areas such as African-American studies, Latin studies, art and music therapy, gay and lesbian counseling, creative writing, multimedia and film studies, intergenerational therapy, bilingual education, special education, English as a second language, men's/women's studies, ecopsychology, theater, ecotourism, East-West spiritual studies, studio arts, literature, social and public policy, journalism, and humanistic or nonprofit management. Education and counseling degrees may be designed to incorporate state-specific certification requirements. The Master of Arts Program is not open to non-degree learners. All learners complete three components to earn their degree: theory, practicum or internship, and the thesis. The thesis may be descriptive, qualitative, or empirical. Most programs can be completed in three semesters but professional certification studies such as counseling psychology or teacher education may require longer to meet state-specific licensing requirements. Applicants without an undergraduate theory background in their chosen master's study area may also choose to complete four semesters of study.

PURDUE UNIVERSITY

School of Pharmacy
Continuing Education Division
1335 Heine Pharmacy Building
West Lafayette, IN 47907-1335
317-494-5757 (Certificate)
317-494-1361 (Doctorate)
E-mail: n/a
URL: n/a

Campus Visits

Certificate applicants are required to attend monthly four-hour discussion workshops for each learning module completed. Certificate programs require completion of from seven to ten learning modules. Discussion workshops are held at various locations throughout Indiana. Doctoral candidates must attend frequent faculty-led discussions at sites around Indiana and complete required clerkships at participating facilities.

Admission

Applicants must hold pharmacy bachelor's degrees from regionally accredited and pharmacy accredited colleges with a minimum 2.7 GPA in the last sixty semester credits of study.

Programs

145 CEUs (10 course modules)
Consultant Pharmacist Certificate Program (CPCP)
125 CEUs (7 course modules)
Geriatric Pharmacy Practice Certificate (GPPC)
Varies
Nontraditional Doctor of Pharmacy

Tuition & Fees

Basic Tuition:	$156–$222 per credit (Indiana); $334 per credit (others)
Certificate Tuition:	$800
Doctorate Tuition:	Varies with clerkship requirements
Financial Aid:	Certificate payment plans, doctoral student loans

Notes

Purdue University is a government-supported college founded in 1869. A variety of undergraduate, graduate, and professional programs are offered on campus. Distance learning programs operate as extensions of on-campus offerings. The low-residency pharmacy program is administered in accordance with the guidelines of the American Council on Pharmaceutical Education (ACPE). Purdue University is approved as a provider of continuing pharmaceutical education by the American Council on Pharmaceutical Education. Printed media, videotapes, and short faculty-led workshops are used to deliver the program.

PURDUE UNIVERSITY—KRANNERT GRADUATE SCHOOL

Executive Master's Program
Krannert Graduate School of Management
1310 Krannert Graduate Center for Executive Management
West Lafayette, IN 47907-1310
765-494-7700
E-mail: rapisarm@mgmt.purdue.edu (Martin Rapisarda, Director)
URL: http://www2.mgmt.purdue.edu/ExecEd/

Campus Visits

Studies begin with a four-day on-campus orientation in the summer. Six two-week residencies are attended on campus during the two-year degree program.

Admission

Applicants are expected to meet the following standards: a GMAT score above the sixtieth percentile, a bachelor's degree with a minimum 3.0 (B) GPA, at least five years of professional work experience, current employment with a position of significant responsibility, and three letters of reference. Applicants must have a computer, a modem, and Internet access to participate via an electronic conferencing between campus residencies and to access the computer-based business applications curriculum. International applicants are welcome. Applicants have attended from Brazil, Canada, Dubai, England, Mexico, Puerto Rico, Singapore, Taiwan, and Thailand.

Programs

48 credits (3 modules)
Executive Master of Science in Management

Tuition & Fees

Basic Tuition:	$11,000 per module (includes campus residencies)
Master's Tuition:	$33,000 (includes campus residencies)
Financial Aid:	None

Notes

Purdue University is a comprehensive, government-supported institution founded in 1869. The Krannert Graduate School of Business has offered instruction on campus for over three decades. The Executive master's is accredited by the American Assembly of Collegiate Schools of Business (AACSB) and follows a curriculum that meets the standards of this accrediting board. Distance learning programs operate as extensions of on-campus offerings. The Executive Master's distance program is cohort based. Learners enter the program with a selected class of a maximum of fifty-five executives or mid-career managers; they then complete a common set of curricula together following a three-module plan. Each module covers four courses (a semester of study) and lasts twenty-six weeks. The final module includes a mandatory two-week residency abroad with the cohort study group in either Europe or the Pacific Rim to study international business techniques. The curriculum is largely computer-based. Learners communicate with faculty and their cohorts using electronic mail and conferencing systems between campus residencies. Tuition includes on-campus residencies except for the international residency. An estimated additional $4,000 may apply to that final residency.

■ REFORMED THEOLOGICAL SEMINARY

Admissions Office
P.O. Box 945120
Maitland, FL 32794-5120
407-875-8388
800-752-4382
E-mail: rts@rts.edu
URL: http://www.magicnet.net/rts

Campus Visits

The summer/winter low-residency degree program requires attendance at one-week courses in January, then again in the summer months. Learners complete self-study courses in the interim periods.

Admissions

A bachelor's degree is generally required for regular admission to the master's degree program.

Programs

32 credits
Certificate in Biblical Studies
Certificate in Cultural Studies
Certificate in Historical Studies
Certificate in Theological Studies

66 credits
Master of Arts/Biblical Studies
Master of Arts/Theological Studies

Tuition & Fees

Basic Tuition:	$190 per credit
Certificate Tuition:	$6,080
Master's Tuition:	$12,540
Financial Aid:	Inquire directly

Notes

Reformed Theological Seminary is a private Christian evangelical graduate seminary. The Florida campus opened in 1989 and provides ministry and Christian training to more than 600 students studying in five separate degree programs. The summer/winter low-residency study options are intended for ministers, youth workers, Christian educators, pastors, church workers, and lay people wanting to enhance their understanding of religion and the ministry through a limited residency option. Courses are delivered primarily through surface mail. Faculty mentors are available through E-mail for some courses.

REGENT UNIVERSITY

College of Communication & the Arts
Online Degree in Communication and the Arts
Dr. Robert Schihl, Director
1000 Regent University Drive
Virginia Beach, VA 23464
804-579-4243
E-mail: nettbom@beacon.regent.edu
URL: http://www.regent.edu:80/acad/schcom/

Campus Visits

A four-week summer orientation is required as a beginning residency. Subsequent summer residencies are also required. Campus visits are required for the defense of comprehensive examination or thesis.

Admission

Applicants to the master's program should hold a bachelor's degree. Applicants to the doctorate program should hold a master's with a 3.0 GPA preferably in communications or a closely allied field such as social psychology or popular culture. All applicants spend an intensive orientation workshop on-campus to qualify for admission. Applicants should be committed to integrating a Judeo-Christian view of the world in their chosen academic disciplines. Application materials include a writing sample and at least one letter of recommendation from a member of the clergy. Computer literacy and Internet access are required, as the program is delivered online. The GRE is required. International applicants are welcome with TOEFL scores at 550 or above. Applicants are required to use the online application provided by Regent University on their World Wide Web page. A computer, high-speed modem, and Internet access are required to participate in the program. Application deadline for the master's program is May 1. Application deadline for the doctorate program is February 15.

Programs

38–42 credits
Master of Arts in Communication
Master of Arts in Journalism
42–52 credits post-master's
Doctor of Philosophy in Communication

Tuition & Fees

Basic Tuition:	$320 per credit
Master's Tuition:	$12,920–$14,280
Doctorate Tuition:	$14,280–$17,680
Financial Aid:	Dooner scholarships for Roman Catholics, Azuza Street scholarships for African-Americans, Stafford loans

Notes

Regent University is a private ecumenical Evangelical Christian university founded in 1978 by Pat Robertson. Regent was originally known as the Christian Broadcasting Network University (CBNU) and remains a Christ-centered university. The master's program was launched in 1978 and the doctoral program was launched in 1991. The online program is delivered using the Internet and E-mail principally. On-campus versions of the distance master's and doctoral program require two consecutive full-time semester residencies on campus.

REGENT UNIVERSITY—MBA

School of Business
Distance Learning Programs
1000 Regent University Drive
Virginia Beach, VA 23464-9853
804-579-4096
800-477-3642
E-mail: michra@beacon.regent.edu (Mike Cray)
URL: n/a

Campus Visits

Applicants attend two one-week residencies, one at mid-degree and one at degree completion.

Admission

Regent University is a Christ-centered university. Applicants should adhere to the Christian beliefs that are integrated in all degree offerings. A special Accelerated Scholars and Professionals Program (ASAP) allows professionals with at least ninety semester credits or 135 quarter credits of undergraduate work who do not hold an earned bachelor's degree from a regionally accredited college to enter the master's program. The GMAT is required for those entering through ASAP and is used as a financial aid rating tool for other applicants. Bachelor GPAs should be 3.0 or better for nonprovisional admission. Applicants with undergraduate GPAs below that may be provisionally accepted. Those with bachelor's degrees in areas other than business or management may be required to complete a standard set of course prerequisites such as accounting, marketing, and finance, prior to beginning required master's-level courses. Applicants may petition to have prerequisite courses waived. International learners are welcome with TOEFL scores at or above 550.

Programs

39–57 credits

Master of Business Administration/Entrepreneurship
Master of Business Administration/Financial Planning
Master of Business Administration/Management
Master of Business Administration/Nonprofit (Ministry) Management

30–39 credits

Master of Arts in Management
Master of Arts in Management/Entrepreneurship
Master of Arts in Management/Financial Planning
Master of Arts in Management/Nonprofit (Ministry) Management

Tuition & Fees

Basic Tuition:	$325 per credit
Master's Tuition:	$9,750–$18,525
Financial Aid:	Government loans, veteran's benefits, minority scholarships, scholarships, honors awards for leadership skills, payment plans

Notes

Regent University is a private Christian college founded in 1978 by Pat Robertson. Regent was originally known as the Christian Broadcasting Network University (CBNU) and remains a Christ-centered university. Distance learning programs operate as extensions of campus offerings. Business learners receive audiotapes of course lectures and communicate with faculty and staff using audio, video, and phone conferencing techniques. Learners who enter without undergraduate preparatory courses may be required to complete more credits to include the required prerequisite study. Learners may petition to have undergraduate prerequisites waived. A maximum of twenty-one credits of any business administration degree or twelve credits of any management degree may be earned through a combination of waiver or transfer credits earned within ten years at another regionally accredited school.

REGENTS COLLEGE OF THE UNIVERSITY OF THE STATE OF NEW YORK

MA in Liberal Studies
7 Columbia Circle
Albany, NY 12203-5159
518-464-8500 x1323
E-mail: malibstu@regents.edu
URL: http://www.regents.edu

Campus Visits

None

Admission

Applicants must hold a bachelor's degree from a regionally accredited institution and write an acceptable admissions essay.

Programs

33 credits
Master of Arts in Liberal Studies

Tuition & Fees

Basic Tuition:	$230 per credit
Master's Tuition:	$4,500–$8,000
Financial Aid:	Private educational loans, New York State Tuition Assistance Program (TAP) for residents, veteran's benefits (probable), federal loan deferments.

Notes

Regents College of the University of the State of New York is a government-sponsored institution. Regents has offered undergraduate distance degrees since 1971 and was specifically chartered by the University of the State of New York to offer external studies and assessment for adult learners. The Master of Arts in Liberal Studies is the first graduate degree offered by Regents and is expected to begin enrollment of its first formal class in 1998. As a new program, the degree has provisional approval from the Middle States Association regional accreditation body. The program allows for the interdisciplinary study of the humanities, social sciences, or natural and physical sciences. It is appropriate to the study of any topic that can be approached through a philosophical, cultural, historical, scientific, or sociological perspective. It is not appropriate for the study of vocational and career subjects such as accounting, engineering, and business. Master's learners may join in with online study cohorts to prepare for assessments and exams. Online faculty serve as mentors and guides for study. Online learning is asynchronous and optional. Printed, audio, and video materials are also used in program delivery. The interdisciplinary program is divided into three study tiers. Tier one, the common core, counts for six credits and introduces learners to the interdisciplinary study of selected topics in Western Civilization. Tier two involves the completion of fifteen credits in two or more liberal arts disciplines. Tier three is a six-credit capstone project or thesis which emerges from tier-two study and involves the examination of a key question from an interdisciplinary perspective. Learners may design a capstone project that is theoretical, creative or performance based. Up to fifteen credits may be reviewed for transfer toward tier-two requirements.

REGIS UNIVERSITY

School for Professional Studies
Office of Graduate Programs
3333 Regis Boulevard
Denver, CO 80221-1099
303-458-4080
800-677-9270
E-mail: admarg@regis.edu (Community Leadership)
Email: paulalex@regis.edu (Nonprofit Management)
URL: http://www.regis.edu

Campus Visits

Applicants to the community leadership program will be required to spend a total of nine weeks on campus over three summer sessions. Applicants to the Master of Arts in Liberal Studies must attend a brief orientation on campus to begin the degree followed by up to five one-day campus seminars throughout the degree program. Nonprofit management learners may study through guided independent study with optimal attendance at a special summer intensive for from one to eight days each summer.

Admission

Applicants must hold accredited bachelor's degrees from regionally accredited colleges but the bachelor's need not be in the same area as the proposed graduate degree. Applicants should be able to use an independent study format that relies heavily on personal motivation and discipline. A computer, modem, and Internet access will facilitate learning. No special exams are required for admission. International learners are welcome.

Programs
24 credits
Certificate in Community Leadership
Certificate in Nonprofit Management
36 credits
Master of Arts in Community Leadership
Master of Arts in Community Leadership/Pastoral Administration
Master of Arts in Community Leadership/Religious Education
Master of Arts in Community Leadership/Spiritual Direction
Master of Arts in Community Leadership/Family Ministry
48–52 credits
Master of Arts in Liberal Studies/Education
Master of Arts in Liberal Studies/Language & Communication
Master of Arts in Liberal Studies/Psychology
Master of Arts in Liberal Studies/Social Science
Master of Arts in Liberal Studies/Professional Counselor
Master of Arts in Liberal Studies/Teacher Education
36 credits
Master of Nonprofit Management

Tuition & Fees

Basic Tuition:	$245–$260 per credit
Certificate Tuition:	$5,880
Master's Tuition:	$8,820–$13,520
Financial Aid:	Government loans

Notes

Regis University is a private Jesuit college founded in 1877 that is open to students of all religious denominations. Regis has provided adult education and distance learning low-residency degrees as extensions of their on-campus undergraduate and graduate programs since the 1970s. The community leadership degree emphasizes Christian (ecumenical) leadership development. The liberal studies degree is an individually designed degree that allows students to study any specialty within the areas of education, psychology, social science, teacher education, language and communication, or counselor education. Recent liberal studies degrees have been designed to focus on adult education, organizational communication, technical writing and communication, communication in health care, music therapy, literacy education, speech, and social psychology. The nonprofit management program requires the completion of a 400-hour practicum in nonprofit management. The professional counseling degree may be designed to meet the licensing requirements for a Licensed Professional Counselor (LPC) in Colorado. Teaching degree programs may be designed to cover public school certification needs in Colorado or Wyoming. Certification areas covered may include early childhood, elementary, middle school, secondary, English as a second language, or special education. Applicants interested in meeting teacher certification or counselor licensing requirements in other states should inquire directly. Courses are delivered using surface mail, voice mail via faculty boxes, E-mail, and Internet Relay Chat (IRC). Additional information on the nonprofit management courses and degree program may be accessed online at http://www.usa.net/~faccur. Up to six credits completed in the last ten years may be accepted in transfer toward a Regis master's degree.

REGIS UNIVERSITY—MBA

School for Professional Studies
External MBA
9417 Princess Palm Avenue, Suite 175
Tampa, FL 33619-8317
888-MBA-REGIS
E-mail: mba@mbaregis.com
URL: http://www.mbaregis.com

Campus Visits

None

Admission

Applicants should hold regionally accredited bachelor's degrees, but the bachelor's need not be in business. Applicants are, however, expected to meet specific undergraduate core competency requirements in business. Prerequisite courses include accounting, marketing, statistics, and finance. Scores on CLEP or DANTES exams may suffice instead of formal prerequisite courses. The GMAT is required for admission unless the applicant has at least ten years of significant career experience. Two essays may replace the GMAT for experienced learners.

Programs

10 courses
Master of Business Administration

Tuition & Fees

Basic Tuition:	$975 per course
Degree Tuition:	$9,800
Financial Aid:	None

Notes

Regis University is a private Jesuit college, founded in 1877, open to learners of all religious denominations. Regis has provided adult education and low-residency distance programs as extensions of their Colorado-based on-campus programs since the 1970s. The no-residency MBA program was launched in 1996 with the assistance of Bisk Publishing. Courses use a multimedia learning format. Audiotaped lectures, videotaped tutorials, and textbooks are used for teaching. Students interact with other class participants and their evaluating faculty member via the Internet. Courses are accelerated, lasting only eight weeks each.

ROCHESTER INSTITUTE OF TECHNOLOGY

Office of Part-Time & Graduate Enrollment Services
Bausch & Lomb Building
58 Lomb Memorial Drive
Rochester, NY 14623-5603
716-475-2229
1-800-CALL-RIT
E-mail: opes@rit.edu
URL: http://www.rit.edu

Campus Visits

No campus visits are required for the information technology master's. Other master's programs require up to eight weeks of on-campus residency spread out across summers and one-week long executive seminars.

Admission

Applicants must hold regionally accredited bachelor's degrees. Applicants to the health systems administration degree program should have at least three years of career management experience or be able to complete a local internship in health care management. Instructional technology applicants should have five years of experience in training development and submit GMAT or GRE scores. An undergraduate GPA of 3.0 (B) is generally required for admission. GRE scores will be required for applicants with lower GPAs. Undergraduate prerequisites in computer science and health administration are offered through the distance learning program for applicants who need them. Significant career experience can be used to waive undergraduate course prerequisites. International students are accepted with TOEFL scores at or above 550. All students should have a computer, modem, and Internet access as well as a VCR for home play of videotaped course lectures.

Programs

48–52 quarter credits
Master of Science in Career & Human Resource Development
Master of Science in Hospitality—Tourism Management
Master of Science in Packaging Science
Master of Science in Service Management

48–52 quarter credits
Master of Science in Information Technology/Telecommunications Technology
Master of Science in Information Technology/Telecommunications Management
Master of Science in Instructional Technology
Master of Science in Software Development & Management

57 quarter credits
Master of Science in Health Systems Administration

Tuition & Fees

Basic Tuition:	$507 per quarter credit
Master's Tuition:	$24,336–$28,899
Financial Aid:	New York State Tuition Aid Program for residents, government loans, credit card payments, payment plans, limited scholarships, veteran's benefits

Notes

The Rochester Institute of Technology is a private college founded in 1829. The seventeenth largest independent university in the United States, RIT has been cited as one of the nation's best comprehensive colleges by independent analysts in *U.S. News & World Report*. Over 200 undergraduate, graduate, and professional programs are offered on campus. Distance learning programs operate as an extension of on-campus offerings and were first offered in telecourse form in 1979. The Executive Leader Program (ELP) uses a distance learning course format combined with brief, intensive on-campus seminars for the study and application of advanced management practices. Colleagues may earn from nine to twelve credits of some RIT master's through a portfolio documentation process. A $100 per credit fee applies to the portfolio review process. Nine to twelve quarter credits of some master's degrees may be earned through transfer of credits previously earned. A thesis project is required in most programs. More than 3,000 students study at the undergraduate and graduate level each year through RIT's distance learning networks. Course delivery systems include videotaped lectures, online interactive modes, and telephone conference forums.

SAINT JOSEPH'S COLLEGE

278 Whites Bridge Road
Standish, ME 04084-5263
207-892-7841
800-752-4723
E-mail: n/a
URL: http://www.sjcme.edu

Campus Visits

Two two-week summer residencies are required for the Master in Health Services Administration degree. One two-week summer residency is required for the Master of Science, Nursing major. No residency is required to earn the graduate level Certificate in Health Care Finance.

Admission

Three years of substantive experience in a health-related field and an accredited bachelor's degree are required to enter the Health Services Administration degree program. Applicants to the nursing majors must be graduates of a National League for Nursing (NLN) bachelor's program with at least a 3.0 GPA and hold current RN (Registered Nurse) licenses. Applicants with lower GPAs (2.5–2.9), or those with a bachelor's degree in another field and who hold nursing diplomas or associate degrees from NLN schools may be considered for conditional admission. Either the GRE or the MAT is required for Master of Science/Nursing major admission. Saint Joseph's also offers the undergraduate courses required as prerequisites to graduate-level courses through faculty-directed independent study. International applicants are welcome with TOEFL scores at 500 or above.

Programs

18 credits
Certificate in Health Care Finance
48 credits
Master of Science in Health Services Administration
42 credits
Master of Science, Major in Nursing/Nursing Administration
Master of Science, Major in Nursing/Nursing Education

Tuition & Fees

Basic Tuition:	$220 per credit
Certificate Tuition:	$3,870
Master's Tuition:	$9,030–$10,320
Financial Aid:	Payment plans, tuition guarantee plan, DANTES military approval, veteran's benefits

Notes

Saint Joseph's is a Catholic liberal arts college founded in 1912 by the Sisters of Mercy of Portland, Maine. It is open to all applicants. Bachelor's degrees in eighteen majors are offered to 1,000 students on campus. The college is especially well known for its distance education programs in health care. Undergraduate programs in health care, business, and liberal studies currently enroll more than 4,000 students worldwide. More than 6,500 learners from all fifty states and many foreign countries have completed degrees in the distance education programs since they began in 1976. Up to six credits may be transferred in toward a graduate-level degree or certificate. Alumni of degree programs may take courses tuition-free for five years after their graduation. Courses are delivered primarily through print and surface mail, with E-mail also used. Up to six credits may be transferred in toward a degree.

SAINT MARY-OF-THE-WOODS COLLEGE

Graduate Program in Pastoral Theology
Saint Mary-of-the-Woods, IN 47876
812-535-5206
800-926-SMWC
E-mail: wedadms@woods.smwc.edu
URL: http://www.woods.smwc.edu

Campus Visits

Studies begin with an eight-day summer session. Two summer sessions are required to complete the master's degree. Degree seekers must also attend weekend orientations at the beginning of each semester in January, May, and September.

Admission

Applicants should hold bachelor's degrees from accredited colleges. Applicants may be required to take foundation studies in religion if prior undergraduate studies and experience have not prepared them for graduate-level work. Though Saint Mary's is a women's Roman Catholic college, men and non-Catholics of the Christian faith are welcome in the graduate theology program. Most applicants are already involved in the ministry. No special exams are required for admission but applicants must submit three references concerning their suitability for a general Christian ministry.

Programs

21 credits
Certificate in Youth Ministry
36 credits
Master of Arts in Pastoral Theology

Tuition & Fees

Basic Tuition: $272 per credit
Certificate Tuition: $5,712
Master's Tuition: $9,792
Financial Aid: Government loans

Notes

Saint Mary's, founded in 1840, is America's oldest Catholic liberal arts college for women. On-campus programs include an array of undergraduate liberal arts degrees. At the undergraduate level, the Women's External Degree program (WED) has served adult learners since the 1970s. In 1970, Saint Mary's began offering a professional series of Christian conferences. These conferences evolved in the 1980s into the low-residency Master's in Pastoral Theology program. Courses are delivered through multiple modalities including video and audiotapes, surface mail, and E-mail for those with Internet access. Up to fifteen credits of graduate work may be transferred toward the master's degree.

SAINT MARY-OF-THE-WOODS COLLEGE—ELM

Earth Literacy Master's
External Degree Program
Saint Mary-of-the Woods, IN 47876
812-535-5160
E-mail: elm@woods.smwc.edu
URL: http://www.woods.smwc.edu

Campus Visits

Six of the degree courses are anchored in intensive five-day, on-campus residencies that promote community building and collaborative learning.

Admission

The degree program is open to women and men who advocate and care for planetary concerns. Applicants should hold bachelor's degrees from accredited institutions with a GPA of 2.5 or higher, and submit two letters of reference along with a 200–300 word application essay that discusses their reasons for applying to the program.

Programs

36 credits
Master of Arts Earth Literacy

Tuition & Fees

Basic Tuition:	$278 per credit
Master's Tuition:	$10,008
Financial Aid:	Tuition payment plans

Notes

Saint Mary-of-the-Woods, founded in 1840, is America's oldest Catholic liberal arts college for women. The college has successfully offered distance learning programs for undergraduates since 1973, and for graduates since 1984. The Master's in Earth Literacy grounds applicants in the theory and practice needed to create a just and sustainable Earth community. The curriculum includes 24 credits of team-taught courses that explore Earth literacy from the perspective of the natural and social sciences, the humanities, the arts, and spirituality. The remaining 12 credits are dedicated to internship and practicals in the student's area of interest. Degree-seekers must complete at least two internships (6 credits) with at least one of them focused on the student's own region. Saint Mary's operates on a rolling admissions policy and accepts applications throughout the year. Housing is available in dormitories on campus for the required 5-day residencies at a cost of $13–$26 per night.

SAINT MARY'S UNIVERSITY OF MINNESOTA

Campus Box 78
700 Terrace Heights
Winona, MN 55987-1399
612-471-0708
E-mail: harry.d.hurley@cdev.com
URL: n/a

Campus Visits

None

Admission

This is a non-degree professional certification program. No special credentials or degrees are required to enter the program but applicants to the videoconferencing program should have access to a videoconferencing site or be able to arrange an alternative through Saint Mary's. Applicants to the telecommunications certification programs must have from one to three years of career experience in the selected certification area.

Programs

Noncredit

Certificate in Basic Telecommunications
Certificate in Data Telecommunications
Certificate in Voice Telecommunications
Certificate in Videoconferencing

Tuition & Fees

Basic Tuition:	$600 (Videoconferencing); $330 (Telecommunications)
Certificate Tuition:	$600 (Videoconferencing); $990 (Telecommunications, all three areas)
Financial Aid:	None

Notes

Saint Mary's is a small private liberal arts college, affiliated with the Roman Catholic Church, founded in 1912. Saint Mary's primary program goal is the testing and certification of professionals in telecommunications. Applicants for the videoconferencing program should have access to videoconferencing equipment and facilities. Applicants without videoconferencing facilities may arrange for special sessions. The program includes a three-hour videoconferencing teaching seminar with Saint Mary's followed by a one-hour certification exam. The program teaches applicants how to use videoconferencing technology and manage videoconferenced meetings. The telecommunications program provides learners with a study guide to review in their chosen certification areas. Learners self-study, then take the final certification exam in a local, proctored sitting. A passing score (70 percent minimum) on any two of the three telecommunications areas will entitle individuals to use the professional designation, Certified Telecommunications Professional (CTP).

SALVE REGINA UNIVERSITY

Admissions Office
Graduate Extension
100 Ochre Point Avenue
Newport, RI 02840-4192
401-847-6650, ext. 2908
800-637-0002
E-mail: mistol@salve3.salve.edu
URL: http://www.salve.edu

Campus Visits

Five-day intensive seminars are required on campus in June for all degree-seekers. All correctional studies students must attend a two-week summer institute to begin their studies.

Admission

Applicants should hold bachelor's degrees from regionally accredited colleges. Access to a computer, modem, and the Internet will facilitate studies. One of the following is required for admission: the Graduate Management Admission Test (GMAT), the Graduate Record Examination (GRE), or the Miller Analogies Test (MAT). International applicants are welcome if they have taken the TOEFL.

Programs

36 credits
Master of Science in Management
36 credits
Master of Arts in Correctional Administration
Master of Arts in Human Development
Master of Arts in International Relations

Tuition & Fees

Basic Tuition:	$300 per credit
Master's Tuition:	$10,800
Financial Aid:	Veteran's benefits

Notes

Salve Regina is a private, independent college affiliated with the Roman Catholic Church, established in 1934. A variety of bachelor's, master's, and doctorate degrees are offered on campus. The extension, or adult studies program, was launched in 1984. Distance learning programs operate as extensions of on-campus programs. Over 200 learners from thirty-eight states and nine countries enroll each year. Management students may receive up to twelve-degree credits for professional certifications such as Associated Risk Management (ARM) and the Chartered Property Casualty Underwriter (CPCU) designations. At least twenty-four credits of the thirty-six-credit management degree must be completed as formal course work through Salve Regina. E-mail will be used for some course work and communications.

SAN FRANCISCO THEOLOGICAL SEMINARY

Advanced Pastoral Studies
2 Kensington Road
San Anselmo, CA   94960-2905
415-258-6565
800-447-8820, ext. 565
E-mail: aps@sfts.edu
URL: n/a

Campus Visits

Clergy will attend one four-week and one six-week summer intensive in San Anselmo, California.

Admission

Applicants should hold Master of Divinity degree or the equivalent from accredited theological schools and have at least three years' experience in the ministry.

Programs

30 semester (40 quarter) units
Doctor of Ministry

Tuition & Fees

Basic Tuition: $1,900 per year
Doctorate Tuition: $5,700
Financial Aid: Government loans, veteran's benefits

Notes

The San Francisco Theological Seminary is a seminary of the Presbyterian Church (USA) founded in 1871. The Advanced Pastoral Studies Program welcomes groups under-represented in mainstream Protestant ministry and thought. Learners and faculty come from more than fifty religious denominations. Extension sites and programs may be available in Europe and the Far East. Women and racial/ethnic minorities are welcome.

SAYBROOK INSTITUTE

Graduate School & Research Center
450 Pacific, 3rd Floor
San Francisco, CA 94133-4640
415-433-9200
800-825-4480
E-mail: rhessling@igc.apc.org
URL: n/a

Campus Visits

A one-week summer conference is required each year, plus a one-week winter conference each year.

Admission

Applicants to the master's program should hold regionally accredited bachelor's degrees in psychology, human services, or a closely related field. Applicants who hold bachelor's degrees in majors unrelated to psychology or human services may be asked to submit GRE scores. Most applicants are already working in human services or counseling areas when they enter the program. Access to a computer and modem will facilitate communication with faculty and staff. International applicants are welcome.

Programs

31 credits
Master of Arts in Psychology
Master of Arts in Human Service

76 credits post-master's
Doctor of Philosophy in Psychology
Doctor of Philosophy in Human Service

Tuition & Fees

Basic Tuition: $11,025 per academic year
Financial Aid: Government loans, dissertation grants, California state fellowships for residents who intend to teach, Saybrook scholarships, veteran's benefits

Notes

Saybrook is a private graduate school, originally founded in 1971 as the Institute for Humanistic Studies. Saybrook promotes the study of the art and science of being human according to a tradition of humanistic inquiry established by Rollo May, Abraham Maslow and others of the Human Potential Movement. The human science program offers an individualized interdisciplinary approach to the study of psychological and social problems. Areas of key study within the human sciences department include the following: clinical studies (Eastern therapies, existential therapy, shamanism); consciousness studies (Buddhism, dream work, altered states); health studies (holistic and alternative); social and systems inquiry (sociology and psychology, gender studies, social manufacture of insanity); organizational inquiry (management and organizational change and conflict resolution); peace and conflict studies. Psychology learners may opt to study from the above areas or follow a more traditional program designed to meet clinical and counseling licensing requirements. Applicants with considerable life and career experience may petition to challenge selected required courses, thereby reducing the time it takes to complete a degree. Up to twelve credits may be transferred in toward the master's. Up to eighteen credits may be transferred in toward the doctorate. Learners studying toward professional clinical or counseling certifications should be prepared to complete longer programs of study, including supervised clinical internships in their local communities. Saybrook graduates have been admitted to licensing exams in clinical and counseling psychology in seventeen states and two Canadian provinces. Learners and faculty communicate via surface mail, phone, and electronic mail.

SKIDMORE COLLEGE

Master of Liberal Arts
Saratoga Springs, NY 12866-1632
518-584-5000, ext. 2261
E-mail: lries@skidmore.edu (Dr. Lawrence Reis, Director)
URL: http://www.skidmore.edu

Campus Visits

An admissions interview is required on campus. A five-day entrance seminar begins all studies. An on-campus presentation of the student's academic plan is required.

Admission

All applicants should hold accredited bachelor's degrees and be able to give evidence of their ability to succeed at self-designed graduate study. The application essay and admissions interview are important factors in admission. No standardized exams are used in the selection process.

Programs

30 credits
Master of Arts in Liberal Studies

Tuition & Fees

Basic Tuition:	$4,100 annual fee; plus $450 for each course tutorial
Master's Tuition:	$8,000–$12,100
Financial Aid:	Stafford loans

Notes

Skidmore is a private, independent college, established in 1903. A variety of bachelor's and master's degrees are offered on campus. Skidmore has offered a self-designed bachelor program through distance education via an innovative University Without Walls (UWW) program since the 1970s. The Master of Arts in Liberal Studies (MALS) is Skidmore's first master's program. The MALS program is especially designed for adult, part-time learners, most of whom will continue working while earning their degrees. The MALS programs allows adult learners to work with two faculty advisors to develop and complete an individualized curriculum that embodies the learner's interests and experiences. All studies are self-designed, often combining the use of community resources, such as formal graduate classes at local universities, work internships, and creative or investigative projects. Primary areas of study will vary but have previously included interdisciplinary projects across the curriculum areas of arts administration, communications, counseling, creative arts, education, health studies, historical studies, journalism, sociology, environmental sciences, Latin American studies, literature, media studies, management, multicultural studies, museum studies, organizational change and development, public policy, philosophy, religion, social science, sociology, and women's studies. Any program rooted in the interdisciplinary study of the three liberal arts areas of humanities, social science, and the natural sciences, may be proposed. All learners complete a three-credit entrance, orientation, and degree-planning seminar, a twenty-four-credit concentration, and a final three-credit thesis/project. Tuition and fees will vary widely depending on the options individual learners use to complete degrees. All learners pay an annual fee to Skidmore for assistance in designing and evaluating their individualized degrees. Up to six credits may be awarded for documented prior work experience that is relevant to the degree plan. The Skidmore program is a member of the Association of Graduate Liberal Studies Programs.

SOUTHEASTERN UNIVERSITY

Distance Learning Degree Programs
501 Eye Street, SW
Washington, D.C. 20024-2715
202-488-8162, ext. 205
E-mail: dldp@admin.seu.edu
URL: n/a

Campus Visits

Attendance is required at a one-week residency where learners complete the requirements for two courses or six credits of study.

Admission

Applicants should hold bachelor's degrees from accredited colleges but the bachelor's need not be in business. Applicants should have a 3.0 GPA from their undergraduate studies. Those with lower GPAs may petition for admission. The GMAT is not required for admission to the degree program but scores on the GMAT can be submitted and will be considered. All applicants must pass a computer literacy test or complete through Southeastern's distance program an undergraduate level course in computer literacy prior to beginning the MBA. International applicants are welcome with TOEFL scores at 550 or above.

Programs

45 credits
Master of Business Administration in Management

Tuition & Fees

Basic Tuition: $216 per credit; plus a one-time $170 registration fee
Master's Tuition: $9,720–$10,470
Financial Aid: Veterans' benefits, payment plans

Notes

Southeastern is a private, independent university established in 1879. A variety of degrees are offered on campus. A distance learning undergraduate program has been in operation for several years. The distance MBA operates as an extension of on-campus offerings and was launched in 1994–1995. Up to nine graduate credits may be accepted in transfer toward the forty-five credit master's degree. Transfer credits may include credit for evaluated work experience, ACE credits, or military credit awards, as well as formal classes taken elsewhere. A $250 fee is charged to review and transcript each three-credit course earned through a review of one's career expertise. Course delivery and instructional support occurs primarily via surface mail and phone.

SOUTHERN CHRISTIAN UNIVERSITY

Extended Learning
1200 Taylor Road
P.O. Box 240240
Montgomery, AL 36124-0240
334-277-2277
800-351-4040
E-mail: scuniversity@mindspring.com
URL: http://www.southernchristian.edu

Campus Visits

None

Admissions

Applicants should hold qualifying bachelor's degrees. All graduate learners must take either the GRE or the MAT. The Doctor of Ministry degree is an advanced professional degree program intended for the experienced minister. Applicants to the doctorate program will need to earn the master's degree first.

Programs

54 quarter credits
Master of Arts in Biblical Studies

120 quarter credits
Master of Divinity

48 quarter credits
Master of Science in Ministry

50 quarter credits
Master of Science in Counseling

45 quarter credits post-master's
Doctor of Divinity

Tuition & Fees

Basic Tuition:	$192 per quarter credit (Extended Learning Master's); $3,000 per year (doctorate)
Master's Tuition	$9,216–$23,040
Doctorate Tuition	$9,000
Financial Aid:	Government loans, scholarships, veteran's benefits, payment plans

Notes

Southern Christian University is a private, Christian university, first accredited in 1989. Extended learning programs operate as extensions of on-campus offerings. Extended learning students are held to the same assignments in the same time period as their on-campus peers. Extended learners receive videotapes of on-campus classroom sessions. A toll-free phone line, fax, and E-mail are also used to enhance instructional communication. SCUnet, a website and Internet gateway, is under development as a way to enhance computer-mediated communications between students and distance learners. The Master of Science in Ministry is intended for those involved with or making a career change into the Christian ministry. The Master of Arts in Biblical Studies is designed for those intending to pursue doctoral study later; as such it requires both Greek or Hebrew language and a thesis. The Master of Science in Counseling degree program is designed to meet the State of Alabama's requirements for those intending to sit for the state exam to be a licensed professional counselor. Students from other states wishing to meet counseling requirements should inquire directly to their state's licensing division about meeting licensing requirements. Students in the counseling program must locate and complete counseling internships in their local communities. The counseling program is taught from a Christian perspective, using Biblical foundations. Southern Christian may award credit for ministry work or practicums currently being completed for selected degree programs.

SOUTHERN METHODIST UNIVERSITY

School of Engineering & Applied Science
Distance Learning—Videotape Program
P.O. Box 7500335
Dallas, TX 75275-0335
214-768-1452
E-mail: rmk@seas.smu.edu (Michael Kirkpatrick, Director)
URL: http://www.seas.smu.edu/disted

Campus Visits

No on-campus attendance is required to complete any of the degree programs. All courses are available by videotape. Students must make arrangements for a test proctor, usually someone at their place of employment.

Admission

All degree applicants must hold accredited bachelor's with a minimum 3.0 GPA. Telecommunications majors must hold a bachelor's degree in engineering, computer science, business, liberal arts, or science; a course background in physics and integral calculus is helpful, but not required. Hazardous Waste majors must hold bachelor's degrees in engineering, mathematics, or a natural science, with a one-year course background in chemistry and calculus. Engineering Management majors must hold a bachelor's in engineering. Manufacturing Systems majors should hold a bachelor's in engineering or a quantitative science, but other majors will be evaluated. Software Engineering majors must hold a bachelor's in quantitative science, mathematics, computer science, or an engineering discipline, with at least one year of background in calculus plus one year of experience in software development and maintenance. System Engineering majors must hold a bachelor's in engineering, mathematics, or a physical science. International learners are welcome. Applicants have enrolled from Canada, Europe, Asia, and South America.

Programs

30–36 credits
Master of Science/Engineering Management
Master of Science/Hazardous & Waste Materials
Master of Science/Manufacturing Systems Management
Master of Science/Software Engineering
Master of Science/Systems Engineering
Master of Science/Telecommunications

Tuition & Fees

Basic Tuition: $600 per credit; $250 per semester videotape fee
Master's Tuition: $18,000–$21,600
Financial Aid: Government loans, veteran's benefits, military discounts

Notes

Southern Methodist University is a private, comprehensive university, founded in 1911 by what is now the United Methodist Church. The university has been ranked as among the top 100 American universities by *U.S. News & World Report*. For more than three decades, the School of Engineering and Applied Science (SEAS) has operated a distance learning program, working in partnership with corporations in the Dallas-Forth Worth metropolitan area. SEAS offers distance learning in three formats: the TAGER television system provides for live broadcast to specially equipped corporate sites in the Texas viewing area; SMU offers satellite-based graduate engineering courses and degrees to more than 300 corporate sites nationwide through partnership with the National Technological University (NTU); the videotape program records lectures in color during live broadcast, which are then mailed to remote learners worldwide. The videotape master's degrees are interdisciplinary in nature, intended for a professional audience. Up to six credits may be transferred in toward a master's degree.

SOUTHERN POLYTECHNIC STATE UNIVERSITY

Master of Science in Quality Assurance
1100 South Marietta Parkway
Marietta, GA 30060-2896
770-528-7243
E-mail: MSQA@spsu.edu
URL: http://www.msqa.edu/degree.html

Campus Visits

The final course in the degree sequence (Research Methods) requires students to attend two separate on-campus sessions. These symposiums take place during Saturday sessions. At the first symposium, students meet program faculty and listen to presentations made by other degree students. At the second symposium, students have the opportunity to make 45-minute presentations themselves.

Admission

Applicants should possess a bachelor's degree in business, social science, education, or other non-technical majors and either be working in a quality-related field (e.g., human resources or training), or want to work in a quality-related field. Students are required to take the GRE. Students must have a computer with a modem and access to the Internet.

Programs

36 credits
Master of Science in Quality Assurance/Quality Systems Concentration

Tuition & Fees

Basic Tuition:	$260 per course (Georgia); $950 per course (others)
Master's Tuition:	$2,340 (Georgia); $8,550 (others)
Financial Aid:	None

Notes

Located in suburban Atlanta, Southern Polytechnic State University is a government-supported unit of the University System of Georgia. The Master of Science in Quality Assurance has been offered on campus since 1992. The Industrial Engineering Technology Department offers the program in an effort to meet the needs of students in both the manufacturing and service industries. The program focuses on total quality management and analytical methods such as statistics, process, analysis, and problem-solving techniques. The program has been established to meet the needs of individuals who are currently practicing in the field, but who have not had any formal technical education in the discipline. The Internet-based master's degree program employs the same professors who teach in the on-campus program, but offers only the non-thesis degree option. (Only on-campus students may opt for and complete the thesis-based degree tract.) The online degree program is designed to be completed in a two-year cycle. Course syllabi, outlines, and assignments are posted on the program's home page on the World Wide Web. Professors deliver courses online, and they are available several times each week in a live chat room for students to ask questions or receive learning assistance with readings and classroom assignments. Chat rooms are always available for students to use to communicate with each other. Students have written assignments due every two weeks, which are typically submitted directly to professors via E-mail. About halfway through each course, students take proctored midterm exams. The proctor may be an approved company manager or personnel officer, or a state certified high school or college teacher. Some courses will require teamwork and team projects.

SOUTHWEST MISSOURI STATE UNIVERSITY

Master of Science in Computer Information Systems
359 Glass Hall
Springfield, MO 65804
417-836-4131
E-mail: mscs@mail.smsu.edu
URL: http://www.mscis.smsu.edu

Campus Visits

Students must attend four on-campus sessions. These intensive seven-and-a-half-day sessions take place every six months, and include lecture and discussion classes, as well as group activities. Classes meet from 8 a.m. to 5 p.m. daily, with evening computer labs and tutorials.

Admission

Applicants should have three years of professional experience in computer information systems, a bachelor's degree with a minimum GPA of 2.75 for the last two years or 60 semester credits of work, and acceptable GMAT scores. An IBM-compatible computer with a modem and Internet access is required of all applicants. Applicants should have completed at least one undergraduate course in the areas of databases, systems analysis and design, and computer programming. Applicants should have a background in business administration, including exposure to accounting, finance, economics, and management. Candidates who possess an undergraduate or graduate degree in business administration, or have completed at least nine credit hours of courses in the three basic business areas will be considered. Students who do not meet the normal admission requirements but who otherwise appear to be excellent candidates for the degree program will be considered for admission on a case-by-case basis.

Programs

36 credits
Master of Science/Computer Information Systems

Tuition & Fees

Basic Tuition:	$295 per credit (Missouri); $395 per credit (others)
Degree Tuition:	$10,620–$14,220
Financial Aid:	Federal Stafford loans, payment plans

Notes

Southwest Missouri State University, a government-supported university, is Missouri's second largest university, with an on-campus undergraduate and graduate enrollment of more than 17,000 students. The College of Business Administration (COBA), home of the Computer Information Systems (CIS) Department, is one of the strongest business schools in the country. It has approximately 2,500 students, more than 600 of which study in CIS. COBA also holds the distinction of being among the top 10 percent of schools in the nation holding accreditation by the American Assembly of Collegiate Schools of Business (AACSB). All of COBA's degree programs, including the Master's in CIS, are fully accredited by the AACSB. The Computer Information Systems Department is one of the largest in the nation. The Master of Science in Information Systems degree requires the completion of 30 credit hours of core course work plus six credits of electives. No thesis is required. Off-campus instruction occurs using E-mail and computer conferencing via the Internet. Students can access assignments and participate in online course discussions and case analyses with their professors and classmates worldwide. Up to six semester credits of graduate credit earned at another accredited university may be reviewed for transfer toward the Missouri master's degree. Lodging costs while on campus are not included in the tuition and fees.

SPERTUS INSTITUTE OF JEWISH STUDIES

Distance Learning Admissions
618 South Michigan Avenue
Chicago, IL 60605
312-922-9012
E-mail: college@spertus.edu
URL: n/a

Campus Visits

Learners attend one or two short intensive seminars on campus each year. Summer seminars are usually one week long, while academic-year seminars last two or three days.

Admission

Master's applicants should hold an accredited bachelor's degree in any subject area. To qualify for doctoral admission, applicants must have a master's degree in Jewish Studies from an accredited college or a rabbinical ordination or certificate as a Hazzan from a recognized Jewish institution of learning. Applicants must also be able to demonstrate advanced proficiency in reading classical and modern Hebrew texts. A personal interview and essay, along with a review of professional experience, are heavily weighted in the admission process. International applicants are accepted.

Programs

50 quarter credits
Master of Science in Jewish Studies
54 quarter credits
Doctor of Jewish Studies

Tuition & Fees

Basic Tuition:	$150 per quarter credits (master's); $200 per quarter credit (doctoral)
Master's Tuition:	$7,500
Doctorate Tuition:	$10,800
Financial Aid:	Scholarships, payment plans

Notes

Spertus Institute of Jewish Studies is a private, independent, post-baccalaureate institute of higher learning, operating under Jewish auspices. Founded in 1924 as Chicago's Jewish College, Spertus supports an on-campus library, the Asher Library, that contains more than 100,000 books, periodicals, and microfilm holdings. The Spertus Museum, founded in 1968, contains the largest collection of Judaica between the American coasts. In 1988, Spertus was ranked as a "best buy" college by *U.S. News & World Report* in a comparative study. Distance graduate programs operate as extensions of on-campus offerings, using faculty-guided independent study. The D.JS (Doctor of Jewish Studies) offered through distance means does not aim at training individuals to pursue a scholarly scientific research career as does the on-campus Doctor of Philosophy (Ph.D.). Unlike the D.Min (Doctor of Ministry), the D.JS program is not clinically oriented. The D.JS program is designed for in-service Jewish clergy, educators, and communal service workers who are committed to building on their knowledge of Judaica. The D.JS consists of three integrated components: seven reading courses in Jewish spirituality, twenty-one credits of intensive study seminars, and a final Project Demonstrating Excellence. Master's learners may opt for a concentration in one of five areas: Jewish Religion, Jewish Social History, Jewish Education, Jewish Communal Service, or a self-designed area of specialty. Up to nine quarter credit hours may be transferred in toward the master's degree. Instruction may occur via telephone, mail, fax, computer, and in-person as the program progresses.

STATE UNIVERSITY OF NEW YORK—ENGINET

Janice Kinzer, EngiNet Information Specialist
T. J. Watson School of Engineering and Applied Sciences
P. O. Box 6000
Binghamton, NY 13902-6000
800-777-4965
607-777-4965
E-mail: jkinzer@binghamton.edu (Janice Kinzer)
URL: http://www.enginet.binghamton.edu

Campus Visits

Thesis and final degree projects may require an on-campus oral defense or seminar presentation. Inquire directly for information on individual program options.

Admission

Computer science applicants should hold bachelor's degrees in computer science or a related field. Applicants whose undergraduate work was not in computer science may be required to complete preparatory work for full admission into the degree program. Electrical engineering applicants may be required to submit GRE scores if they did not graduate from an ABET-accredited engineering college with an electrical engineering (BSEE) degree. The mechanical engineering program accepts applications from those who hold bachelor's degrees in mechanical engineering or a closely related field such mathematics, physics, or other engineering disciplines. Applicants without a mechanical engineering degree may be required to take preparatory course work. The general GRE is required of mechanical engineering applicants but applicants with strong credentials may petition for admission without the GRE. The industrial engineering program accepts applicants with bachelor's degrees in industrial engineering or closely related fields, although applicants with degrees outside the area of industrial engineering may be accepted on the condition that they take preparatory course work. The GRE is required for industrial engineering applicants. A minimum TOEFL score of 550 is required for all international applicants.

Programs

30 credits

Master of Engineering/Specialization in Electrical Engineering
Master of Engineering/Specialization in Industrial Engineering
Master of Engineering/Specialization in Mechanical Engineering

30–36 credits

Master of Science/Computer Science
Master of Science/Electrical Engineering
Master of Science/Industrial Engineering
Master of Science/Mechanical and Aerospace Engineering
Master of Science/Mechanical Engineering
Master of Science/Systems Science

Tuition & Fees

Basic Tuition:	$213 per credit (New York); $351 per credit (others)
Master's Tuition:	$6,930–$8,316 (New York); $10,539–$12,636 (others)
Financial Aid:	Varies by program. Inquire directly.

Notes

The State University of New York (SUNY) is a comprehensive system of government-supported campuses offering an array of undergraduate, graduate, and professional degree programs at campus sites around the State of New York. EngiNet (TM) is a part of the Graduate Education Network of the Statewide Instructional Network of the SUNY Schools of Engineering at SUNY Binghamton, SUNY Stony Brook, SUNY Buffalo, SUNY New Paltz, the College of Environmental Science and Forestry at Syracuse, and the New York State College of Ceramics at Alfred University. Credit-bearing courses are taught from each of these universities via the EngiNet cooperative program. Distance learning students view the actual campus-based courses and electives offered from the six campuses on videotape. EngiNet learners receive videotaped courses and mailed assignments, course notes, and exams on a regular semester schedule at their offices or their homes. EngiNet students can communicate with faculty during live broadcasts (if they can receive them), during faculty phone hours, or via e-mail. Non-degree seekers may audit courses rather than taking them for degree credit. The Master of Engineering (ME) degree, as distinct from the Master of Science Engineering (MSE) degree, is a practice-oriented degree that replaces the research thesis with a two-course applied project sequence. These courses are designed to teach students a rigorous approach for accomplishing projects in an industrial setting. A few EngiNet courses are taught online via the World Wide Web. The program has begun to migrate from a video and broadcast model to an Internet delivery one in the 1997–98 academic year.

STEPHENS COLLEGE

School of Graduate & Continuing Education
Campus Box 2083
Columbia, MO 65215
800-388-7579
573-876-7283
E-mail: GRAD@wc.stephens.edu
URL: http://www.stephens.edu

Campus Visits

Students are required to make two campus visits. Degree-seekers must attend a weekend workshop to begin their program, and spend a week on campus to complete the integrative seminar on Advanced Business Policy and Strategy at the end of the degree program. Applicants who live within commuting distance of the campus may also opt to attend Saturday courses as an alternate.

Admission

Applicants are required to submit GMAT scores, three letters of reference, an essay, and, in certain cases, a personal interview. An undergraduate grade point average of at least 3.0 in the last 60 credit hours of academic work is expected. Applicants should have completed at least eight undergraduate foundation courses (24 semester credits) including Introduction to Information Systems, Microeconomics, Introduction to Statistics, Principles of Management, Principles of Marketing, Accounting I, Accounting II, and Principles of Finance. Two additional foundation courses are required for Clinical Information Systems Management majors: Essentials of Human Anatomy and Physiology, and Physiology and Clinical Applications in Health Information Management. Stephens College offers undergraduate foundation courses via distance learning for applicants who require them. A computer with a modem and Internet access is required of all applicants. International applicants are welcome.

Programs

36 credits
Master of Business Administration/Management
Master of Business Administration/Entrepreneurial Studies
Master of Business Administration/Clinical (Health) Information Systems Management

Tuition & Fees

Basic Tuition:	$230 per credit
Degree Tuition:	$8,280
Financial Aid:	Loans, scholarships, payment plans

Notes

Stephens College is a private university founded in 1833. The School of Continuing Education was founded in 1971, and has helped more than 1,300 adult and nontraditional students to complete their degrees through weekend and distance learning programs. A distance learning bachelor's degree program is also available. The Master's in Business Administration program consists of a traditional nine-course

(27 semester credit) core, with three additional courses (9 semester credits) required to complete a specialty tract. The MBA program offers learners a chance to specialize in three tracts: general management, entrepreneurship, or clinical (health) information systems management. The clinical (health) information systems management tract is appropriate for hospital and health care administrators and consultants wishing to understand the impact and implementation of computerized information and recordkeeping systems in a health care environment. The program is delivered primarily via the Internet.

SYRACUSE UNIVERSITY

Independent Study Degree Programs
700 University Avenue
Syracuse, NY 13244-2530
315-443-4590
800-442-0501
E-mail: suisdp@uc.syr.edu
URL: http://www.maxwell.syr.edu:80/maxpages/students/wzhang17/isdp/

Campus Visits

Three two-week summer intensive seminars are required for most degrees. The business program requires one week on campus at the beginning of each semester. Social science degree candidates can complete their two-week summer intensive seminars in Washington, D.C., London, England, or Syracuse. Information resource candidates begin their studies with one week on campus and may attend two-to-three-day orientations at the beginning of some semesters. Design and illustration learners may meet for special contact days or brief workshops with faculty and other learners throughout the program at cities nationwide.

Admission

All applicants should hold regionally accredited bachelor's degrees. The GMAT is required of business applicants and is never waived. The average GMAT score is competitive at 570. The nursing and library science degrees require the GRE with a minimum score of 1,000. The design degree requires submission of a professional portfolio and is open only to those with three years of career experience in the field. The communications management program is open to public relations practitioners who have at least five years of experience and satisfactory scores on either the GRE or the GMAT. The information resources program requires the GRE or the GMAT, with a minimum score of 1,000 on the GRE. Information resources applicants must have access to a computer, modem, and the Internet, as that program is delivered online. Applicants to the nursing program must hold a Bachelor of Science in Nursing (BSN) from an National League for Nursing-accredited college. Nurses must be employed in a hospital to complete the required clinical programs and have competency in computer use and statistics. Applicants to the library science program must have a computer and Internet access. No special admission exams are required for the social science degree. International learners are welcome with TOEFL scores at 550-600.

Programs

30 credits
Master of Arts in Advertising Design
Master of Arts in Illustration

36–54 credits
Master of Business Administration

36 credits
Master of Library Science

48 credits
Master of Library Science/School Media Specialist

36 credits
Master of Science in Communications Management

42 credits
Master of Science in Information Resources Management
Master of Science in Telecommunications Network Management

36 credits
Master of Science in Nursing/Nursing Administration
Master of Science in Nursing/Nursing Education
Master of Science in Nursing/Nurse Practitioner

30 credits
Master of Social Science
Master of Social Science/Social Studies Teacher Certification

Tuition & Fees

Basic Tuition: $529 per credit
Master's Tuition $15,870–$28,566
Financial Aid: Government loans, veteran's benefits, New York state aid, payment plans

Notes

Syracuse University is a private, independent college established in 1870. The university has been ranked among the nation's top fifty universities in annual ratings by *U.S. News & World Report*. On-campus programs include a variety of undergraduate and professional degrees. Launched in 1966, the Syracuse independent study program is one of the three oldest distance degree programs in the United States. Syracuse uses multiple instructional delivery methods to extend campus programs to distance learners. The information resources management program makes extensive use of the Internet and the World Wide Web. The library science program is accredited by the American Library Association and is a competitive entry professional program. The business administration program is accredited by the American Assembly of Collegiate Schools of Business and is a competitive entry professional program. Design programs are accredited by the National Association of Schools of Art and Design. The nursing program is accredited by the National League for Nursing. Once admitted, nursing students may specialize in many fields, including critical care, psychiatric, pediatric, gerontological, community, maternal-child, or primary care areas. The social science degree is a broad degree in American or European history, international relations and political issues, and war and social issues. Individual social science courses are open to non-degree learners via independent study. The social science degree meets teacher certification requirements in social sciences for New York and many other states. All programs except for the design program will accept up to six graduate transfer credits completed in the last five years. Special waiver exams are available in graduate business course areas. The exams cost $100 each and can reduce the Master's in Business Administration to only thirty-six credits. The school media library program meets teacher certification needs in New York and many other states.

TEXAS A&M UNIVERSITY

Center for Distance Learning Research
615 Harrington Tower
College Station, Texas 77843-3256
409-862-4954
E-mail: mmouzes@acs.tamu.edu (Maria Mouzes, Coordinator)
URL: www-ehrd.tamu.edu/CDLR/

Campus Visits

Two intensive weekends are required on campus to use the distance learning technology labs and videoconferencing studios at Texas A&M University. On-campus sessions may be attended in either San Antonio or College Station. Between weekends, usually a period of four weeks, applicants prepare assignments and practice distance education principles through electronic communication with each other.

Admission

Applicants must have Internet access. No specific educational prerequisites are imposed but most applicants are professional educators or corporate trainers seeking advanced training and certification.

Programs

40 Contact Hours (4 CEUs)
Distance Learning Certification Program

Tuition & Fees

Basic Tuition: $1,200
Financial Aid: None

Notes

Texas A&M University and General Telephone & Electric (GTE) have developed an intensive training program for those involved in developing, delivering, or selecting distance learning technologies for higher education or industry. The competency-based program covers distance learning basics, instructional design, instructional television, effective teaching/training, distance learning technologies, multimedia and desktop publishing, collaboration skills, public relations, presentation skills, graphic design, and distance learning program logistics and administration. Hands-on training takes place during weekend visits to the Center for Distance Learning Research.

TEXAS TECH UNIVERSITY

Office of the Dean of Engineering
Distance Education Program
P.O. Box 43103
Lubbock, Texas 79409-3103
806-742-3451
E-mail: mdigby@coe1.coe.ttu.edu (Mysti Digby)
URL: http://aln.coe.ttu.edu/distance/disted.htm

Campus Visits

None

Admission

Applicants should hold an accredited bachelor's in engineering or its equivalent. Learners with bachelor's degrees in areas other than engineering may be admitted as special cases provided they meet undergraduate course requirements, which will provide them with a solid theory foundation for completing a graduate-level engineering degree. A computer, modem, and access to the Internet is required.

Programs

36 credits
Master of Science in Engineering

Tuition & Fees

Basic Tuition:	$841 per 3-credit course (Texas);
	$1,459 per 3-credit course (others)
Master's Tuition:	$10,092 (Texas); $17,508 (others)
Financial Aid:	None

Notes

Texas Tech University is a government-supported institution founded in 1923. On-campus programs include a variety of undergraduate, graduate, and professional degree programs. Distance programs operate as extensions of on-campus offerings. The university has offered a no-residency, video-based, interdisciplinary, non-thesis master's in engineering to off-campus learners since 1990. The program is intended primarily for practicing engineers who wish to continue their careers while learning. The thirty-six-credit interdisciplinary curriculum requires the completion of six credits in classical analytical and numerical methods; twelve credits in the fundamentals of engineering science; and eighteen credits of electives. Courses are delivered using asynchronous and synchronous Internet modes, coupled with mailed videotapes of lecture materials. Individual courses are open to learners wishing to take them for career enhancement. While there is no thesis, every candidate must pass a final comprehensive exam, which may be written, oral, or a combination of these modes. Up to half the master's may be earned through transfer credits taken at another graduate university upon the review and approval of Texas Tech University. Master of Science degrees in discrete engineering disciplines may be added to the distance learning program in the near future.

TEXAS WESLEYAN UNIVERSITY

Distance Learning Master of Education
1200 Wesleyan
Fort Worth, TX 76105-1536
800-336-4954
817-531-4444
E-mail: joyedwards@aol.com (Joy Edwards, Director of Graduate Studies in Education)
URL: n/a

Campus Visits

A final comprehensive degree exam must be taken on campus.

Admission

Applicants must reside in Texas, teach full time, hold Texas teaching certification, and have completed at least one year of teaching as the teacher of record. The degree program is not approved for delivery outside the state of Texas. Applicants should hold an accredited bachelor's degree and have undergraduate grade point averages of at least 3.0 or a GRE composite score of 900 or higher. A phone interview is required with the Director of Distance Learning. A computer with a modem and Internet access is required, and a videocassette player is required to view course tapes.

Programs

36 credits
Master of Education

Tuition & Fees

Basic Tuition:	$239 per credit
Degree Tuition:	$8,604
Financial Aid:	Guaranteed student loans, teacher scholarships, payment plans, veteran's benefits

Notes

Texas Wesleyan University is a private, comprehensive United Methodist university founded in 1890. The university serves an undergraduate and graduate on-campus population of more than 2,600. The teacher education program is accredited by the Texas Education Agency and is appropriate for elementary or secondary classroom teachers. The distance learning education program was launched in 1996. The Master's in Education degree requires completion of 30 core credit hours (ten courses) and 6 credit hours (2 courses) of electives. Electives may be taken through Texas Wesleyan, or transferred from another approved graduate program. The distance degree program is delivered via videotape and printed study guides. It requires degree-seekers to work in study teams ranging from two to four members to complete their course work. Study teams are coordinated within the state of Texas by the program. Course work includes the mandate that students apply lessons in an actual classroom environment. Course videotapes include footage of actual K–12 classroom lessons taught by master teachers. Faculty support is provided through toll-free phone conferencing (access to a speaker phone is required), E-mail, and the Texas educational Internet.

TEXAS WOMAN'S UNIVERSITY

School of Occupational Therapy
P.O. Box 425648
Denton, TX 76204-3648
817-898-2802
E-mail: n/a
URL: n/a

Campus Visits

Long distance learners may attend the "fly-and-drive" program that meets on the Denton campus one weekend each month. The rehabilitation therapy major is available only at the Houston site with once weekly class attendance.

Admission

The program is a postprofessional program. It is open only to registered occupational therapists. Both men and women are admitted.

Programs

30 credits
Master of Arts in Occupational Therapy
Master of Arts in Rehabilitation Therapy
60 credits
Doctor of Philosophy in Occupational Therapy

Tuition & Fees

Basic Tuition: $54 per credit (Texas); $266 per credit (others)
Master's Tuition: $1,620 (Texas); $7,480 (others)
Doctorate Tuition: $3,240 (Texas); $15,960 (others)
Financial Aid: Government loans, State aid for residents, Southern states tuition discounts

Notes

Texas Woman's University, founded in 1901, is government-supported. Both women and men are admitted to the occupational therapy program. On-campus programs include an array of bachelor's, master's, and doctorate degrees. Applicants from Alabama, Arkansas, Georgia, Kentucky, Louisiana, Maryland, Mississippi, Oklahoma, South Carolina, Tennessee, Virginia, or West Virginia may, under a special "academic common market" agreement, pay the lower Texas state tuition. All distance programs require completion of a thesis. Elective credits may be reviewed for transfer.

THOMAS EDISON STATE COLLEGE

Graduate Studies Program
101 West State Street
Trenton, New Jersey 08608-1176
609-292-5143
E-mail: ammartini@call.tesc.edu
URL: http://www.tesc.edu

Campus Visits

All degree candidates will visit the campus two times. A weekend orientation/residency is required to begin studies, and a final weekend assessment residency closes the program.

Admission

Course work is offered online so applicants need Internet access. A computer with at least 8 megabytes of RAM and a 14.4 bps modem is required. Applicants with regionally accredited bachelor's degrees in all areas are invited to apply. It is recommended that applicants have at least five years of significant supervisory experience. International applicants are welcome with TOEFL scores at or above 500.

Programs

42 credits
Master of Science in Management

Tuition & Fees

Basic Tuition: $289 per credit; plus $1,500 for residency fees
Master's Tuition: $12,150–$14,650
Financial Aid: Inquire directly

Notes

Thomas Edison State College was chartered in 1972 by the State of New Jersey specifically to serve adult distance learners. Undergraduate credentials have been offered via distance means for over three decades. The Master's of Science in Management is the first graduate degree to be offered by the college and opened to its first class of applicants in 1996. Thomas Edison offers computer-assisted undergraduate courses for applicants needing to prepare for graduate study. The program is largely computer-based, with faculty mentors available via E-mail. The program focuses on the development of leadership skills and management competencies. Team, group, and cohort learning are important parts of the program's structure. Up to six credits earned elsewhere may be reviewed for transfer toward the degree.

TRINITY UNIVERSITY

Executive Program
Health Care Administration
715 Stadium Drive
San Antonio, TX 78212
210-736-8107
E-mail: shubenak@trinity.edu
URL: http://www.trinity.edu/departments/health_care/

Campus Visits

Attendance is required at a three-day intensive session on campus at the beginning of each fall and spring semester.

Admission

Trinity's Executive Program is designed for individuals currently holding a responsible position in a health care setting. All applicants must have a bachelor's degree from an accredited college or university. Applicants are required to take either the GRE General Test or the GMAT. Applicants who hold graduate degrees may have these examinations waived. Prerequisite courses include three hours of undergraduate credit in each of the fields of accounting, economics, and statistics. Applicants are evaluated on the basis of transcripts, standardized test scores, letters of recommendation, a resume, and a statement of purpose. Application for the fall should be submitted by June 1.

Programs

42 credits
Master of Science in Health Care Administration

Tuition & Fees

Basic Tuition:	$585 per credit
Master's Tuition:	$24,570
Financial Aid:	Inquire directly

Notes

Trinity is a private, highly selective institution that emphasizes undergraduate liberal arts and select Master of Science programs in professional fields. The University was founded in 1869, but the Skyline Campus was established in 1953. The department has been accredited by the Accrediting Commission on Education for Health Services Administration (ACEHSA) since 1969. Course work is completed during the on-campus session, by written assignments, and using regular telephone conferences. An IBM-compatible PC is required. E-mail may be used. Transfer credit is dealt with on an individual basis in accordance with specific Trinity University guidelines.

THE UNION INSTITUTE

Graduate School
440 East McMillan Street
Cincinnati, OH 45206-1947
513-861-6400
800-486-3116
E-mail: mrobertson@tui.edu (Michael Robertson, Admissions Director)
URL: http://www.tui.edu/

Campus Visits

Attendance is required at a ten-day regional colloquium to begin studies. Colloquia are held nationwide. Fifteen days of seminars are required at regional sites as the degree progresses. Sites are sometimes maintained abroad for foreign applicants. Inquire directly about the site nearest you.

Admission

Applicants should hold master's degrees from accredited institutions. Exceptional applicants who do not hold master's degrees will sometimes be considered by petition. Applicants in the creative arts will be asked to submit a portfolio of their work for review. Because applicants design their own degrees, all applicants should be exceptionally motivated and have some career experience or knowledge in the areas they wish to study. International learners are accepted but should inquire about meeting residency requirements from foreign locations. A computer and modem will facilitate communication with faculty and staff.

Programs

6–8 semesters

Doctor of Philosophy/Emphasis in Creative Arts & Communications
Doctor of Philosophy/Emphasis in Educational Administration
Doctor of Philosophy/Emphasis in Environmental Studies
Doctor of Philosophy/Emphasis in Health & Healthcare
Doctor of Philosophy/Emphasis in Literature & Creative Writing
Doctor of Philosophy/Emphasis in Multicultural Studies
Doctor of Philosophy/Emphasis in Organizational Behavior & Development
Doctor of Philosophy/Emphasis in Peace Studies
Doctor of Philosophy/Emphasis in Philanthropy & Leadership
Doctor of Philosophy/Emphasis in Professional (Clinical/Counseling) Psychology
Doctor of Philosophy/Emphasis in Psychoanalysis
Doctor of Philosophy/Emphasis in Public Policy
Doctor of Philosophy/Emphasis in Racial & Ethnic Studies
Doctor of Philosophy/Emphasis in Social & Political Thought & Action
Doctor of Philosophy/Emphasis in Sociology & Social Work
Doctor of Philosophy/Emphasis in Women's Studies

Tuition & Fees

Basic Tuition:	$3,860 per semester
Doctorate Tuition:	$23,160–$30,880
Financial Aid:	Government loans, discounted early payments, payment plans

Notes

The Union Institute, a private college, was founded in 1964 by a board of ten regionally accredited college presidents seeking to develop an innovative low-residency distance learning university for self-directed adults. The institute awards self-designed bachelor's and doctorate degrees. Doctoral learners combine two or more subject areas to create unique interdisciplinary degrees within the institute's fifteen broad areas of study. For example, art and counseling psychology could be combined to earn a Professional Psychology degree in art therapy; or sociology and criminal justice could be combined to create a Public Policy degree covering rehabilitation in the prison system. Learners interested in completing technical studies should consult with a Union advisor. Union does not commonly support technical or scientific studies, such as engineering or computer science, but may support related degrees such as a self-designed plan to study management in technological areas. Learners must take the initiative to locate local mentors and arrange tutorials and internships in their areas of interest. A final master work, or Project Demonstrating Excellence (PDE), is required of all learners. PDEs may be creative, critical, or based in social action. An internship of at least three months (410 hours) is required for all degree-seekers. Prior professional experience may sometimes be reviewed for direct credit toward the doctorate. Professional psychology (clinical/counseling) graduates have qualified to sit for mental health licensing exams in most states. Psychoanalytical therapy and other therapy orientations are possible areas of study. The Union Institute operates within a three-semester per calendar year format. A minimum of six semesters (two years) is required to earn a degree. The average time actually taken to earn a degree is three years and three months. Professional psychology applicants must complete a minimum of eight semesters, with a required number of clinical/counseling internship hours also required. The academic year begins July 1 of each year. E-mail, an electronic bulletin board system, and the World Wide Web, are used for communication with faculty and other learners.

UNITED STATES SPORTS ACADEMY

Distance Learning Admissions
One Academy Drive
Daphne, Alabama 36526-7055
334-626-3303
800-223-2668
E-mail: academy@ussa-sport.usaa.edu
URL: http://www.sport.usaa.edu

Campus Visits

Students who elect the thesis option must attend a public thesis proposal defense and a final thesis defense on campus. Courses that require laboratory access (sports medicine) must be completed on-campus through resident study, or in conjunction with a certified lab with the approval of the USSA program.

Admission

Admission to the Certification and Continuing Education Programs are open to anyone, regardless of educational level or background. Applicants seeking the master's degree must be graduates of regionally accredited four-year undergraduate colleges with a minimum GPA of 2.75, and composite scores on the GRE of at least 800, or a raw score on the MAT of at least 27. Applicants with other credentials may receive provisional acceptance. Sports Medicine and Sports Fitness Management degree majors will need to meet prerequisite course requirements in the sciences. A computer and modem with E-mail and World Wide Web access is required for the program. International applicants with a minimum TOEFL score of 550 are welcome.

Programs

12–48 CEUs
Certificate in Bodybuilding
Certificate in Personal Training
Certificate in Sport Coaching
Certificate in Sport Management

33 credits
Master of Sport Science/Sport Coaching
Master of Sport Science/Sport Fitness Management
Master of Sport Science/Sport Management
Master of Sport Science/Sport Medicine

Tuition & Fees

Basic Tuition:	$25 per CEU; $300 per credit
Certificate Tuition:	$300–$1,200
Master's Tuition:	$9,900
Financial Aid:	Federal Stafford loans, Alabama state teacher grant-in-aid, veteran's benefits

Notes

The United States Sports Academy was founded in 1972 in direct response to the ever-increasing need for a scientific and academically supported program of sports study. The Academy is the nation's first and only free standing, accredited academic institution dedicated solely to professional graduate studies in sports. In addition to being regionally accredited, the Academy is licensed and approved by the Alabama Department of Education to grant the Master of Sport Science degree. The Alabama State Board of Education (ASBE) has approved the Academy's programs to prepare coaches, sports trainers, and coach-trainers at the master's degree (Class A) certification level. Student who satisfactorily complete the ASBE requirements will be eligible for Class A or master's level certification in Alabama and in other states that have signed the National Association of State Directors of Teacher's Education and Certification (NASDTEC) reciprocity agreements, provided that the state in which the student seeks such reciprocity has a certification program. Students seeking teacher certification in states other than Alabama should check with their local school administration and state Department of Education. Students may earn their degrees and certification credentials through either on-campus or distance learning study. The distance delivery option allows students to earn a degree through a combination of independent and practical applied study with limited travel to the campus. Degree-seekers are required to take 12 semester credits of core theory courses, 15 semester credits in a major area, and 6 credits of mentorship or thesis. In the mentorship option, students must complete a minimum of 360 contact hours of field experience in their local communities. Distance learning requires the student to work with a faculty member using a course syllabus, study guides, required text and readings, and optional teaching technologies such as E-mail, video, telephones, and faxes to receive classes. The special sports certificate/certification programs award continuing education units (CEUs) rather than degree credits.

UNIVERSITY OF ALABAMA

Department of Criminal Justice
Box 870320
Tuscaloosa, AL 35487-0320
205-348-7795
E-mail: cjdept@cj.as.ua.edu
URL: n/a

Campus Visits

Two-week orientations are held in January, May, and August of each year. Degree seekers spend four weeks completing readings, then attend two-week study sessions on campus. Learners then return home to complete a seminar paper or written report, which is evaluated for credit by the faculty. Learners typically attend three two-week on-campus sessions each year.

Admission

Applicants must hold bachelor's degrees from accredited colleges. An undergraduate major in the social sciences or criminal justice is preferred but not required. To be admitted unconditionally, the applicant must have a minimum 3.0 GPA in the last two years of bachelor's work. The GRE or MAT is required for admission. Applicants with undergraduate GPAs below 2.5 should score at least 1500 on the GRE or 50 on the MAT. No minimum exam score is required for those with a 3.0 or above bachelor's GPA. International applicants are welcome with TOEFL. Applicants should be practitioners of criminal justice.

Programs

30 credits
Master of Science in Criminal Justice

Tuition & Fees

Basic Tuition:	$103 per credit
Master's Tuition:	$3,090
Financial Aid:	None

Notes

The University of Alabama, founded in 1831, is government supported. Distance programs operate as extensions of on-campus offerings, which include a variety of undergraduate, graduate, and professional programs. The distance learning criminal justice degree was launched in 1975. The degree may be completed with a research thesis or with a policy and practice paper. Non-degree learners are not admitted. Up to six credits may be transferred in toward the master's after successful completion of at least twelve credits in the program. E-mail may be used to communicate with faculty and other learners.

UNIVERSITY OF ALABAMA—HUNTSVILLE

Engineering Department
Engineering Building 120
Distance Learning
Huntsville, AL 35899
205-890-6976
E-mail: utley@ebs330.eb.uah.edu (Dawn Utley, Assistant Professor)
URL: n/a

Campus Visits

None

Admission

Applicants must hold an ABET-accredited engineering bachelor's with a minimum 3.0 GPA and meet all engineering departmental requirements. Departmental requirements include a minimum score of 1500 on the GRE or the equivalent on the MAT. Two years of career experience as an engineer in a U.S.-based firm is also required. International learners are admitted.

Programs

33–36 credits

Master of Science in Industrial & Systems Engineering/Option in Manufacturing Systems
Master of Science in Industrial & Systems Engineering/Option in Systems Engineering
Master of Science in Industrial & Systems Engineering/Option in Engineering Management
Master of Science in Civil and Environmental Engineering

Tuition & Fees

Basic Tuition:	$550–585 per 3-hour credit (Alabama); $630 (East of Mississippi) $675 (West of Mississippi/East of Pacific); $895 (Pacific Coast); $995 (international)
Master's Tuition:	$18,150–$35,820
Financial Aid:	None

Notes

The University of Alabama is a government-supported institution founded in 1831. The Huntsville campus was founded in the 1950s and became an independent and autonomous campus within the Alabama System in 1969. On-campus programs include a variety of undergraduate, graduate (including Ph.D.), and professional degree offerings. The undergraduate engineering program is accredited by the Accreditation Board for Engineering and Technology (ABET). Distance Learning programs at the graduate level operate as extensions of on-campus offerings and were first introduced in 1992. On-campus courses are videotaped, then mailed second-day delivery to registered distance learners. E-mail and phone conferencing are used to facilitate faculty and learner interaction. The engineering program is delivered to industry partners nationwide, Boeing, Proctor & Gamble, and Saturn Corporation, to name a few.

UNIVERSITY OF ALABAMA—QUEST

Office of Educational Telecommunications
Quality University Extended Site Telecourses
Box 870388
Tuscaloosa, AL 35487-0388
205-348-9278
E-mail: ctingle@ccs.ua.edu
URL: http://ualvm.ua.edu/~estudies/ccs.html

Campus Visits

None

Admission

Applicants to master's study must hold an accredited bachelor's and meet all engineering departmental requirements. Departmental requirements may include the submission of scores on the Engineering GRE. International learners are admitted.

Programs

33–36 credits

Master of Science in Aerospace Engineering
Master of Science in Civil Engineering
Master of Science in Electrical Engineering
Master of Science in Environmental Engineering
Master of Science in Mechanical Engineering

Tuition & Fees

Basic Tuition:	$150 per credit
Master's Tuition:	$4,950–$5,400
Financial Aid:	None

Notes

The University of Alabama is a government-supported institution founded in 1831. On-campus programs include a variety of undergraduate, graduate, and professional degree offerings. Distance programs operate as extensions of on-campus offerings. The QUEST program—Quality University Extended Site Telecourses—began in 1991. QUEST staff videotape on-campus lectures, then mail videotapes to learners nationwide or overseas. Individuals may receive course videotapes and take proctored exams through their local libraries, community centers, military centers, or work sites. Private corporations may apply to be sites and receive QUEST courses. The only special equipment required to become a site is a VCR and a television set. No special fees are charged to individuals or corporations to become sites. A separate program (IITS), utilizes compressed video to deliver courses to specially equipped sites located throughout the state of Alabama. Undergraduate video-based courses are also available on a limited basis in engineering, computer science, business, and professional nursing. Non-degree learners are accepted to QUEST but all who take courses through QUEST must first be officially admitted to the University of Alabama.

UNIVERSITY OF ALASKA—FAIRBANKS

Center for Distance Education and Independent Learning
College of Rural Alaska
P.O. Box 756700
Fairbanks, AK 99775-6700
907-474-5353
E-mail: sycde@orca.alaska.edu
URL: http://www.uafcde.uaflrb.alaska.edu

Campus Visits

No campus visits are required to complete some of the individual courses. The Teacher Credentialing programs and Master of Education degrees require learners to reside in Alaska, spend two weeks on the Juneau, Alaska, campus each summer, and complete student-teaching practicums in the classroom. The Master of Education in Educational Technology requires some on-site study at the Juneau campus.

Admission

A regionally accredited bachelor's degree is required. Selected courses may require a computer. Alaskan teachers who are seeking credits for teacher certification or recertification can generally earn graduate credit through the Alaska program without being admitted to a degree program. Courses may require employment in a school environment to complete practicums. Individual courses may be taken by learners residing anywhere but Teacher Credentialing programs and the Master of Education degree programs only accept applicants who reside in Alaska.

Programs

Credits vary
Certificates/Teaching Credentials:
Early Childhood Teacher Education (Preschool–Third Grade)
Educational Technology
Elementary Education
Principal/Educational Leadership
45 credits
Master of Education in Early Childhood Education
36 credits
Master of Education in Educational Technology

Tuition & Fees

Basic Tuition:	$153 per credit
Certificate Tuition:	Varies
Master's Tuition:	$5,508–$6,885
Financial Aid:	Alaska state aid, veteran's benefits, government loans

Notes

The University of Alaska is a government-supported university founded in 1917. A variety of undergraduate and professional programs are offered on campus at various sites in Juneau, Sitka, and Fairbanks. Distance learning programs operate as extensions of on-campus offerings. The Alaska Independent Learning program has offered correspondence courses for more than three decades. Electronic mail may be used to send lessons for some courses. Surface mail, fax, satellite, cable TV, audioconferencing, and video course delivery methods are used throughout the program. Residents of Alaska may explore Alaska's alternative teacher certification programs. These programs typically combine distance learning with limited site-based study.

UNIVERSITY OF ARIZONA

School of Information Resources and Library Science
Master of Arts in Information Resources and Library Science
1515 East First Street
Tucson, AZ 85721
520-621-3565
E-mail: fsg@u.arizona.edu (Francis Stephen Griego)
URL: http://timon.sir.arizona.edu

Campus Visits

Currently twelve units, four three-unit courses, must be earned at the Tucson campus. The School of Information Resources and Library Science offers three summer sessions by which one may earn as many as fifteen units. The doctorate program requires two consecutive full-time semesters, fall and spring, on campus. All students pay in-state tuition during the summer term.

Admission

Applicants must have a bachelor's degree with a 3.0 GPA. The general GRE is required with preferred scores at the 85th percentile. International applicants must earn 580 on the TOEFL. Graphical web access is required for the virtual education program.

Programs

36 credits
Master of Arts in Information Resources and Library Science
48 credits post-master's
Doctor of Philosophy in Information Resources and Library Science

Tuition & Fees

Basic Tuition:	$320 per 3 credit course (Arizona);
	$1,043 per 3-credit course (others)
Master's Tuition:	$3,840 (Arizona); $12,516 (others)
Doctorate Tuition:	$5,120 (Arizona); $16,688 (others)
Financial Aid:	Government aid, American Library Association scholarships

Notes

The University of Arizona, a research and land grant institution, was founded in 1885. Academic divisions include the following colleges: Agriculture, Architecture, Arts and Sciences, Business and Public Administration, Education, Engineering and Mines, Law, Medicine, Nursing, and Pharmacy. A full range of undergraduate, graduate, and professional programs are offered throughout the academic year and summer school. The School of Information Resources and Library Science is accredited by the American Library Association and offers courses focusing on the study of information and its use as a social phenomenon. The degree is heavily weighted in technology and emphasizes theoretical constructs of information resources. Competence and adaptability in manipulating information and in using advancing technologies are key aims of the curriculum. Individual courses are open to non-degree status learners. Currently the virtual program has distance students in Alaska, Arizona, California, Colorado, Delaware, Florida, Idaho, Iowa, Maryland, Montana, Nevada, New Mexico, Ohio, Oregon, Pennsylvania, South Dakota, Utah, Vermont, Virgin Islands, Washington, Wyoming, the Universidad de las Americas in Puebla, Mexico, and Canada.

UNIVERSITY OF ARIZONA—EXTENDED UNIVERSITY

Distance Learning Program, #301Q
P.O. Box 210158
Tucson, AZ 85721-0158
520-526-2079
800-478-9508
E-mail: villafar@ccit.arizona.edu (Mimi Villafane)
URL: http://w3.arizona.edu/~uaextend/distance.htm

Campus Visits

None

Admission

The program is open to students in the United States who hold a bachelor's degree in engineering, math, or physics. The university highly recommends that students have completed one university introductory course in Probability & Statistics within the last five years. The university offers a distance refresher course in Calculus & Probability for those who need it. International students can not be accommodated.

Programs

15 quarter credits

Professional Certificate in Reliability & Quality Engineering

Tuition & Fees

Basic Tuition:	$1,760 per course, plus $400 videotape fee
Certificate Tuition:	$8,800, plus videotape fees
Financial Aid:	Arizona state resident tuition discounts, Early registration discounts

Notes

The University of Arizona is a state-supported institution founded in 1885. On-campus degree programs include a full array of undergraduate, graduate, and professional offerings. The university has pioneered distance learning programs since 1972. The Reliability & Quality Engineering program draws on the university's internationally renowned departments of Systems & Industrial Engineering (SIE) and Aerospace & Mechanical Engineering (AME). The Professional Certificate in Reliability & Quality Engineering from the University of Arizona College of Engineering and Mines consists of five courses including reliability and engineering testing, experimental design, engineering statistics, and probabilistic mechanical design. Instructors deliver courses primarily via mailed videotapes of on-campus lectures. All courses completed for the certificate can be applied later to the university's Master of Science in Reliability & Quality Engineering. To complete a master's degree, students must spend one semester in residency on campus and complete a minimum of 15 to 18 credits beyond the distance learning certificate. The Professional Certificate is intended for working engineers who want to further their education in the aerospace, military, automotive, electronic, and consumer product manufacturing fields, and for industry and government agencies with a need to train top-grade reliability engineers. The course prepares students for the American Society of Quality Control Certified Reliability Engineer or Certified Quality Engineer exams.

UNIVERSITY OF BRIDGEPORT

Office of Distance Education
126 Park Avenue
Bridgeport, CT 06601-2449
203-576-4851
800-470-7307
E-mail: ubonline@cse.bridgeport.edu
URL: http://www.bridgeport.edu

Campus Visits

Degree-seekers must attend a final comprehensive examination at the university's main campus in Bridgeport, or at a special distance site approved by the university.

Admission

A bachelor's degree from an accredited college with a GPA of 3.0 or better is required of applicants. An IBM-compatible or Macintosh computer with a modem and Internet access is also required. Applicants are expected to have completed undergraduate prerequisite courses in Human Anatomy and Physiology and Introductory Biochemistry. International applicants with TOEFL at or above 550 are welcome to apply.

Programs

31 credits
Master of Science in Human Nutrition

Tuition & Fees

Master's Tuition:	$320 per credit
Degree Tuition:	$9,920
Financial Aid:	Government loans

Notes

The University of Bridgeport is a private university founded in 1927 that launched its distance learning programs in 1997. The Master's of Science in Human Nutrition program focuses on the role of nutrition in both health and disease. The program is suitable for those with career training or interests in hospital care, chiropractory, nutrition consulting, pharmacy, and other allied health fields. Graduates of the program may qualify for state-specific licensing or certification programs such as Certified Nutrition Specialists (CNS) or Certified Clinical Nutritionists (CCN). Course work is delivered primarily online via an electronic campus on the World Wide Web. Instructors deliver lectures via computer conferencing, video and audiocassettes, and CD-ROM. After completing all nine required courses, students must pass a final examination in-person to earn the degree.

UNIVERSITY OF COLORADO

Executive Program in Health Administration
P.O. Box 480006
Denver, CO 80248-0006
303-623-1888
800-228-5778
E-mail: peter_taffe@together.cudenver.edu
URL: http://www-bus.colorado.edu/execed/home.htm

Campus Visits

Every six months, learners are required to attend intensive campus residencies. A total of nine weeks must be spent on campus to complete the twenty-five month degree program.

Admission

A bachelor's degree from an accredited college is required for admission. A significant number of applicants already hold higher degrees in medical or health care fields. Applicants should be practicing health care professionals with a minimum of three years of professional responsibility in a health care agency. Applicants must have access to a computer and modem. A telephone interview is required. Applicants with GMAT or GRE scores may submit them for consideration. Canadian residents are currently enrolled. Applicants from other countries should inquire directly about the feasibility of completing the program.

Programs

48 credits
Master of Science in Health Administration

Tuition & Fees

Basic Tuition: $28,000 for the two-year program
Master's Tuition: $28,000 (comprehensive tuition and fees; includes books)
Financial Aid: Government loans, educational loans, half-tuition scholarships

Notes

The University of Colorado was founded in 1876 and is a government-supported university. Distance programs operate as extensions of on-campus offerings. The health degree program is fully accredited by the Accrediting Commission on Education for Health Services Administration (ACEHSA). Instruction takes place through printed media and electronic conferencing. A comprehensive program fee, charged to all applicants, includes conferencing software, textbooks, and reading material. Up to six credits may be reviewed for transfer toward the master's degree. Individual courses are not open to non-degree students. No thesis is required for the degree.

UNIVERSITY OF COLORADO—CATECS

Center for Advanced Training in Engineering & Computer Science
Campus Box 435
Boulder, CO 80309-0435
303-492-6331
E-mail: micucciv@spot.colorado.edu
URL: http://www.colorado.edu/CATECS

Campus Visits

Most degrees require a final visit to campus to orally defend either the final project report (Master of Engineering) or the final thesis (Master of Science). Learners may arrange to receive mailed videotapes of on-campus lectures. Learners in Colorado may opt to attend public broadcast sites to receive live interactive lectures in Littletown, or attend interactive broadcasts at their place of employment if their employers participate in the CATECS program. The Master of Science, as opposed to the Master of Engineering, may require campus classes in some departments depending on course offerings.

Admission

An undergraduate engineering degree from an accredited college is typically required for admission. Admission requirements and course prerequisites vary with department. Applicants are expected to have strong academic backgrounds in science and math, if not engineering, with a 3.0 undergraduate GPA and some professional experience. The GRE may be required for those with undergraduate GPAs below 3.0. No special exams are required for admission but because more learners apply than can be accommodated in some programs, learners are encouraged to submit their GMAT or GRE scores for consideration. International applicants are accepted.

Programs

30 credits
Master of Engineering/Aerospace Engineering
Master of Engineering/Computer Science
Master of Engineering/Electrical and Computer Engineering
Master of Engineering/Engineering Management
Master of Engineering/Telecommunications

30–32 credits
Master of Science/Aerospace Engineering
Master of Science/Electrical and Computer Engineering
Master of Science/Telecommunications

Tuition & Fees

Basic Tuition:	$332 per credit
Master's Tuition:	$9,960–$10,624
Financial Aid:	Government loans, scholarships, minority scholarships, fellowships, veteran's benefits

Notes

The University of Colorado was founded in 1876 and is a government-supported university. The Center for Advanced Training in Engineering & Computer Science (CATECS) began broadcasting courses to work sites in 1983 to help fill the need for site-based engineering training in the Rocky Mountain region. CATECS still sends live, interactive microwave lectures to equipped public and corporate sites in Colorado but has expanded to offer video-based lectures to learners nationwide, and as far away as Saudi Arabia and Australia. The Internet is used to facilitate learning and communication. Either the Master of Engineering (ME) or the Master of Science (MS) degree can be earned in most engineering departments. The Master of Engineering is an interdisciplinary degree, allowing learners to take courses from departments other than engineering, such as management.

University of Colorado—JEC

C/O JEC College Connection
9697 East Mineral Avenue
P.O. Box 6612
Englewood, CO 80155-6612
800-777-6463
E-mail: edcenter@meu.edu
URL: http://www.jec.edu

Campus Visits

None

Admission

An accredited bachelor's degree is required. The certificate is intended for those who teach reading in the public schools. Some courses may require learners to practice tutoring in a local classroom. Some courses require E-mail communication. Applicants should either have access to JEC Cable TV or have a VCR for viewing mailed videotapes of lectures.

Programs

8 credits
Certificate in Early Reading Instruction

Tuition & Fees

Basic Tuition:	$350 per 3-credit course
Certificate Tuition:	$935
Financial Aid:	None

Notes

JEC College Connection, formerly known as Mind Extension University (ME/U), is an educational company that assists colleges and universities in presenting their curriculum and degrees via a variety of electronic distance learning platforms. Cable broadcasts, mailed videotapes, E-mail, the World Wide Web, electronic forum conferencing, fax and toll-free phone advising are used for program delivery. The University of Colorado at Colorado Springs was founded in 1965 and is a government-supported learning institution offering a variety of undergraduate, graduate, and professional degrees on-campus. Distance learning programs operate as extensions of on-campus degrees, offering the same curriculum and faculty. The School of Education is accredited by the North Central Association of Teacher Education and the Colorado Department of Education. The reading certificate is for those interested in developing early literacy in children. Remedial and literacy techniques for the preschool and elementary school population are covered. Courses meet teacher certification needs in Colorado and other states. Individual courses are open to enrollment by non-certificate learners. Learners without cable access may rent videotapes of course lectures, which are then mailed to them for a variable fee.

UNIVERSITY OF COLORADO—MBA

C/O JEC College Connection
9697 East Mineral Avenue
Post Office Box 6612
Englewood, CO 80155-6612
800-777-6463
E-mail: edcenter@meu.edu
URL: http://www.jec.edu

Campus Visits

None

Admission

Applicants should possess regionally accredited bachelor's degrees. Applicants to the Master of Business Administration program must submit scores on the GMAT. Applicants to the Master of Public Administration program may submit scores on either the GMAT or the GRE. Public administration majors will be required to complete an internship as a part of their degree if they enter the program without significant career experience in public administration or nonprofit management. A computer, modem (at least 14.4 bps), and Internet access are required. Learners need access to video equipment to view taped course lectures or access to JEC Knowledge TV broadcasts. International learners who submit a TOEFL score are welcome.

Programs

36 credits
Master of Business Administration
Master of Public Administration

Tuition & Fees

Basic Tuition: $650 per 3-credit course
Master's Tuition: $7,800
Financial Aid: Loans, payment plans

Notes

JEC College Connection, formerly known as Mind Extension University (ME/U), is an educational company that assists colleges and universities in presenting their curriculum and degrees via a variety of electronic distance learning platforms. Cable broadcasts, mailed videotapes, E-mail, the World Wide Web, electronic forum conferencing, fax, and toll-free phone advising are used for program delivery. The University of Colorado at Colorado Springs was founded in 1965 and is a government-supported learning institution offering a variety of undergraduate, graduate, and professional degrees on campus. Distance learning programs operate as extensions of on-campus degrees, offering the same curriculum and faculty. The MBA program is accredited by the American Assembly of Collegiate Schools of Business (AACSB). The Graduate School of Public Affairs is accredited by the National Association of Schools of Public Affairs and Administration. The MBA and MPA have a common eighteen-credit core business curriculum and are designed to be completed in a two-year cycle.

UNIVERSITY OF GUELPH

Independent Study/OAC ACCESS
Room 010
Johnston Hall
Guelph, Ontario
Canada N1G 2W1
519-767-5050
E-mail: handbook@access.uoguelph.ca
URL: http://www.uoguelph.ca/istudy

Campus Visits

None

Admission

Applicants to the post-diploma horticulture certificate program should hold an appropriate degree or diploma in horticulture, agriculture, landscape design, forestry, or a closely related field, and may be required to write an entrance exam in their chosen subject area prior to beginning study.

Programs

5 course minimum, plus qualifying exams
Post-diploma Horticulture Certificate/Specialization Commercial Floriculture
Post-diploma Horticulture Certificate/Specialization Landscape Contracting
Post-diploma Horticulture Certificate/Specialization Landscape Design
Post-diploma Horticulture Certificate/Specialization Landscape Maintenance
Post-diploma Horticulture Certificate/Specialization Nursery Management
Post-diploma Horticulture Certificate/Specialization Park Horticulture
Post-diploma Horticulture Certificate/Specialization Small Business Management
Post-diploma Horticulture Certificate/Specialization Turf Management
Post-diploma Horticulture Certificate/Specialization Urban Forestry

Tuition & Fees

Basic Tuition: $250 average (courses vary widely in cost)
Certificate Tuition: $1,250–$2,500
Financial Aid: None

Notes

The University of Guelph is a provincially administered member of the Association of Universities and Colleges of Canada, the association charged with monitoring accredited learning in Canada. All independent study horticulture and landscaping programs, including the post-diploma certificate program, are approved by the senate of the University of Guelph. Independent study registers more than 6,000 active learners annually from across North America in self-directed learning opportunities, ranging from a single course to a certificate or a diploma program. All independent study offerings can be taken for personal enrichment or for professional development. Most courses are print-based with supplementary video materials. Assignments are returned by learners to the university by mail, by fax, or by E-mail for assessment and returned with detailed comments. All post-diploma certificate candidates must complete a minimum of five independent study courses, plus a final qualifying examination in their area of specialization. Additional fees for examinations apply.

Tuition fees are in Canadian dollars.

UNIVERSITY OF IDAHO—ENGINEERING OUTREACH

Jansen Engineering Building
Moscow, ID 83844-1014
208-885-6373
800-824-2889
E-mail: outreach@uidaho.edu
http://www.uidaho.edu/evo/

Campus Visits

After completion of all courses, master's degree candidates are required to come to campus to take a final comprehensive exam or present a thesis. Doctoral students must spend a minimum of the last academic year on-campus doing research.

Admission

Admission to the computer science program is highly competitive. Computer science applicants are expected to have strong undergraduate backgrounds in computer theory and applications, a minimum 3.0 undergraduate GPA, and a minimum score of 1700 on the general GRE. Most engineering programs accept applicants with bachelor's degrees related to engineering and a minimum undergraduate GPA of 2.8. Some engineering programs require the GRE. The GREs are generally required for applicants who have not attended ABET-accredited engineering programs. Some engineering programs will review applicants who have earned bachelor's degrees from non-regionally accredited or non-ABET-accredited engineering colleges. International applicants are welcome with TOEFL scores at or above 550.

Programs

36 credits (thesis)
Master of Arts in Teaching/Mathematics
Master of Engineering/Agricultural
Master of Engineering/Civil
Master of Engineering/Computer
Master of Engineering/Electrical
Master of Engineering/Geological
Master of Engineering/Mechanical
Master of Science in Engineering/Agricultural
Master of Science in Engineering/Civil
Master of Science in Engineering/Computer
Master of Science in Engineering/Electrical
Master of Science in Engineering/Geological
Master of Science in Engineering/Mechanical
Master of Science in Engineering/Mining
Master of Science in Engineering/Metallurgical
Master of Science in Psychology/Human Factors

30 credits (non-thesis); 36 credits (thesis)
Master of Science in Computer Science

78 credits
Doctor of Science in Computer Science

Tuition & Fees

Basic Tuition: $292 per credit (non-degree), $319 per credit (graduate students)
Master's Tuition: $9,570–$11,484
Doctorate Tuition: $24,882
Financial Aid: Veteran's benefits, Federal family loans

Notes

The University of Idaho is a government-supported institution founded in 1889. The Engineering Outreach program videotapes on-campus lectures, then mails the videotapes to learners. Videotapes are mailed to the homes of individual learners or to company site locations. Electronic conferencing is desired. Non-degree learners are welcome. Learners who take courses for undergraduate credit may pay a lower tuition: $292 per credit. Tuition and fees are reduced if two or more students share videotapes. Up to twelve credits may be transferred in toward most degree programs.

University of Illinois at Urbana–Champaign

Graduate School of Library & Information Science
LEEP 3—Excellence in Online Education Program
501 East Daniel Street
Champaign, IL 61820-6211
800-982-0914
E-mail: leep@alexia.lis.uiuc.edu
URL: http://alexia.lis.uiuc.edu/leep3/

Campus Visits

A two-week summer orientation must be attended on-campus in July. Applicants are required to attend at least one three-day weekend session on-campus each semester.

Admission

Applicants should hold an accredited bachelor's degree, with a preferred GPA of 3.0 (B) on the last sixty semester credits or junior and senior years of undergraduate study. Applicants must submit scores on the general GRE, a personal statement, and three references. A computer with a CD-ROM and a modem as well as Internet access are required. Preference will be given to applicants who have strong technological abilities, support from their workplace, and a willingness to work with faculty to pioneer new curriculum delivery methods. Applicants not familiar with online access and research methods will be given an on-campus orientation to the technology prior to beginning studies. International applicants are welcome with TOEFL scores at or above 620.

Programs

40 credits
Master of Science in Library & Information Science

Tuition & Fees

Basic Tuition:	$3,150 per full-time year (Illinois); $8,580 per full-time year (others)
Master's Tuition:	$6,300–$17,160
Financial Aid:	Government loans, Illinois State library scholarship for Illinois residents

Notes

The University of Illinois at Urbana–Champaign is a comprehensive, government-supported educational institution founded in 1867. The distance learning online LEEP degree program was launched in 1996 and operates as an extension of on-campus offerings through the Graduate School of Library and Information Science. The program is accredited by the American Library Association (ALA). Local applicants may combine on-campus courses with Internet-based distance learning as needed to complete the degree. Courses are delivered using multiple methods, including asynchronous computer discussions and synchronous computer chats as well as research and informational access via the World Wide Web. Course work includes theoretical independent study, a community library practicum, and a final thesis. Up to four credits earned at another ALA-accredited graduate school may be accepted in transfer toward the master's degree.

UNIVERSITY OF ILLINOIS AT URBANA-CHAMPAIGN— CCEE

University of Illinois at Urbana-Champaign—CCEE
Off-Campus Courses and Degree Programs
College of Continuing Engineering Education
Division of Extramural Programs
301 John Street, Suite 1405
Champaign, IL 61820
217-333-1320
800-252-1360, ext. 3-9806
E-mail: gustin@ntx1.cso.uiuc.edu (Dr. Ken Gustin, Program Director)
URL: http://www.engr.uiuc.edu/OCEE

Campus Visits

No campus or site visits are generally required, however, faculty reserve the right to require brief visits for selected courses offered within the program. During the 1997–98 academic year, applicants were required to study in clusters of at least five engineers at company-sponsored sites in the United States. Any company may become a site by assigning an individual in the human resources department to distribute and return course videotapes, proctor course exams, and make sure a VCR is available to play course videotapes. The program is migrating from video-based delivery to an Internet platform during the 1997–98 academic year. The Internet delivery program will allow individual engineers to study on their own, outside the small-group format that has been required for the video-based program. Alternatively, the program is also offered at public and corporate study sites throughout the state of Illinois.

Admission

Degree seekers must hold the equivalent of a regionally accredited bachelor's degree with a minimum undergraduate GPA of 3.0 on a 4.0 = A scale for admission to most degree programs. The Mechanical Engineering program requires applicants to hold at least a bachelor's degree from an ABET-accredited engineering program and have a minimum undergraduate GPA of 3.0, with a 3.25 minimum for the last 60 credits hours. Individual departments may enforce varying admissions standards. Internet and World Wide Web access is required to complete some courses in the program.

Programs

32–36 credits

Master of Science/Electrical and Computer Engineering
Master of Science/General Engineering
Master of Science/Mechanical Engineering
Master of Science/Theoretical and Applied Mechanics

Tuition & Fees

Basic Tuition:	$198 per credit
Master's Tuition:	$6,336–$7,128
Financial Aid:	Veteran's benefits

Notes

The University of Illinois at Urbana-Champaign is a government supported university founded in 1867. On-campus programs serve more than 36,000 full-time students each year at the undergraduate, graduate, and professional level. The off-campus, distance learning engineering program uses the same standards, faculty, and degree content as the on-campus program. On-campus courses are videotaped and surface mailed to students for viewing. Faculty support students via telephone and E-mail. The program is migrating to an Internet delivery platform to accommodate student/faculty interaction online. For most degrees, a thesis or non-thesis option may be taken. Thesis degrees generally require completion of approximately 32 semester credits (8 units), while non-thesis degrees require a minimum of 36 semester credits (9 units). Applicants not seeking the degree but wishing to complete individual courses are eligible for enrollment. The university is a member of the Association for Media-Based Continuing Education for Engineers (AMCEE). In addition to the tuition rates given, off-campus students are charged an additional $30 fee for each course enrollment.

UNIVERSITY OF LA VERNE

Graduate & Professional Studies
1950 Third Street
La Verne, CA 91750
909-593-3511, ext. 4382/4385
E-mail: n/a
URL: n/a

Campus Visits

Applicants must join study clusters at one of fourteen established sites in California. Clusters meet on Saturdays or once weekly. At the beginning of each semester applicants must attend a weekend Road Show at one of three specific sites in California.

Admission

The program is open to practicing school administrators, K–12 who hold master's degrees. Applicants must attend meetings once a week at an established site in California. The GRE or the MAT is required for admission. Minimum recommended score on the GRE is 1,000. The minimum recommended score on the MAT is 50.

Programs

36–48 credits
Certificate of Advanced Study in Educational Management
54 credits (post-master's)
Doctor of Education in Educational Management

Tuition & Fees

Basic Tuition:	$455 per credit
Certificate Tuition:	$16,400–$21,900
Doctorate Tuition:	$24,600
Financial Aid:	Payment plans, government loans, California state grants, scholarships

Notes

The University of La Verne is a private, comprehensive college established in 1881. On-campus programs include a variety of bachelor's, master's, and professional degree options. The limited residency educational doctorate is intended for those who administer K–12 schools and programs. Studies will meet the Preliminary or Professional Administrative Services Credential requirement for the California Board of Education. The certificate program allows applicants to complete all studies but the research thesis. It is essentially a non-thesis doctoral option for advanced studies. Individual independent study courses are not open to non-degree learners because all studies are site-based at one of thirteen California sites.

UNIVERSITY OF LONDON—BIRBECK COLLEGE

External Programme
Senate House, Room 3W
Malet Street
London
United Kingdom WCI E 7HU
44-01-71-636-8000, ext. 3150
E-mail: s.gidman@eisa.lon.ac.uk (Susan Gidman, Deputy Director, Marketing)
URL: http://www.lon.ac.uk/external

Campus Visits

None

Admission

Applicants to master's study in psychology must be qualified through the possession of a good honors degree in psychology or the possession of a good honors degree in which half the assessment was in psychology. Applicants to organizational behavior master's study should possess a good honors undergraduate degree in any area. Applicants to diploma study should hold a good honors degree in any subject or have sufficient previous education and experience to demonstrate a level of proficiency equivalent to a good first honors degree. Diploma applicants without first honors degrees who do exceptionally well on their diploma exams may be invited to continue their registration into the master's program. Applicants must have access to local libraries and study resources to undertake these programs. International applicants are encouraged. Instruction is self-guided, leading to annual competency exams.

Programs

6 modules
Diploma in Organizational Behavior
9–12 modules
Master of Science in Organizational Behavior
Master of Science in Occupational Psychology

Tuition & Fees

Basic Tuition:	585 British Pounds Sterling (Registration Fee) ($936 US);
	677 British Pounds Sterling (Study Modules) ($1,083 US)
Diploma Tuition:	1,939 British Pounds Sterling ($3,102 US)
Master's Tuition:	3,293 British Pounds Sterling ($5,268 US)
Financial Aid:	Aid to United Kingdom residents only

Notes

The University of London, founded in 1836, has provided tutoring and instruction to external learners since 1858. Operating under Royal Charter, the university is recognized as the equivalent of a regionally accredited university in the United States. More than fifty colleges are affiliated with the university, providing lead instruction in various topics. Birbeck College is the lead or sponsoring college for the occupational psychology program. The external programs listed in this profile provide only study syllabus and recommended reading programs. They do not provide one-on-one instruction from faculty. In October of each year, learners have the option of submitting written assignments, on which they will receive written feedback from tutors in preparation for their exams. The written assignments do not count toward the grade or success of any course. Success is determined solely by a written three-hour final exam taken in each course. Applicants self-study, then take annual proctored competency examinations at approved testing sites worldwide to earn the final degree. The organizational behavior and occupational psychology programs are made available through the faculty of Birbeck College and qualify learners in the United Kingdom to apply for registration as a Chartered Occupational Psychologist.

A conversion rate of 1 United States dollar to .60 British Pound Sterling is used. Conversion rates may vary.

UNIVERSITY OF LONDON—CIEE

**Centre for International Education in
Economics, SOAS
Thornhaugh Street
London
United Kingdom WC1H OXG
44-01-71-637-7075 (fax)
Email: cieeuol@soas.ac.uk
URL: http://www.soas.ac.uk/Centres/CIEE**

Campus Visits

None

Admission

The Postgraduate Diploma in Economic Principles is designed for non-economists in need of a conversion or preparatory course to pursue further studies in graduate economics and finance by distance learning. Applicants to the Postgraduate Diploma program must have a good undergraduate degree with some work experience. Applicants who successfully achieve the Postgraduate Diploma in Economic Principles will be invited to continue on for their master's degree in one of the discrete departments. For direct entry into a master's program, applicants should possess a good first degree in economics, or, alternatively, appropriate professional qualifications that include economics. International learners are welcome.

Programs

4 courses
Postgraduate Diploma in Economic Principles
Postgraduate Diploma in Development Finance
Postgraduate Diploma in Financial Economics
Postgraduate Diploma in Financial Policy

7 courses
Master of Science in Development Finance
Master of Science in Financial Economics
Master of Science in Financial Management

Tuition & Fees

Basic Tuition:	720 British Pounds Sterling per course ($1,152 US)
Diploma Tuition:	3,450 British Pounds Sterling ($5,520 US)
Master's Tuition:	5,870 British Pounds Sterling ($9,392 US)
Financial Aid:	None

Notes

The University of London was founded in 1836 and is one of Britain's top three universities, together with Oxford and Cambridge. The university has provided tutoring and instruction to distance or external learners for more than 100 years. The university operates under Royal Charter, recognized as the equivalent of regional accreditation in the United States. The School of Oriental and African Studies (SOAS), founded by Royal Charter in 1916, is one of fifty colleges that comprise the University of London system. This school houses the economics, finance, and development external study programs. Course instruction takes place using multiple delivery systems, including computer software, specially written learning guides, videotaped lectures, and traditional textbook readings. Tutors and faculty are accessible via E-mail. A "fast-track" option allows learners to complete master's course modules in eight-week stretches over two years.

The grade in each course is determined through grades earned on assignments (30 percent) and final exam grades (70 percent). Final exams are held in proctored settings worldwide each September through November and typically last three hours. Exam pass rates worldwide are 94 percent. Master's degree requirements include completing seven courses or six courses and a dissertation. Up to two individual courses may be taken by learners who wish to sample the program. The development finance program focuses on the special study of economics in developing countries. Tuition given includes all texts and study materials. Winner of the Queen's Anniversary Prize for Higher and Further Education 1996, CIEE has around 1,000 students worldwide.

A conversion rate of 1 U.S. dollar to .60 British Pound Sterling is used. Conversion rates may vary.

University of London—King's College

External Programme
Senate House, Room 3W
Malet Street
London
United Kingdom WCI E 7HU
44-01-71-636-8000, ext. 3150
E-mail: s.gidman@eisa.lon.ac.uk (Susan Gidman, Deputy Director, Marketing)
URL: http://www.lon.ac.uk/external

Campus Visits

None

Admission

Applicants to master's study should possess a good first undergraduate honors degree in geography or a related cognate. Applicants without honors degrees may be given undergraduate qualifying exams in geography to determine special eligibility. Applicants will be individually assessed and may be deemed qualified for master's study without holding a first degree by special examination or by virtue of their career or professional background. Applicants should have access to local libraries, study resources, and a possible fieldwork site to undertake this program. International applicants are encouraged. Instruction is self-guided, leading to a two-part competency exam and a dissertation.

Programs

2 competency exams plus a dissertation
Master of Arts in Geography

Tuition & Fees

Basic Tuition:	1,000 British Pounds Sterling (Fees) ($1,600 US)
Master's Tuition:	1,000 British Pounds Sterling (Fees) ($1,600 US)
Financial Aid:	Aid to United Kingdom residents only

Notes

The University of London, founded in 1836, has provided tutoring and instruction to external learners since 1858. Operating under Royal Charter, the university is recognized as the equivalent of a regionally accredited university in the United States. Over fifty colleges are affiliated with the university, providing lead instruction in various topics. King's College is the lead or sponsoring college for the geography program. King's College was founded in 1829 by King George IV and the Duke of Wellington. This century, five scientists from King's College have been awarded Nobel Prizes. The external programs listed in this profile provide only study syllabi and recommended reading programs. They do not provide one-on-one direct instruction from faculty. Applicants may wish to register for structured courses at local colleges to supplement or structure their studies. Tuition stated is only an estimate of the exam and dissertation reading fees charged by King's College. Degree success is determined solely by scores on a two-part written comprehensive exam and a dissertation of 10,000 words. Applicants study alone, then take annual proctored competency examinations at approved testing sites worldwide to earn the final degree.

A conversion rate of 1 United States dollar to .60 British Pound Sterling is used. Conversion rates may vary.

UNIVERSITY OF LONDON—WYE COLLEGE

Wye College
External Programme
Wye, Ashford
Kent
United Kingdom TN25 5AH
44-01-23-381-3555
E-mail: ep@wye.ac.uk
URL: http://www.wye.ac.uk

Campus Visits

None

Admission

Applicants to the master's program should hold a first or second class honors bachelor's from an accredited college or have professional qualifications suitable for advanced study. Applicants without undergraduate degrees who perform well on their diploma exams may be invited to continue on for the master's degree. Applicants are encouraged worldwide. A TOEFL score of 500 is expected for all non-native English speakers.

Programs

4 courses
Postgraduate Diploma in Agricultural Development
Postgraduate Diploma in Agricultural Development & Environmental Management
Postgraduate Diploma in Agricultural Economics
Postgraduate Diploma in Applied Environmental Economics
Postgraduate Diploma in Environmental Management
Postgraduate Diploma in Food Industry Management & Marketing

7 courses
Master of Science in Agricultural Development
Master of Science in Agricultural Development & Environmental Management
Master of Science in Agricultural Economics
Master of Science in Applied Environmental Economics
Master of Science in Environmental Management
Master of Science in Food Industry Management & Marketing

Tuition & Fees

Basic Tuition: 790 British Pounds Sterling per course ($1,264 US)
Diploma Tuition: 3,500 British Pounds Sterling ($5,600 US)
Master's Tuition: 5,950 British Pounds Sterling ($9,520 US)
Financial Aid: Overseas research student award (non-UK)

Notes

The University of London was founded in 1836 and is one of Britain's top three universities, together with Oxford and Cambridge. The university has provided tutoring and instruction to distance or external learners for more than 100 years. The university operates under Royal Charter, the equivalent of regional accreditation in the United States. Wye College operates as a postgraduate college of the University of London, an affiliation of more than fifty institutions, serving more than 40,000 learners. For over 100 years, Wye College has served as the University of London's center of excellence for research and graduate education relating the natural and social sciences to agriculture, the food industry, and the rural environment and economy. In 1994 Wye College was one of twenty-one prize winners from among 700 competitors for a Queen's Anniversary Prize for Higher and Further Education. Each master's program requires the completion of seven courses or six courses and a dissertation. Learners submit three assignments to their tutors for each course. The assignments are not formally graded, but are used to provide extensive feedback to the learners on their progress. The final assignment in each course is a mock examination paper devised to help learners prepare for the final course exam. To pass each course, learners must pass the final exam, which is taken in a proctored setting. Individual courses are open to learners worldwide who wish to sample the program. Graduates of Wye College's external programs are later eligible to participate in the University of London's research-based distance doctoral program. Tuition given includes all texts and study materials.

A conversion rate of 1 U.S. dollar to .60 British Pound Sterling is used. Conversion rates may vary.

UNIVERSITY OF LOUISVILLE

Department of Special Education
School of Education - Room 158
Louisville, KY 40292
502-852-6421
E-mail: d0edge01@ulkyvm.louisville.edu (Dr. Denzil Edge, Program Director)
URL: http://www.louisville.edu/edu/edsp/distance/

Campus Visits

Students must attend a two-day orientation at the Kentucky School for the Blind to receive an introduction to the program and the electronic delivery systems. Attendance is also required at a summer institute to complete the program.

Admission

Applicants must hold at least a bachelor's degree. Applicants wishing to earn the master's degree must submit satisfactory GRE scores. Students seeking teacher certification in the area of visual impairment must hold certification in early childhood, elementary, middle, or secondary education prior to enrollment, and have access to a local mentor (professional in the field of visual impairment) to participate in the program. Applicants should have access to a local satellite downlink site to receive courses that are broadcast on Kentucky Educational Television, Star Channel 8, or may receive videotapes of courses and participate in them via the Internet and the World Wide Web. Kentucky residents may also access courses on Cable TV. Students are also required to have a fax machine, computer and modem, Internet access, and a Braille machine to complete the program.

Programs

27 credits
Certificate/Teacher Preparation Program in Visual Impairment
33 credits
Master of Special Education/Certificate in Visual Impairment
Tuition & Fees
Basic Tuition: $166 per credit (Kentucky); $459.50 (others)
Certificate Tuition: $4,482 (Kentucky); $12,406.50 (others)
Degree Tuition: $5,478 (Kentucky); $15,163.50 (others)
Financial Aid: WHAS scholarships, ACT scholarships, Bell-Schuman awards

Notes

The University of Louisville is a government-supported university founded in 1798. The School of Education was founded in 1968 and began offering distance learning courses in 1992. The School of Education is accredited by the National Council for Accreditation of Teacher Education. Based on the need for more teacher preparation in the area of visual impairment in the rural areas of Kentucky and nationwide, the Department of Special Education has created a new distance delivery system that combines a short campus orientation and summer institute with electronically delivered distance learning courses to provide teacher training for those who wish to work with the visually impaired. Applicants may earn either the Certificate in Visual Impairment (27 credits) or a master's degree in the field of special education/visual impairment (33 credits). The master's degree requires students to complete two additional courses, one in educational research, and one in the philosophy of education at the University of Louisville or another graduate school. The courses are delivered via interactive TV, the World Wide Web, E-mail, videotapes, and electronic listservs. Candidates must complete a local teaching internship and practicum to graduate.

UNIVERSITY OF MARYLAND UNIVERSITY COLLEGE

Graduate School of Management and Technology
Distance Learning
University Boulevard at Adelphi Road
College Park, MD 20741-0869
301-985-7200
E-mail: gradinfo@nova.umuc.edu
URL: http://www.umuc.edu/prog/gsmt/dist-ed.html/

Campus Visits

None

Admission

Applicants must hold a bachelor's degree or its equivalent from a regionally accredited college with an overall GPA of 3.0 (B) in the last sixty semester credits of the bachelor's program. Applicants with GPAs of 2.5 may be provisionally admitted. All learners must have a computer, modem, and Internet access.

Programs

36–39 credits

Master of Science in Computer Systems Management/Information Resources Management
Master of Science in Technology Management
Master of General Administration/Applied Management
Master of General Administration/Financial Management
Master of General Administration/Health Care Administration
Master of General Administration/Human Resources Management
Master of General Administration/Not-For-Profit Management
Master of General Administration/Procurement and Contact Management
Master of International Management/International Commerce
Master of International Management/International Finance
Master of International Management/International Marketing

Tuition & Fees

Basic Tuition:	$273 per credit (Maryland); $353 per credit (others)
Master's Tuition:	$9,540–$10,335 (Maryland); $12,340–$13,377 (others)
Financial Aid:	Government loans, veteran's benefits, DANTES military benefits, Maryland state scholarships for residents

Notes

The University of Maryland is a government-supported institution founded in 1947. The Graduate School of Management and Technology was founded in 1978. The school is a part of the University of Maryland University College system, which is one of the eleven degree-granting institutions of the University of Maryland System. The first online graduate program, the Master of Science in Computer Systems Management, was launched in the Spring of 1997. The Master of Science in Computer Systems Management (CSMN) is designed for information personnel, including programmers, developers, engineers, and other knowledge workers who are involved in technology development and management. The Graduate school's distance degree programs are designed specifically for midcareer professionals. Each of the degree programs addresses the real challenges facing managers in today's globally competitive business environment and integrates the study of theory with the practical applications of managerial study. Programs are delivered online, using a combination of the University of Maryland's proprietary graphically oriented client/server communication software, Tycho, and the World Wide Web. Tycho allows learners to participate in online conferences, read faculty notes on course material online, upload assignments, receive tutoring, work on group projects online, and access library services electronically.

UNIVERSITY OF MASSACHUSETTS

Video Instruction Program (VIP)
College of Engineering
113 Marcus Hall, Box 35115
Amherst, MA   01003-5115
413-545-0063
E-mail: vip@vip.ecs.umass.edu
URL: http://www.ecs.umass.edu/vip/

Campus Visits

Master's programs require no campus visits. Doctorates require the last academic year be spent engaged in research on campus.

Admission

Applicants should hold bachelor's degrees from recognized colleges with a minimum undergraduate GPA of 2.75 and a strong undergraduate academic background in engineering, math, physics, or a related hard science. Access to the Internet is mandatory. The GRE general exam is mandatory. International scholars are welcome and required to take the TOEFL exam.

Programs

33–36 credits

Master of Science in Computer Science
Master of Science in Electrical & Computer Engineering
Master of Science in Engineering Management
Master of Science in Engineering Management/Quality Control & Reliability

Credits vary

Doctorate in Electrical & Computer Engineering
Doctorate in Industrial Engineering

Tuition & Fees

Basic Tuition:	$1,225 per 3-credit course
Master's Tuition:	$14,700
Doctorate Tuition:	Varies
Financial Aid:	Government loans

Notes

The University of Massachusetts is a government-supported institution founded in 1863. The Video Instruction Program (VIP) has delivered courses to remote sites since 1974. VIP courses may be delivered to students via live broadcasts, videotapes, electronic conferencing means, or the Internet. Videotapes are generally delivered to corporate sites, but may also be delivered to homes. Master's may be completed with a thesis or without one. Professional study courses are also available in engineering, science, math, computer science, and technology and management and are open to non-degree learners. Individual noncredit training courses on various topics are available for rental or purchase.

UNIVERSITY OF MEMPHIS

Department of Journalism
Online Program
Campus Box 52661
Memphis, TN 38152-6661
901-678-4779
E-mail: ewbrody@cc.memphis.edu (Dr. Bill Brody, Journalism Department)
URL: http://umvirtual.memphis.edu/

Campus Visits

Only those who elect to complete a thesis need to visit the campus to defend it.

Admission

Applicants to the program must have a minimum composite GRE score of 900, with a minimum score of 500 on the verbal portion, or a minimum score of 40 on the MAT. A minimum undergraduate GPA of 3.0 is required. Applicants should hold bachelor's degree in journalism or mass communication from programs accredited by the Accrediting Commission on Education in Journalism and Mass Communications (ACEJMC) or earn grades of "C" or better on the following undergraduate courses from an ACEJMC-accredited undergraduate program: Survey of Mass Communications, Media Writing, and any third journalism course. Applicants who do not hold an undergraduate degree from an accredited department of journalism may, under certain circumstances, be admitted to the degree program on a conditional basis. Applicants must have access to a computer with a modem and the Internet. A VCR is required to view course videotapes. International applicants with a minimum TOEFL score of 600 are welcome to apply.

Programs

30–36 credits
Master of Arts in Journalism/General Journalism
Master of Arts in Journalism/Journalism Administration

Tuition & Fees

Basic Tuition:	$1,113 per course fee (includes tuition, videotape rentals, and books)
Master's Tuition:	$11,113–$13,356
Financial Aid:	Tuition discounts for employees of National Newspaper Association

Notes

The University of Memphis is a comprehensive government-supported university, founded in 1912, that serves more than 20,000 students each year. It is one of forty-six institutions of the Tennessee Board of Regents system, and the seventh largest system of higher education in the United States. On-campus programs include an array of bachelor's degree, master's degree, and doctoral offerings. The Master of Arts in Journalism program is delivered via videotape, online through CompuServe, and the World Wide Web for those without access to CompuServe. For those with CompuSeve access, the Journalism Forum (JFORUM) and the Public Relations and Marketing Forum (PRSIG) archive course materials and discussions. Instructors also mail videotapes of their course lectures directly to student's homes. The degree program is appropriate for practicing professionals in print, broadcast, advertising, and public relations as well as individuals who lack career experience but hold undergraduate degrees in journalism or communications. Applicants may complete a thesis degree (30 credits), a course work-only degree (36 credits), or a degree that includes an applied professional project (33 credits). Journalism Administration majors are required to take a minimum of four courses (12 credit hours) or the MBA core of study from the College of Business and Administration.

UNIVERSITY OF MINNESOTA

Carlson School of Management
ISP—Executive Program
University Office Plaza
2221 University Avenue SE, Suite 110
Minneapolis, MN   55414-3074
612-625-1555
E-mail: chris180@gold.tc.umn.edu
URL: http://ispweb.csom.umn.edu

Campus Visits

A two-week summer intensive is required each year. Participation is required in regional one-day seminars and regional study groups. The master's degree requires a final three to five weeks on campus.

Admission

Applicants must be currently employed in health care administration. Applicants to the master's program must submit scores on the GRE with preferred minimum combined scores at the 50th percentile. A 3.0 undergraduate GPA is preferred for master's applicants. International learners are welcome.

Programs

55 quarter credits
Credential of Advanced Studies in Health Services Administration

30 quarter credits
Credential of Management Studies in Health Services Administration

70 quarter credits
Master in Healthcare Administration/Ambulatory Care Administration
Master in Healthcare Administration/Hospital Administration
Master in Healthcare Administration/Patient Care Administration

Tuition & Fees

Basic Tuition: $189 per quarter credit average
Credential Tuition: $5,700–$10,400
Master's Tuition: $13,000
Financial Aid: Veteran's benefits

Notes

The University of Minnesota is a government-supported institution founded in 1848. The Executive Healthcare Program has been in operation since 1969. The program is fully accredited by the Accrediting Commission on Education for Health Services Administration (ACEHSA) and the Council on Education for Public Health (CEPH). Once registered for the program, learners may join special interest groups to focus on areas of specialized interest like elder health services or dental group management. Learning takes place according to the multi-method model, which emphasizes the integration of management theory with practice. More than 2,700 health care executives from thirty nations have enrolled in the program since its inception.

UNIVERSITY OF MISSOURI—COLUMBIA

Continuing Engineering Education
W1000 EBE
Columbia, MO 65211
800-776-1044
E-mail: eastinb@ext.missouri.edu (General); rpotter@ecn.missouri.edu (Richard Potter,
College of Engineering)
URL: http://www.missouri.edu/~ceeewww/courses/online.html

Campus Visits

None

Admission

Applicants should hold a bachelor's degree from an accredited institution and submit
their GRE scores. Additional program requirements may apply. Students must have a
computer with a Windows operating system and Internet access to participate in online
course work. International applicants are welcome, and should submit their TOEFL
scores.

Programs

36 credits
Master's in Environmental Engineering

Tuition & Fees

Basic Tuition: $598.80 per 3-credit course
Master's Tuition: $7,186
Financial Aid: Inquire directly

Notes

The University of Missouri—Columbia, the oldest university west of the Mississippi River,
is a comprehensive government-supported university. Distance learning programs
operate as extensions of on-campus and continuing education offerings. The university
launched the online graduate degree program in environmental engineering in 1996
under a grant from the Alfred P. Sloan Foundation. Engineers from around the world may
participate in this degree program via the Internet. The program is delivered using a
combination of printed textbooks, videotapes, World Wide Web presentations (for
lecture notes, exam reviews, links to online learning resources, and homework
assignments), and asynchronous computer conferencing is used for classroom
discussions, project and team presentations, and case studies. The program is accessible
through FirstClass software, which is made available to registered students.

UNIVERSITY OF NEBRASKA LINCOLN—CHRFS

College of Human Resources & Family Sciences
Distance Learning Masters in Human Resources & Family Sciences
P.O. Box 830800
Lincoln, NE 68583-0800
402-472-2913
E-mail: agri030@unlvm.unl.edu
URL: http://ianrwww.unl.edu/ianr/chrfs/EXTEDUC.htm

Campus Visits

None

Admission

Applicants should hold a bachelor's degree with a minimum GPA of 3.0 and a minimum of 12 semester credits of undergraduate course work related to the primary area of interest (i.e., consumer affairs, home economics education, housing, human development, family science, textiles, design, clothing, or nutrition). Those who need to take undergraduate prerequisite course work may do so through the University of Nebraska undergraduate correspondence program or any other regionally accredited distance learning program. Applicants are required to submit GRE scores and a written statement addressing the reasons they want to undertake graduate studies. Students must have a computer with Internet access to complete the online course work and a VCR to view taped mini-lectures.

Programs

36 credits
Master of Science in Interdepartmental Human Resources and Family Sciences

Tuition & Fees

Basic Tuition:	$156 per credit
Master's Tuition:	$5,607
Financial Aid:	None

Notes

The University of Nebraska—Lincoln is a government-supported university. On-campus programs include a full array of undergraduate, graduate, and professional degree options. The university delivers the interdepartmental Master of Science degree via the World Wide Web and videocassettes of lectures that are mailed directly to students. Students view the lectures and read assigned books and materials, then go online to interact with students and faculty via asynchronous message boards and E-mail. The virtual classroom supports multi-way interaction with the instructor, other students, and learning teams ranging from three to six students who complete group projects or hold electronic classroom discussion groups. The degree program provides a general human resources and family sciences background. It is designed to be completed through part-time study over a four-year period, with a final written exam and critical research paper. The degree consists of the following components: 18 credit hours in the Family and Consumer Sciences department; 6 credits hours in the Textiles, Clothing, and Design department; 6 credit hours in the Nutritional Science and Dietetics department; 3 credit hours in Research Methods; and 3 credit hours in Statistics. Individual courses can be audited for half the regular tuition fee, or can be taken for credit by non-degree students.

UNIVERSITY OF NEBRASKA—LINCOLN

Department of Educational Administration
1204 Seaton Hall
P.O. Box 880638
Lincoln, NE 68588-0638
402-472-3726
800-742-8800
E-mail: fwendel@unlinfo.unl.edu (Frederick Wendel, Professor)
URL: http://www.unl.edu/tcweb

Campus Visits

On-campus attendance is required for a minimum of two ten-week periods during the summer sessions in years one and two, or at two regular semesters, preferably consecutive ones.

Admissions

Applicants should hold regionally accredited bachelor's degrees. A master's degree and current employment in a collegiate setting are desirable, as the program is built on a practitioner's model. Applicants are required to have a computer, modem, and Internet access. The Graduate Record Exam (GRE) is required for admission along with a 500-word essay. International learners are welcome with TOEFL scores at or above 550.

Programs

56–92 credits

Doctor of Education in Administration, Curriculum, & Instruction/Educational Leadership & Higher Education

Doctor of Philosophy in Administration, Curriculum, & Instruction/Educational Leadership & Higher Education

Tuition & Fees

Basic Tuition:	$99 per credit (Nebraska); $245 per credit (others); Additional distance learning fees may apply
Doctorate Tuition:	$5,558–$9,131 (Nebraska); $13,734–$22,563 (others)
Financial Aid:	Government loans

Notes

The University of Nebraska—Lincoln is a comprehensive government-supported university, founded in 1869. A variety of undergraduate, graduate, and professional programs are offered on campus. The distance learning doctorate option operates as an extension of on-campus offerings and is designed to allow educational practitioners currently working in community colleges and public and private four-year educational institutions to pursue advanced studies while remaining employed. The program uses a "collaborative learning-reflection on practice approach" conducted through interactive computer-based communications and "journaling" methodologies. Distributed collaborative learning takes place through virtual groups whose members are widely distributed geographically but who study together primarily using asynchronous computer means. A Lotus Notes platform is used in program delivery online. A guiding principle is that learning is the responsibility of the student, with faculty facilitating learning through encouragement, guidance, and leadership. Interactive television and video may be used to deliver some courses to those located in the Nebraska reception area. The three-year program (fifty-six credit minimum) assumes a master's is held at entry. A longer program (up to ninety-two credits) may be required for those lacking a master's at entry or needing to take additional foundation work in educational theory or practice.

UNIVERSITY OF NEW ENGLAND

Distance Learning Master's Program
Hills Beach Road
Biddeford, ME 04005
207-283-0171, ext.2848
800-604-6088
E-mail: msed@mailbox.une.edu
URL: http://www.une.edu/cpcs/msedhm.html

Campus Visits

Applicants attend a half-day orientation session. Inquire directly about the orientation session nearest you. Applicants must attend a one-week integrating seminar on campus in Maine.

Admission

A bachelor's degree from a regionally accredited college is required for admission. All applicants must have at least one year of teaching experience and be either employed as K-12 teachers or able to submit evidence that they have a sponsoring school that will support a teaching internship on their behalf. A study team or study partner is a required part of the degree program. Applicants should have access to E-mail to facilitate learning and program communication.

Programs

33 credits
Master of Science in Education

Tuition & Fees

Basic Tuition:	$235 per credit ($60 per course materials; $55 one-time fee)
Master's Tuition:	$8,400
Financial Aid:	Loans, veteran's benefits

Notes

The University of New England (UNE) is a comprehensive, private, independent college founded in 1978. UNE recently merged with Westbrook College, a small liberal arts college in Portland, Maine. The university now recognizes Westbrook College's 1831 charter date as the University of New England's founding date. The university has been ranked by *U.S. News & World Report* as one of the best regional liberal arts colleges in the country. Distance learning programs operate as extensions of on-campus offerings. The distance learning education degree meets the requirements for permanent New York State teaching certificate (K–12) and may assist students in other states to meet teacher credentialing standards. The program uses videotapes and print materials, which are surface mailed to all registrants. E-mail, fax, and a toll-free telephone system are used to facilitate communication. Students may transfer up to six credits into the program. Currently students are accepted from the six New England states and New York State. Additional states and foreign countries may be added soon. Call for details.

UNIVERSITY OF NORTH CAROLINA—CHAPEL HILL

School of Public Health, Department of Health Policy and Administration
Executive Master's Program
CB #7400 McGavran-Greenberg Hall
Chapel Hill, NC 27599-7400
919-966-7364
E-mail: emp@unc.edu
URL: http://www.sph.unc.edu/hpaa/

Campus Visits

A three-day orientation is required to begin studies. A six-week intensive session is required each summer. A two-week on-campus study session is required in January. North Carolina residents may attend one day of classes each week at various North Carolina extension sites rather than attend the intensive summer sessions.

Admission

The executive program admits mid-career professionals in health care who hold accredited bachelor's degrees with a minimum 3.0 GPA. To complete required courses and practicums, all applicants must be employed in a health or human services agency. Applicants should have at least three years of career experience unless a terminal graduate degree (MD, DDS, JD) has been earned. E-mail and conferencing capabilities are required of all learners. Applicants should have knowledge of both accounting and statistics prior to applying. The GRE or the GMAT is required for admission unless a terminal doctorate has been earned. GRE scores for verbal and quantitative sections combined should be at 1000 or above. International applicants are welcome with the TOEFL.

Programs

39 credits
Master of Public Health with Concentration in Management
Master of Public Health with Concentration in Public Health Dentistry
51 credits
Master of Healthcare Administration with Concentration in Health Services Management

Tuition & Fees

Basic Tuition:	$160 per credit (North Carolina); $360 per credit (others)
Master's Tuition:	$6,240–$8,160 (North Carolina); $14,040–$18,360 (others)
Financial Aid:	None

Notes

The University of North Carolina, founded in 1795, is a state-supported institution. The low-residency executive master's program has been serving mid-career professionals worldwide for the last twenty-six years. The distance program operates as an extension of the on-campus program, which has served learners for the last forty years. Applicants must have access to an IBM-compatible computer and the Internet to communicate with faculty and study peers. Because all learners study part time, no financial aid or student loan programs are offered. Individual courses are generally not open to non-degree learners. Learners may pursue either the MPH or MHA degree and must state their intent to pursue one or the other in the second year of studies. Up to six credits from an accredited university may be reviewed for transfer toward a master's degree. The MPH program is accredited by the Commission on Education in Public Health (CEPH). The MHA program is accredited by the Accrediting Commission on Education for Health Services Administration (ACEHSA).

UNIVERSITY OF NORTH DAKOTA

Distance Education Coordinator
Department of Space Studies
P.O. Box 9008
Grand Forks, ND 58202-9008
701-777-2480
800-828-4274
E-mail: info@space.edu
URL: http://www.space.edu

Campus Visits

A two-week capstone seminar must be attended on campus before graduation.

Admission

Applicants should hold accredited bachelor's degrees in one of the following fields—engineering, science, communications, business, social science, or information systems—with at least one course in statistics, calculus, or computer programming, and one course in the social sciences and hard sciences. Applicants need access to a computer, modem, and Internet connection. International learners are welcome with English fluency (TOEFL required). Previous applicants have come from Australia, Cambodia, Canada, Columbia, France, Germany, Spain, and Sri Lanka.

Programs

32 credits
Master of Science in Space Studies

Tuition & Fees

Basic Tuition:	$258.08 per credit
Master's Tuition:	$8,258.56
Financial Aid:	NASA fellowships, graduate assistantships, government loans, DANTES tuition assistance

Notes

The University of North Dakota is a state-supported institution founded in 1883. The Graduate School is a member of the Midwest Association of Graduate Schools, the Western Association of Graduate Schools, and the Council of Graduate Schools. The Space Studies program is listed in the DANTES Extended Degree Catalog. The Department of Space Studies was founded in 1987. The Space Studies degree is interdisciplinary in nature, drawing on space law, technology concerns, and human factors in space. It is the only program of its kind in the world. Learners receive videotapes of classroom lectures, attend classes online using Internet Relay Chat software, and take tests and submit papers electronically.

UNIVERSITY OF OKLAHOMA

Master of Liberal Studies
1700 Asp Avenue, Suite 226
Norman, OK 73072-6400
405-325-1061
E-mail: cls@ou.edu
URL: n/a

Campus Visits

Attendance at three on-campus seminars is required of all students. The introductory seminar is offered as a two-week seminar and also on a split session format. The split session seminars meet Thursday through Sunday with a break of several weeks between the two four-day sessions. A mid-point colloquium of two weeks is required the second year. A final seminar of two weeks, during which the student defends a thesis, is required to complete the degree.

Admission

Applicants should hold accredited bachelor's, with a preferred 3.0 GPA over the last two years or sixty credits of undergraduate study, and be willing to engage in the creative and critical design of their own interdisciplinary degree. Conditional admission may be granted if the undergraduate GPA approaches 3.0. Museum applicants will be asked to submit reference letters from two professional associates. Preference will be given to individuals who have two years of professional museum or collections experience.

Programs

32 credits
Master of Liberal Studies
Master of Liberal Studies/Administrative Leadership
Master of Liberal Studies/Health Care
Master of Liberal Studies/Interdisciplinary Education
Master of Liberal Studies/Museum Emphasis

Tuition & Fees

Basic Tuition: $82 per credit (Oklahoma); $240 per credit (others)
Master's Tuition: $2,600 (Oklahoma); $7,720 (others)
Financial Aid: Scholarships, government loans, veteran's benefits

Notes

The University of Oklahoma, established in 1890, is a government-supported institution. On-campus offerings include undergraduate, graduate, and professional programs. Distance programs operate as extensions of on-campus offerings. The liberal studies program was launched in the 1960s as America's first bachelor's degree program specifically designed for part-time adults. The College of Liberal Studies is one of the twelve colleges of the University of Oklahoma at the Norman campus. The Master of Liberal Studies (MLS) option was added in 1967. In 1981, the Master of Liberal Studies with an emphasis in museum studies was added to serve active museum professionals. The MLS degree can be a self-designed program or students can opt for career tracks in Administrative Leadership, Interdisciplinary Education and Health Care as well as the Museum Emphasis program. Liberal Studies degree seekers design their own interdisciplinary degrees around one of the three broad areas of the liberal arts: humanities, natural science, or social science. Recent interdisciplinary degrees have covered, but not been limited to, projects in the social sciences (anthropology, economics, geography, history, political science, psychology, sociology, organizational behavior and change, alternative teaching and education models, international conflict, Native American studies), humanities (critical art studies, cultural history, literature, multicultural awareness, philosophy, women's studies, music), and the natural sciences (environmental policy studies, pollution studies, biology, physical science, earth science). Museum students study anthropology, zoology, art history, history, education, or another academic field of their choice. The program delivery is a combination of self-directed, print-based home study, short intensive on-campus seminars, and the research and writing of a thesis. Studies are undertaken tutorial style with faculty guidance. Electronic mail will facilitate student and faculty interaction. Seminars have grades of satisfactory (equivalent of B or better in graduate work) or unsatisfactory. All students complete a thesis.

UNIVERSITY OF PHOENIX—CDE

Center for Distance Education
4605 East Elwood Street, 7th Floor
Phoenix, AZ 85040
602-921-8014
800-366-9699
E-mail: cdeinfo.oramail@apollogrp.edu
URL: http://www.uophx.edu/cde.html

Campus Visits

None

Admission

Master's degree applicants are expected to hold a bachelor's degree from colleges that are regionally accredited or are candidates for regional accreditation. A minimum undergraduate GPA of 2.5 over the last two years is expected. Master of Nursing degree applicants must be Registered Nurses, employed in the United States, with at least three years of nursing experience, and have valid liability insurance. Nurses with non-nursing undergraduate degrees from regionally accredited colleges must complete a special ten-credit "bridge" program. At least three years of career experience is required to enter most master's programs. Applicants to the MBA/Technology program should have worked in technology-intensive environments and have held significant responsibility for the development, diffusion, production, or marketing of technology. International applicants are welcome with TOEFL scores at 580 or above.

Programs

51 credits
Master of Business Administration
Master of Business Administration/Technology Management
40 credits
Master of Arts in Organizational Management
38–40 credits
Master of Arts in Education/Administration (K–12)
Master of Arts in Education/Diverse Learner
39–40 credits
Master of Nursing

Tuition & Fees

Basic Tuition:	$325 per credit
Master's Tuition:	$12,350–$16,575
Financial Aid:	Government loans, DANTES military benefits, alumni scholarships

Notes

The University of Phoenix is a private college founded in the 1970s to provide bachelor's, master's, and professional education to adult learners. The campus includes forty-seven site learning centers in ten states and the Commonwealth of Puerto Rico. The Center for Distance Education (CDE) offers non-residency independent study via surface mail, fax, fax/mail, and E-mail. Programs follow a model that merges theory with practice concerns to better accommodate the adult learner. Education degrees may meet teacher licensing or certification needs for K–12 public school teachers in different states. The "diverse learner" option focuses on special education—gifted students as well as those with special needs. Selected individual courses are open to non-degree learners.

UNIVERSITY OF PHOENIX–ONLINE

100 Spear Street, Suite 110
San Francisco, CA   94105
415-541-0141
800-388-5463
E-mail: klbertne.oramail@apollogrp.edu (Kevin Bertness, Enrollment Supervisor)
URL: http://www.uophx.edu/online

Campus Visits

None

Admission

All applicants should hold bachelor's degrees from regionally accredited colleges or colleges which are candidates for regional accreditation, with a preferred undergraduate GPA of 2.5. Applicants should have a minimum of three years of career experience in their chosen study areas. Applicants are individually assessed to determine the need for undergraduate prerequisite study. Those seeking the MBA without a bachelor's degree in business may be required to take undergraduate foundation studies in accounting, finance, economics, and statistics. Undergraduate prerequisites are offered online by the university. A computer, modem, and Internet access are required. All courses are taught through an online electronic conferencing system. International learners are welcome with TOEFL scores at 580 or above.

Programs

45 credits
Master of Science in Computer Information Systems
41 credits
Master of Arts in Organizational Management
41 credits
Master of Business Administration/Global Management
51 credits
Master of Business Administration
Master of Business Administration/Technology Management

Tuition & Fees

Basic Tuition:	$425 per credit
Master's Tuition:	$17,425–$21,675
Financial Aid:	Government loans, tuition freeze guarantee on entry

Notes

The University of Phoenix is a private college established in 1976 to offer professional outreach programs to adult learners. The University of Phoenix is one of the largest and earliest enrollers of distance MBA learners in the United States, and the largest private business school in the United States. The online program is delivered through asynchronous computer conferencing. The MBA is a classic seventeen-course program. The technology and management major is intended for anyone involved in managing industries or operations that are technically driven—information systems managers, manufacturers, engineers, operations managers, and scientists. The Computer Information Systems degree is intended for those wishing to integrate the different aspects of information technology in a business applications context. The Global Management MBA provides learners with a broad-based understanding of the economics of international and global enterprises and prepares them to deal with cultural, political, and legal aspects of doing business abroad. Courses are accelerated, designed to be completed in six to eight weeks, or half the time of a regular semester system. New courses begin each month so learners need not wait for a new semester to begin their program of study. Courses are delivered via asynchronous computer conferencing with learners studying in interactive peer groups with no more than thirteen members. Up to nine credits of transfer work may be accepted toward a master's degree.

UNIVERSITY OF SAN FRANCISCO

College of Professional Studies
Institute for Nonprofit Organization Management
4306 Geary Boulevard, Suite 201
San Francisco, CA 94118
415-750-5180
800-281-5180
E-mail: komitod@usfca.edu (David Komito, Director of Education Programs)
URL: http://www.cps.usfca.edu/fundraising

Campus Visits

On-campus attendance is required every seventh week of the ten-month program.

Admissions

Applicants must demonstrate evidence of ability to do quality professional work comparable to graduate-level work. Evidence of career commitment to development and management work in a nonprofit setting is also required. Possession of a bachelor's degree from an accredited university or evidence of two years of college work coupled with evidence of professional work in fundraising will qualify as evidence of program preparedness. Applicants are required to have a computer, modem, and Internet access.

Programs

15 CEUs
Development Director Certificate

Tuition & Fees

Basic Tuition:	$5,600
Certificate Tuition:	$5,600
Financial Aid:	Scholarships

Notes

The University of San Francisco is a comprehensive private university, founded in 1855. A variety of undergraduate, graduate, and professional programs are offered on campus. The College of Professional Studies was founded in 1975 to meet the continuing and professional educational needs of older adults. The Institute for Nonprofit Management, a pioneer in the field of nonprofit administration, was founded in 1983. The distance learning Development Director Certificate is offered in conjunction with the on-campus Master of Nonprofit Administration (MNA) degree program. Applicants who complete the certificate and later attend the on-campus MNA program may be awarded up to twelve semester credits toward that professional degree. Courses are delivered using asynchronous conferencing, readings and lectures posted to the World Wide Web, E-mail, and phone conferencing. The program provides in-depth preparation for people interested in the role of chief fund-raiser for a nonprofit organization or for other professionals who want to develop their understanding of the fundraising function. The program covers marketing, annual giving, corporation and foundation philanthropy, major gifts, planned giving, and capital campaigns. On-campus residencies include presentations, lectures, and special projects by leaders in the fundraising field. A completely online, no-residency Executive Certificate in Nonprofit Management is under development for 1998.

UNIVERSITY OF SARASOTA

Graduate Admissions
5250 17th Street
Sarasota, FL 34235
941-379-0404
800-331-5995
E-mail: univsasr@Compuserve.com
URL: http://www.sarasota-online.com/university/graduate.html

Campus Visits

One- to two-week intensive sessions are held on campus throughout the year. Master's candidates usually attend a minimum of three two-week sessions during a two-year program. Doctoral candidates usually attend a minimum of six two-week sessions during a three-year program.

Admission

Master's applicants should hold regionally accredited bachelor's with a minimum undergraduate GPA of 3.0. Doctoral applicants should hold appropriate master's degrees from regionally accredited colleges with a minimum GPA of 3.0. Either the GRE or the MAT may be required for admission. International learners are welcome with TOEFL scores at or above 550 for doctoral study and at or above 500 for master's study. A computer and modem with access to the Internet will facilitate learning.

Programs

45–48 credits
Master of Arts in Guidance Counseling
Master of Arts in Human Services Administration
Master of Arts in Mental Health Counseling

39 credits
Master of Arts in Education/Curriculum & Instruction
Master of Arts in Education/Educational Leadership

60 credits post-master's
Doctor of Education/Counseling Psychology
Doctor of Education/Curriculum & Instruction
Doctor of Education/Educational Leadership
Doctor of Education/Human Services Administration
Doctor of Business Administration/Management
Doctor of Business Administration/Marketing
Doctor of Business Administration/(Computer) Information Systems
Doctor of Business Administration/International Business

Tuition & Fees

Basic Tuition:	$317 per credit
Master's Tuition:	$12,363–$15,216
Doctorate Tuition:	$19,020
Financial Aid:	Government loans, payment plans, veteran's benefits

Notes

The University of Sarasota is a private, independent graduate school founded in 1969 to provide higher educational opportunities to professionals working in education and business. Faculty and learners communicate via phone, E-mail, asynchronous computer conferencing, and surface mail. Counseling degrees require supervised internships or placements in counseling facilities as a part of the degree program. Applicants seeking to meet state or professional licensing requirements in counseling should speak with an advisor directly. Up to twelve credits earned at previous graduate programs may be reviewed for transfer toward a Sarasota master's degree. Up to twelve credits previously earned at regionally accredited programs may be accepted in transfer toward a Sarasota doctorate.

UNIVERSITY OF SOUTH CAROLINA

APOGEE Program
College of Engineering
Columbia, SC   29208
803-777-4192
803-777-3340 (fax)
E-mail: coleman@sc.edu
URL: http://www.sc.edu/deis

Campus Visits

Four Saturday visits are required each semester for master's learners to speak with faculty, present homework, and take examinations. The doctorate may require one year on campus to complete the required research dissertation.

Admission

The APOGEE program is open to applicants with ABET-accredited engineering bachelor's. Applicants without ABET-accredited bachelor's degrees may be required to complete extensive remedial work. The GRE is required for admission for those without ABET-accredited engineering degrees.

Programs

30 credits

Master of Science/Chemical Engineering
Master of Science/Civil and Environmental Engineering
Master of Science/Computer Engineering
Master of Science/Electrical Engineering
Master of Science/Mechanical Engineering

Credits vary

Doctorate in Engineering/Chemical Engineering
Doctorate in Engineering/Civil and Environmental Engineering
Doctorate in Engineering/Computer Engineering
Doctorate in Engineering/Electrical Engineering
Doctorate in Engineering/Mechanical Engineering

Tuition & Fees

Basic Tuition: $648 per course (South Carolina); $1,209 per course (others)
Master's Tuition: $19,440 (South Carolina); $36,270 (others)
Financial Aid: Veteran's benefits

Notes

The University of South Carolina is a government-supported institution founded in 1801. A comprehensive array of undergraduate, graduate, and professional degrees are offered on campus. The College of Engineering is one of the founding members of the Association for Media-Based Continuing Education for Engineers (AMCEE) and National Technological University (NTU). APOGEE (A Program of Graduate Engineering Education) operates as an extension of the on-campus engineering program. Registrants receive videotapes of on-campus lectures and complete the same assignments at the same time as on-campus learners. Courses are delivered via mailed videotapes to learners at a distance and via closed circuit television broadcasts to established college and corporate sites throughout South Carolina. Individual courses are open to non-degree students. Short courses are also offered.

UNIVERSITY OF ST. AUGUSTINE FOR HEALTH SCIENCES

Division of Distance Education
170 Malaga Street
Saint Augustine, FL 32084
904-826-0084
800-241-1027
E-mail: TKBaker@aug.com (Patricia King Baker)
URL: http://www.use.edu

Campus Visits

Master's applicants in physical therapy are required to attend a minimum of two three-week residencies at separate times, with additional short-term residency seminars of two-to-five days during the degree. Doctoral students also attend brief residencies

Admission

The Master's are advanced post-professional degrees for practicing physical therapists. Applicants should hold bachelor's degrees from accredited colleges and be licensed physical therapists at application. The GRE is required. International applicants are welcome.

Programs

45 quarter credits
Master of Science in Physical Therapy/Advanced Post-Professional Degree
36 quarter credits
Master of Business Administration/Health Care
26 quarter credits post master's
Doctorate of Physical Therapy

Tuition & Fees

Basic Tuition:	$329 per credit (Physical Therapy); $225–$495 per credit (MBA)
Master's Tuition:	$14,805
Financial Aid:	Loan program; Tuition reduction for physical therapists also admitted to the year-long, campus-based clinical residency program.

Notes

The University of St. Augustine for Health Sciences is a private school for health studies founded in 1966. The program is accredited by the Distance Education and Training Council. Distance learning courses have been offered since 1990. A campus-based Master of Physical Therapy (MPT) is offered for those seeking to become certified physical therapists. The distance degree is an advanced post-professional program. The program accepts only practicing physical therapists. While the distance program emphasizes orthopedics and manual therapy, learners may also focus on sports physical therapy, or industrial rehabilitation or neurology. The master' of Business Administration/Health Care is offered jointly by St. Augustine and ISIM University. Both colleges are DETC accredited schools. Up to twelve quarter credits may be transferred toward the degree. Learners and faculty communicate using surface mail, videotapes, and E-mail. Individual courses may be open to non-degree learners.

UNIVERSITY OF SURREY

M.Sc. Applied Professional Studies in Education & Training
Department of Educational Studies
Guildford, Surrey
United Kingdom GU2 5XH
01-48-325-9757
01-48-325-9519 (fax)
E-mail: E.Oliver@surrey.ac.uk (Elizabeth Oliver)
URL: http://www.surrey.ac.uk

Campus Visits

None

Admission

Normal entry is based on the possession of a British first honors degree or the equivalent such as a regionally accredited American bachelor's degree. Applicants who wish to enter based on career experience or the possession of nontraditional academic credentials are welcome. The program is intended primarily for those in leadership, program development, or teaching, tutoring, or training roles in industry. Individuals involved in community social services or post-secondary education are also welcome, as are international and overseas applicants.

Programs

4 course modules
Postgraduate Certificate in Applied Professional Studies in Education and Training
8 course modules
Postgraduate Diploma in Applied Professional Studies in Education and Training
12 course modules
Master of Science in Applied Professional Studies in Education and Training

Tuition & Fees

Basic Tuition:	310 British Pounds Sterling per course module ($456 US)
Certificate Tuition:	1,070 British Pounds Sterling ($1,600 US)
Diploma Tuition:	2,480 British Pounds Sterling ($3,200 US)
Master's Tuition:	3,720 British Pounds Sterling ($4,800 US)
Financial Aid:	None

Notes

The University of Surrey is a chartered university and a vocational and professional institute with more than 2,000 postgraduates enrolled in the areas of science, engineering, and human and educational studies. A regular residency program is available. More than 700 overseas learners are engaged in distance self-study through the sponsorship of Surrey faculty. Distance learning course modules cover the essentials of teaching and learning theory, curriculum design, assessment and evaluation of training and learning, management issues, organizational policy, the educational role of the trainer, and leadership in education. Distance learners may take specialized course modules in areas such as continual education, distance learning, higher education, youth and community education, teaching English as a second language, and gerontological education. Applicants who have appropriate academic experience/qualifications may request exemption from up to three course modules at the diploma or master's level. Courses are delivered primarily through print, mail, and audiocassettes, with some E-mail communication possible. Registrants complete and return two marked assignments for each course module. The master's requires a research thesis. Registrants not wanting to complete a thesis may terminate the program at the professional diploma level.

Fees are stated in British Pound Sterling and include most course module materials. A conversion rate of 1 United States dollar to .60 British Pound Sterling is used. Conversion rates may vary.

UNIVERSITY OF SURREY—ED.D

School of Educational Studies
Guildford, Surrey, GU2 5XH
United Kingdom
01-48-325-9757
01-48-325-9519 (fax)
E-mail: E.Oliver@surrey.ac.uk (Elizabeth Oliver)
URL: http://www.surrey.ac.uk

Campus Visits

None

Admission

Normal entrance qualification is a master's degree from a UK university or an overseas qualification of an equivalent standard, in education or a related field, plus at least four years' relevant professional experience. Applicants without a master's degree would normally be expected to complete eight modules from the University of Surrey master's program prior to commencement of doctoral program. Students completing program at a distance need access to a research library and the Internet.

Programs

9 course modules
Doctor of Education (Ed.D)

Tuition & Fees

Doctorate Tuition:	6,070 British Pounds Sterling ($9,712 US)
Financial Aid:	None

Notes

The University of Surrey is a chartered university and a vocational and professional institute with more than 2,000 postgraduates enrolled in the areas of science, engineering, and human and educational studies. A regular residency program (leading to M.Phil/Ph.D) is available. More than 700 overseas learners are engaged in distance self-study through the sponsorship of Surrey faculty. Students entering with a master's degree complete four modules in research methodology, four optional modules (from a wide choice), one research proposal module, one research seminar, and a thesis of approximately 50,000 words. There is an intermediate exit point (with an 18,000-word dissertation) leading to award of M.Sc. (Research).

A conversion rate of 1 United States dollar to .60 British Pound Sterling is used. Conversion rates may vary.

UNIVERSITY OF TENNESSEE

Engineering Management Program Office
UT Space Institute
Tullahoma, TN 37388
615-393-7378
888-822-UTSI, ext. 293
E-mail: ggarriso@utsi.edu
URL: n/a

Campus Visits

Applicants in Tennessee who reside close to a public or corporate equipped broadcast site are expected to attend a site and participate in the interactive video classroom environment. Applicants residing elsewhere may complete the degree through mailed videotapes. International learners are not accommodated.

Admission

Applicants should hold bachelor's degrees from ABET-accredited engineering programs with a minimum 2.7 GPA. Applicants should have at least two years of professional engineering experience, and meet all regular engineering departmental requirements. Applicants without ABET-accredited or the equivalent engineering bachelor's may be admitted with remedial prerequisite study that includes, at a minimum, engineering economics, engineering statistics, and proven computer proficiency.

Programs

33 credits
Master of Science/Industrial Engineering
36 credits
Master of Science/Engineering Management

Tuition & Fees

Basic Tuition:	$526 per 3-credit course (Tennessee); $1,134 (others)
Master's Tuition:	$4,900 (Tennessee); $13,000 (others)
Financial Aid:	None

Notes

The University of Tennessee, founded in 1794, is a government-supported institution. An array of undergraduate, graduate, and professional degrees are offered on campus. The distance engineering program operates as an extension of on-campus offerings, which include engineering degrees at the bachelor's, master's, and doctoral levels. Distance learning programs began in the 1960s. In the 1990s, the university began to use specially equipped remote broadcast classrooms to deliver course lectures and classes at interactive sites around Tennessee and to videotape engineering courses for mail delivery nationwide. The University of Tennessee at Knoxville and the Space Institute cooperate in the delivery of the engineering management and industrial engineering programs via distance means. The degree program is delivered to individuals and to receptive industrial sites nationwide. The curriculum is designed to ally theory with practice. Participants should have access to a computer and the Internet. A capstone project allows learners to apply course methods to problems or issues drawn from the real world of work. Learners must present an oral defense of their capstone project.

UNIVERSITY OF TENNESSEE—PEMBA

College of Business Administration
Physician Executive MBA Program
721 Stokley Management Center
Knoxville, TN 37996-0570
423-974-5061
888-446-5458
E-mail: mstahl@utk.edu (Michael J. Stahl, Program Director)
URL: http://www.pemba.utk.edu

Campus Visits

Physicians are required to spend four one-week residencies on campus—one every three months. Residencies are held in January, April, August, and December. Additionally, they must be able to log onto forty 3-hour, real-time interactive audio and data classes over the Internet on Saturday mornings throughout the program.

Admission

The program accepts applications from physicians only and admits applicants on a competitive basis. Applicants must submit all previous transcripts as well as a one-page essay that addresses why they wish to be a part of the program and what they hope to gain from it. Applicants must have access to a notebook computer and the Internet to participate in required course work online.

Programs

4 modules plus a yearlong project
Physician Executive Master of Business Administration

Tuition & Fees

Basic Tuition:	$40,000 (comprehensive degree fee)
Master's Tuition:	$40,000 (comprehensive degree fee)
Financial Aid:	None

Notes

The University of Tennessee at Knoxville is a state-assisted university founded in 1794. The American Assembly of Collegiate Schools of Business (AACSB) accredits all degree programs of the University of Tennessee—Knoxville College of Business Administration. The Physicians Executive Master's in Business Administration (PEMBA) was designed based on interviews with physicians and physician leaders to teach them the basic business skills and knowledge that will allow them to keep pace with the constant changes taking place in health care today. The PEMBA program was launched in January 1998, with a class of twenty-five physicians from ten different states. It is designed to be completed in a twelve-month period with study groups of no more than twenty-eight physicians. The PEMBA program is built around four curriculum module themes: Fundamentals of Business in the Healthcare Industry; Analyzing the Healthcare Firm; Continuous Improvement of Healthcare Systems; and Preparing for the Future of Healthcare. A final yearlong project helps physicians to apply their studies to real-life practice concerns. The results of the yearlong project are presented at the end of the program in oral and written form. Course work is delivered live via the Internet in interactive audio and data mode between the four required weeklong campus residencies. The program uses "WebWorks" to deliver 24-hour asynchronous access to online assignments that may include downloadable course materials, short audio and video units, and classroom discussion boards. Real-time Saturday morning sessions are delivered via "CyberClass," an Internet system that allows for real-time audio interactions, shared electronic whiteboard access for group collaboration, online pop quizzes, and the synchronized playback of PowerPoint multimedia presentations. The comprehensive $40,000 program fee covers textbooks and course materials in addition to academic tuition.

UNIVERSITY OF VICTORIA

Division of Continuing Studies
Certificate in Adult & Continuing Education (CACE)
P.O. Box 3010
Victoria, British Columbia
Canada V8W 3N4
250-721-7860
E-mail: danderson@uvcs.uvic.ca (Diane Anderson, Coordinator)
URL: http://www.uvcs.uvic.ca/csie/cace/cace.htm

Campus Visits

None

Admission

Applicants should be high school graduates with at least three years of career experience in adult education program design or delivery. Applicants typically hold professional positions as instructional designers, trainers, educational planners, personnel officers, or career counselors. International applicants are welcome.

Programs

8 noncredit courses
Certificate in Adult & Continuing Education (CACE)

Tuition & Fees

Basic Tuition: $295 per course
Certificate Tuition: $2,360
Financial Aid: None

Notes

Administered through the University of Victoria, a provincially sponsored institution, the Certificate in Adult and Continuing Education (CACE) program is developed and delivered through the combined efforts of several provincially supported Canadian universities: University of Alberta, University of Saskatchewan, and the University of Manitoba. All participating universities are members of the Association of Universities and Colleges of Canada. The Certificate in Adult & Continuing Education is a professional program for those involved in adult education offered both on campus and through distance means to those in colleges and corporations. Applicants complete four common core courses, then select four electives. Electives are commonly offered in instructional design, corporate training, literacy instruction, marketing, advising/counseling and women in adult education. Courses are delivered with administrative and instructional support through print, mail, audiocassettes, videotapes, and an optional bulletin board system accessible on the Internet. Individual courses are open to non-certificate learners, if space allows. Applicants may attend optional face-to-face short summer sessions on campus in July and August to enrich their learning if they wish.

Tuition and fees are stated in Canadian dollars. A $40 administrative fee per course is applied for students outside Canada.

UNIVERSITY OF WASHINGTON

**School of Public Health and
Community Medicine
Extended MPH Degree Program
Department of Health Services
Box 357660
Seattle, WA 98195-7660
206-685-7580
E-mail: n/a
URL: http://weber.u.washington.edu/~larsson/edp94/edphome.html**

Campus Visits

Four-week intensive summer sessions are required for three consecutive summers, and four intensive on-campus weekend (Friday-Saturday) seminars during the academic year for the first two years. The Health Education Pathway requires additional time on campus.

Admission

The Extended Degree Program is designed specifically for employed public, community, and environmental health professionals with a minimum of three years' experience. A baccalaureate degree from an accredited college is required, and at least a 3.0 grade point average in the last graded 90 quarter/60 semester hours. The GRE, taken within six years, is required. Applicants with MD or DO degrees from an accredited U.S. college or university may be able to waive the GRE requirement if they have successfully completed (with a grade of B or better) a college-level algebra or basic statistics course within the past five years.

Programs

63–66 quarter credits

Master in Public Health in Health Services
Master in Public Health in Health Services/Health Education
Master in Public Health in Health Services/Maternal and Child Health

Tuition & Fees

Basic Tuition:	$272 per quarter credit
Master's Tuition:	$17,136–$17,952
Financial Aid:	Government loans, public traineeships, veteran's benefits

Notes

The University of Washington, founded in 1861, is the oldest state-assisted institution of higher education on the Pacific Coast. Distance learning and extended programs operate as extensions of on-campus offerings. The Extended MPH Degree Program was established in 1980 and is accredited by the Council on Education for Public Health (CEPH). The EDP curriculum is designed to provide advanced knowledge and skills in the planning, organization, and evaluation of health services or environmental health services, and the management of public, community, or environmental health programs. The three-year program is offered through a combination of intensive four-week summer sessions on campus at the University of Washington, four intensive on-campus weekend seminars during the academic year for the first two years, directed independent study, and electives taken at the University of Washington and/or other institutions. In addition to required course work, students are required to complete a practicum and a thesis or agency-related project.

UNIVERSITY OF WASHINGTON EXTENSION

Distance Learning
5001 25th Avenue NE
Seattle, WA 98105-4190
206-543-2320
800-543-2320
E-mail: jhilov@u.washington.edu (Jack Hilovsky, Public Health Program)
URL: http://www.edoutreach.washington.edu/extinfo

Campus Visits

Project management applicants must attend a total of six Saturday sessions on campus over the course of the five module program. Public health applicants must attend three two-week on-campus sessions in July, January, and the following July, to complete the certificate program.

Admission

The Certificate in Project Management requires either a bachelor's degree and two years of work experience, two years of college and four years of project management work experience, or six years of project management experience. Applicants with prior project management experience will receive priority. The Certificate in Public Health requires a bachelor's degree and three to five years of experience in the public health field. Public health applicants must also be able to complete a three-credit public health practicum in a local setting. Students are required to have a computer and Internet access to complete selected courses.

Programs

5 modules
Certificate in Project Management

33 quarter credits
Certificate in Public Health/Administration and Management
Certificate in Public Health/Community Development
Certificate in Public Health/Epidemiology and Information
Certificate in Public Health/Policy Development and Program Planning

Tuition & Fees

Basic Tuition:	$273 per quarter credit
Certificate Tuition:	$2,054 (Project Management); $9,009 (Public Health)
Financial Aid:	None

Notes

The University of Washington Extension is the continuing education division of the government-supported University of Washington, founded in 1861. The campus-based extension program offers over sixty professional and continuing education certificate options with evening and weekend attendance in a classroom setting. The distance learning program offers more than 120 courses each session. The certificates in Project Management and Pubic Health operate as extensions of classroom offerings. The project management program consists of five course modules: What Is Project Management; Project Planning I: Scope, Risk, and Scheduling; Project Planning II: Cost Estimating and Budgeting; Organization and Team Processes; Implementation and Close Out: Procurement, Contract, Monitoring and Change Management. The program provides information about the PMP (Project Management Professional) certification program and presents students with a chance to develop, present, and evaluate a project management plan of their own. Participants in the fifteen month-long Certificate in Public Health program will gain 33 graduate quarter credits that may later be used toward the University of Washington's low-residency Extended Master's in Public Health program. The first half (16 credits) of the public health program, which begins in July each year, emphasizes fundamental subjects. The second half, the specialty track, begins in January, and allows students to specialize by completing a 14-credit track specialty. All public health applicants must complete a final 3-credit practicum in public health at a local site. Programs are delivered using printed texts and study guides in conjunction with E-mail and the use of the World Wide Web.

UNIVERSITY OF WASHINGTON—PHARMACY

UW/WSU External Doctorate of Pharmacy
5001 25th Avenue, NE
Seattle, WA 98105-4190
800-543-2320
206-543-2320
E-mail: distance@u.washington.edu
URL: http://weber.u.washington.edu/~instudy

Campus Visits

Periodic weekend workshops held at sites throughout Washington State will need to be attended throughout the degree program.

Admission

The program admits only licensed Washington State pharmacists who wish to continue their education while they remain employed in their local communities.

Programs

63–66 quarter credits
Doctor of Pharmacy

Tuition & Fees

Basic Tuition: $265 per course module; $640 per clerkship
Doctorate Tuition: $5,085 (estimate)
Financial Aid: Government loans

Notes

The University of Washington is a comprehensive, government-supported institution founded in 1861. Washington State University is a comprehensive, government-supported institution founded in 1890. Permanent faculty members from both institutions serve as faculty for the jointly developed and delivered external, limited-residency Doctor of Pharmacy (Pharm.D) program. The program is accredited by the American Council on Pharmaceutical Education. Both institutions began offering the Pharm.D as the sole professional pharmacy degree in 1995. Based on an assessment of prior knowledge, education, and experience gained through pharmacy practice, applicants may qualify for transfer credit standing toward the degree. The curriculum is divided into three required phases. Phase one requires the completion of three courses in basic knowledge. Phase two requires the completion of nine independent study modules in advanced therapeutics ($265 each). Phase three requires the completion of nine required clerkships, each four weeks long. Prior knowledge and experience may count toward the required clerkships. Distance courses are delivered using predesigned modules, which are enhanced with E-mail and Internet chat room discussions and assignments. Weekend workshops held at site locations across Washington State augment distance learning with face-to-face instruction.

UNIVERSITY OF WISCONSIN—DISTANCE EDUCATION

Distance Education Professional Development
Department of Continuing & Vocational Education
225 North Mills Street, Room 112
Madison, WI 53706
608-262-8530
E-mail: cholgren@macc.wisc.edu (Christine Olgren)
URL: http://www.uwex.edu/disted/depd/certpro.html

Campus Visits

None

Admission

Applicants need not hold any special degrees or credentials to enter the program, but most applicants are professionally involved in distance education or training delivery.

Programs

15 Continuing Education Units (CEUs)

Certificate of Professional Development in Distance Education

Tuition & Fees

Basic Tuition: $145–$420 per course
Certificate Tuition: $2,250 (payment in advance); $2,500 (partial payment in advance); $3,200 (one course at a time)
Financial Aid: Payment plans

Notes

The University of Wisconsin at Madison is a government-supported university founded in 1849. The University of Wisconsin system has been a pioneer in the development and delivery of distance education in the United States since 1891. The distance education professional certificate program is suited to those in corporate training, K–12 media and learning, or higher education program development and delivery. Four self-paced modules form the core curriculum for certificate learners: Learning at a Distance, Distance Education Technology, Instructional Systems Design, and Evaluation in Distance Education. Electives are then chosen from print-based learning modules, audioconference seminars, online Internet seminars, individualized learning contracts, or optional attendance at seminars or Wisconsin's annual conference on distance learning and technology. The program covers print, electronic, and audio and video technology and delivery, and features application-based self-study modules that allow learners to integrate career projects with their studies. Individual courses are open to non-certificate seekers wishing to enhance their professional skills.

UNIVERSITY OF WISCONSIN—ENGINEERING OUTREACH

1415 Engineering Drive, Room 1147
Madison, WI 53706-1691
608-262-5516
E-mail: outreach@engr.wisc.edu
URL: http://www.engr.wisc.edu/services/oeo

Campus Visits

To earn one of the two video-based master's degrees, applicants must attend a campus course that is offered every summer. This is a three-week lab experience.

Admission

The program is designed for practicing engineers who wish to extend their education but cannot attend courses on campus. A bachelor's degree in a suitable area is required for admission. A 2.75 undergraduate GPA is required. Additional exams or entrance requirements may be imposed by individual engineering departments.

Programs

24 credits

Master of Science in Electrical & Computer Engineering (Power Electronics)
Master of Science in Mechanical Engineering (Controls)

Tuition & Fees

Basic Tuition: $275 per credit (Wisconsin); $830 per credit (others)
Master's Tuition: $6,600 (Wisconsin); $19,920 (others)
Financial Aid: Veteran's benefits

Notes

The University of Wisconsin at Madison is a government-supported college founded in 1849. The College of Engineering has delivered off-campus studies since the 1970s. About 13,000 registrants nationwide take over 400 off-campus courses each year from the College of Engineering. Courses are delivered via video, audio conference, Internet, print and surface, or satellite to corporate or public downlinks. Master's programs are primarily video based. Learners receive videotapes of on-campus lectures and communicate with faculty and other learners through E-mail and phone conferencing. A maximum of six credits may be transferred toward the degree. Individual courses are open to non-degree learners. Undergraduate courses are also available in some engineering areas. Corporations may arrange to rent or purchase selected courses for in-house use.

University of Wisconsin—Professional Development in Engineering

Department of Engineering Professional Development
432 North Lake Street, Room 313
Madison, WI 53706-1498
608-262-0133
800-462-0876
E-mail: karena@epd.engr.wisc.edu
URL: http://epdwww.engr.wisc.edu

Campus Visits

The professional degree can be completed by choosing courses that require no on-campus residency.

Admission

A bachelor of science degree in engineering from an ABET-accredited program is required for non-provisional admission to the Professional Development (PD) degree. Applicants with bachelor of science degrees in areas other than engineering from an ABET-accredited college should have completed at least 100 undergraduate credits that would be equivalent to a University of Wisconsin ABET-accredited bachelor of science in engineering degree or have passed the Professional Engineer (PE) registration exam. In general, graduates of "engineering technology programs" have not been judged sufficiently prepared to enter the PD program. The PD degree is an advanced alternative to the theoretical master's for practicing engineering professionals. Forty percent of applicants already hold master's or doctoral degrees. International applicants are welcome.

Programs

120 Continuing Education Units (CEUs)
Professional Development Degree in Engineering

Tuition & Fees

Basic Tuition:	Varies
PD Tuition:	$2,500–$4,500
Financial Aid:	Veteran's benefits

Notes

The University of Wisconsin—Madison is a land grant institution founded in 1849. The College of Engineering has delivered off-campus courses since the early 1970s, and is a charter member of the National Technological University, whose courses are delivered via satellite. Additionally, the College offers off-campus seminars and short courses; about 13,000 participants attend more than 400 of these each year. The College of Engineering Outreach also offers graduate level engineering courses via videotape, audioconference, Internet, audiographics, and satellite. Undergraduate-level correspondence courses in engineering and other topics are offered through the University of Wisconsin—Extension. The Extension, established in the 1890s, currently offers more than 400 courses annually in many different content areas. The Professional Development degree is a post-baccalaureate degree offered as an alternative to the traditional research-based master's degree. The PD Degree program, offered since 1971, allows practicing engineers to transfer in up to one-half of the CEUs needed for the degree. A required independent study project, supervised by a faculty advisor, constitutes part of the degree program. Each candidate designs a curriculum based on individual professional needs; applicants from all areas of engineering are invited to participate.

University of Wisconsin—Graduate School of Banking

Graduate School of Banking at UW—Madison
5315 Wall Street, Suite 280
Madison, WI 53704-7939
608-243-1945
800-755-6440
E-mail: akleist@gsb.org
URL: http://www.gsb.org

Campus Visits

Two weeks are required on campus each August for three consecutive summers.

Admission

The program is open to professional bankers, regulatory agency officials, bank directors, savings institution employees, and professionals from other financial service institutions and from firms providing services to banks. Applicants should be executive officers. Non-officers may be accepted with the appropriate letters of reference from their executive officers. Applicants without bachelor's degrees will be considered if they have executive-level bank management experience. International applicants are accepted.

Programs

18 courses, plus electives
Diploma of Advanced Studies in Bank Management

Tuition & Fees

Basic Tuition:	$1,950 per year
Certificate Tuition:	$6,000 includes on-campus residency room and board
Financial Aid:	None

Notes

The University of Wisconsin is a government-supported college founded in 1849. The Central States Conference of Bankers Associations has sponsored the special Graduate School of Banking program for mid-career bankers since its inception in 1945. Over 17,000 bankers and regulatory officials have graduated from the University of Wisconsin's Graduate School of Banking program. The twenty-five-month, three-year program covers bank marketing, performance analysis, monetary policy, investments, lending, asset/liability management, human resources management, bank law, loan portfolio management, and retail banking. Applicants complete independent readings, case studies, and banking projects between the summer residency sessions.

UNIVERSITY OF WISCONSIN—STOUT

Graduate Vocational Education
Dr. Orville Nelson, Program Director
Room 19, Student Health Services Building
Menomonie, WI 54751
715-232-1382
E-mail: nelson@uwstout.edu
URL: n/a

Campus Visits

At least one summer session or one regular semester must be spent on campus. Up to twenty credits of the thirty-credit master's program may be taken through individualized independent study via surface mail or the commercial online service, America Online.

Admission

Applicants must hold a bachelor's degree from an accredited college, with at least a 2.75 overall GPA. Applicants with undergraduate studies not related to vocational education may be required to take preparatory or foundations course work. International learners are welcome with TOEFL.

Programs

30 credits
Master of Science in Vocational Education

Tuition & Fees

Basic Tuition:	$1,419 per semester (Minnesota),
	$1,407 per semester (Wisconsin),
	$4,287 per semester (others)
Master's Tuition:	$4,200–$5,700 (Minnesota),
	$4,200–$5,600 (others),
	$12,900–$17,100 (others)
Financial Aid:	Government loans, Wisconsin and Minnesota state aid for residents, veteran's benefits

Notes

The University of Wisconsin at Stout is a government-supported institution founded in 1891. An array of undergraduate, graduate, and professional degrees are offered on campus. The graduate Vocational Education program is suitable for those seeking teacher certification in vocational education in Minnesota or Wisconsin. Up to one-third of the master's may be earned through transfer credits completed in the last seven years. Some courses may allow for "test-outs" or for learners to take exams, earn credit, and be exempt from certain formal courses. Higher tuition rates may apply for courses taken individually through self-study or with an E-mail lesson option.

VERMONT COLLEGE OF NORWICH UNIVERSITY

Graduate Studies Division
Montpelier, VT 05602
802-828-8500
800-336-6794
E-mail: VCAdmis@Norwich.edu
URL: http://www.norwich.edu/grad

Campus Visits

The Master of Arts offers self-designed programs within the humanities and social sciences and requires attendance at one three-to-five-day colloquium in Montpelier, Vermont, or Santa Barbara, California. European students must attend two colloquia held in Europe to complete the degree. Also required are quarterly regional meetings that are held at various sites in North America and at a site in Europe or Israel. Students in the Master of Arts in Art Therapy program are required to attend two three-month, on-campus summer residencies and an interim thirty-five-week, community-based internship. Students in the Master of Fine Arts in Visual Art, Creative Writing, or Children's Writing programs are required to attend nine- and eleven-day campus residencies every six months. The Master of Fine Arts in Music Performance can be completed in two years and requires two fourteen-day summer residencies and two four-day winter residencies to complete the degree.

Admission

An open admission policy is maintained for qualified candidates who hold accredited undergraduate degrees.

Programs

36–60 credits
Master of Arts/Art & Art History
Master of Arts/Counseling Psychology
Master of Arts/Education
Master of Arts/Health Care Management
Master of Arts/History
Master of Arts/Human Resources
Master of Arts/International Relations
Master of Arts/Literature & Writing
Master of Arts/Management & Organizational Development
Master of Arts/Multicultural Studies
Master of Arts/Philosophy & Religion
Master of Arts/Political Science
Master of Arts/Psychology
Master of Arts/Public Policy Administration
Master of Arts/Sociology
Master of Arts/Women's Studies

45 credits
Master of Art in Art Therapy

60 credits
Master of Fine Arts in Creative Writing
Master of Fine Arts in Children's Writing
Master of Fine Arts in Music Performance
Master of Fine Arts in Visual Arts/Craft as Fine Art
Master of Fine Arts in Visual Arts/Drawing
Master of Fine Arts in Visual Arts/Nontraditional Media
Master of Fine Arts in Visual Arts/Painting

Master of Fine Arts in Visual Arts/Photography
Master of Fine Arts in Visual Arts/Printmaking
Master of Fine Arts in Visual Arts/Sculpting

Tuition & Fees

Basic Tuition: $4,143–$6,860 per semester
Master's Tuition: $12,429–$25,600
Financial Aid: Government loans, scholarships, veteran's benefits, DANTES
                            military benefits, payment plans

Notes

Vermont College is a division of Norwich University, a private, comprehensive university, founded in 1819. Norwich University is the largest private institution of higher learning in Vermont. Vermont College of Norwich University is one of the few campuses in the United States dedicated exclusively to adult learners and is home to one of the oldest distance learning programs in the United States. The individually designed undergraduate Adult Degree Program has been in operation for more than three decades. The degree model at Vermont College uses an inquiry-based, mentor-style format where adult learners design much of their own degrees with faculty assistance. The integration of theory and practice through the use of local internships and practicums is encouraged. The individualized Master of Arts program invites applicants to design their degrees in the humanities, arts, or social sciences. Studies in technical or professional areas such as engineering, nursing, physics, or accounting cannot be accommodated. Counseling and clinical psychology degrees may be designed to meet state-specific mental health licensing requirements in Vermont and other states. Counseling applicants usually must complete a longer forty-eight- or sixty-credit program to meet licensing content and internship requirements. Master of Fine Arts (MFA) applicants may take a structured course of study or may design their own degrees. Because learners design their own degrees, working directly with faculty mentors, individual courses are not open via correspondence. Students and faculty communicate via U.S. mail, fax, and E-mail. A small number of graduate credits from other accredited institutions that are relevant to the study undertaken at Vermont College may be transferred and applied toward the degree.

■ VIRGINIA COMMONWEALTH UNIVERSITY

Executive Program in Health Administration
Department of Health Administration
Grant House
1008 East Clay Street
P.O. Box 980203
Richmond, VA 23298-0203
804-828-0719
E-mail: vcu-grad@vcu.edu
URL: http://www.vcu.edu/haeweb/had/dept.htm

Campus Visits

Five one- to two-week campus visits are required over a two-year period. Campus sessions are held in July and January.

Admission

Applicants to the executive program in Health Administration should hold bachelor's degrees from regionally accredited colleges with an overall GPA of at least 2.75. All applicants should have at least five years of professional experience in health care. Applicants must have access to a computer and modem, as instruction takes place over Execunet, a computer conferencing system. Applicants with limited formal business education will be required to complete programmed independent study modules in microeconomics, accounting, and quantitative analysis prior to beginning their graduate studies. Either the GRE or the GMAT is required for admission unless the applicant already holds a doctorate.

Programs

45 credits
Master of Science in Health Administration

Tuition & Fees

Basic Tuition:	$3,567 per semester (Virginia), $7,187 per semester (others)
Master's Tuition:	$14,268 (Virginia), $28,748 (others)
Financial Aid:	Government loans

Notes

Virginia Commonwealth is a government-supported institution founded in 1838. An array of undergraduate, graduate, and professional degree programs are offered on campus. The distance program operates as an extension of the on-campus program, which was first offered in 1949. The degree program is accredited by the Accrediting Commission for Education in Health Services Administration (ACEHSA), and is designed to be completed by working professionals in twenty-four months of study. Delivery methods include computer conferencing, videotaped instruction, programmed computer-aided instruction, and self-study modules. Applicants who reside in a Southern Academic Common Market state, such as Georgia, may qualify to pay lower in-state tuition.

WALDEN UNIVERSITY

Institute for Advanced Studies
801 Anchor Rode Drive
Naples, FL 33940
941-261-7277
800-444-6795
E-mail: info@waldenu.edu
URL: http://www.waldenu.edu

Campus Visits

Master's degree applicants attend a five-day summer or December residency and one three-week summer residency. A four-day regional residency workshop is required to begin doctoral studies. To complete doctoral studies, at least one three-week summer residency or one four-day regional intensive must be attended each year. International learners may meet doctoral residency requirements by attending two three-week summer sessions. Summer sessions are held at Indiana University in Bloomington, Indiana.

Admission

Applicants to the master's educational technology program should hold regionally accredited bachelor's degrees and have a minimum of two years of teaching or the equivalent experience in an educational setting. Applicants to doctoral study should hold master's degrees from regionally accredited colleges and have at least three years of career experience in their intended field of study. Applicants to the professional psychology program should hold master's degrees in a mental health specialty, and have practiced for at least three years in a mental health setting. Learners of exceptional promise who hold regionally accredited bachelor's degrees, but not master's degrees, may submit a work portfolio to petition for admission to doctoral study without a master's. Walden maintains an electronic campus on the Internet, the Walden Information Network (WIN). Applicants must have access to a computer and modem and the Internet to communicate with faculty and staff. A minimum of two seminars must be completed online to earn a Walden doctoral program. International learners are welcome with TOEFL scores at or above 550.

Programs

48 credits
Master of Science in Educational Change & Technology Innovation (K–12)

60 credits post-master's
Doctor of Philosophy in Administration/Management
Doctor of Philosophy in Education
Doctor of Philosophy in Health Services
Doctor of Philosophy in Human Services
Doctor of Philosophy in Human Services/Professional Psychology

Tuition & Fees

Basic Tuition:	$2,950 per quarter
Master's Tuition:	$10,100, $210 per credit
Doctorate Tuition:	$29,500–$35,400
Financial Aid:	Government loans, dissertation awards, veteran's benefits, payment plans, private educational loans, 25% spouse doctoral tuition reduction, 50% tuition reduction at doctoral degree candidacy

Notes

Walden is a private graduate and professional university that has served adult distance learners since 1970. Learners and faculty communicate via the Walden Information Network (WIN), a bulletin board and electronic conferencing system that includes online access to the research libraries at Indiana University. Training is offered on Internet access for novices. The master's in educational change is designed for teachers, administrators, media specialists, or resource center librarians at the K-12 levels. At the doctoral level, except for the professional psychology specialty, discrete independent study courses are not offered. Instead, learners must pass a series of eight competency modules in their main degree area, then work with faculty to design a plan of study for the specialty area that interests them. Learners may design their own professional specialties within the four broad degree areas. For example, a management/administration degree seeker might opt to complete a specialty in human resources, personnel management, or international business. An education degree seeker might opt to complete a specialty in distance learning, instructional technology, or educational management. A health services degree seeker might design specialties in women's health care or holistic health. Professional psychology or education students may design their degrees to meet state specific licensing requirements. Counseling specialties, such as substance abuse, feminist therapy, or vocational counseling, may be developed. Clinical internships of up to two years may be required for counseling majors. Applicants seeking the Ed.D. rather than the Ph.D. may complete an approved work project in lieu of a research thesis. Ph.D. learners must complete a thesis. Regardless of transfer credits, all degree candidates must complete a minimum of ten quarters of study through Walden University. The professional psychology program requires a minimum of twelve quarters to complete the requirements of most state licensing boards.

WARREN WILSON COLLEGE

MFA Program for Writers
P.O. Box 9000
Asheville, NC 28815-9000
704-298-3325, ext. 380
E-mail: n/a
URL: http://www.warren-wilson.edu/mfa

Campus Visits

Five ten-day residencies are required. Residencies are held in July and January.

Admission

An essay and critical book analysis are required for admission. Ten pages of original poetry or twenty-five pages of short fiction must be submitted with the application. Admission is based largely on the creative quality of the writing samples submitted. Extremely accomplished writers may petition to enter the MFA program without a bachelor's degree or with a bachelor's in an area other than writing or literature.

Programs

60 credits
Master of Fine Arts in Fiction
Master of Fine Arts in Poetry

Tuition & Fees

Basic Tuition:	$3,800 per semester
Master's Tuition:	$15,200
Financial Aid:	Government loans, MFA grants, Holden minority scholarships, Eric M. King scholarship

Notes

Warren Wilson is a private, comprehensive liberal arts college, founded in 1894. The Master of Fine Arts (MFA) program was designed by Ellen Bryant Voigt at Goddard College in 1976, and moved to Warren Wilson College to become its first graduate program in 1981. The low-residency MFA program currently accepts only 10–15 percent of its applicants each year. The program, which consists of four six-month semesters, emphasizes the study of literature from within—from the writer's, not the critic's or scholar's perspective. Degree candidates must complete critical analysis papers, a degree essay, and a master's creative manuscript, teach a class, and give a public reading of their work. Non-degree learners may attend the ten-day summer residencies in poetry or fiction as noncredit writer's workshops. Ten-day residency fees, which cover room and board, are $475 for each session. Program alumni are eligible for the Joan Beebe Graduate Teaching Fellowship.

WARWICK BUSINESS SCHOOL

Distance Learning MBA
The University of Warwick
Coventry
United Kingdom CV4 7AL
44-01-20-352-4100
E-mail: dmbainf@wbs.warwick.ac.uk
URL: http://www.wbs.warwick.ac.uk/

Campus Visits

Attendance at an eight-day compulsory campus seminar is required in September of each year.

Admission

Normal admission is based on possession of a first- or second-class British honors undergraduate degree or an accredited bachelor's with at least two years of career experience. Admission may be granted to applicants who demonstrate professional qualifications plus a minimum of two years of career experience. Applicants not meeting normal admission criteria may be asked to submit scores on the GMAT. International applicants are welcome.

Programs

1 stage
Certificate in Business Administration
2 stages
Diploma in Business Administration
3 stages, plus a dissertation
Master of Business Administration

Tuition & Fees

Basic Tuition:	2,000 British Pounds Sterling per stage, plus 900 pounds dissertation ($3,200 US)
Certificate Tuition:	2,000 British Pounds Sterling ($3,200 US)
Diploma Tuition:	4,000 British Pounds Sterling ($6,400 US)
Master's Tuition:	7,000 British Pounds Sterling ($11,200 US)
Financial Aid:	Career development loans, AMBA loans (UK residents only)

Notes

The University of Warwick has operated under Royal Charter, the equivalent of America regional accreditation, since 1965. The distance MBA program admits about 350 learners each year, half of them located outside the United Kingdom. The program has accepted learners from more than seventy countries worldwide. The Higher Education Funding Council of the United Kingdom has recognized Warwick with an "excellent" rating for teacher quality. The distance MBA program began in 1986 and was the first distance MBA to be recognized by the European Association of MBAs (AMBA). The distance program adheres to the same teaching, text, and examination procedures as are employed on campus. The Warwick MBA by distance learning is based on a study scheme of specially commissioned study notes, complemented by textbooks, articles, case studies, and assignments. These self-contained study modules offer a structured yet flexible learning experience, which emphasizes the relevance of theory to management practice. Registrants may exit the program at any stage, earning either a certificate or a diploma in business administration for shorter studies with no dissertation. The final dissertation is a research-based project that focuses on an applied management problem. While instruction has historically occurred via surface mail, an E-mail and E-mail listserv option now provides learners with access to tutors and program services. The required September seminar provides for case study analyses and group orientation to each learning stage. Formal assessment is by written examination, together with a final dissertation based on a project normally undertaken in the student's employing organization. Costs given include study guides and texts. No exemptions or transfer credits are allowed. All applicants must take the Warwick exams for each stage of their educational process.

A conversion rate of 1 United States dollar to .60 British Pound Sterling is used. Conversion rates may vary.

WESTERN SEMINARY

Department of External Studies
5511 SE Hawthorne Blvd.
Portland, OR 97215
800-547-4546
503-233-8561
E-mail: n/a
URL: n/a

Campus Visits

None

Admission

Normally, applicants must hold an accredited bachelor's degree with a minimum 2.5 GPA. Provisional admission may be considered for candidates presenting qualifying credentials other than an accredited bachelor's degree or who have lower GPAs. Applicants for enrichment study only may be admitted without holding an undergraduate degree.

Programs

12 credits
Certificate in Theology
Certificate in Church Ministry
30 credits
Diploma in Theological Studies
Diploma in Ministerial Studies

Tuition & Fees

Basic Tuition: $225 per credit
Certificate Tuition: $2,700
Diploma Tuition: $6,750
Financial Aid: Group discounts, spouse discounts, payment plans

Notes

Western Seminary, founded in 1927, is a private evangelical seminary dedicated to developing Godly leaders committed to Christ's redemptive purpose throughout the world. The seminary is a candidate for accreditation from the Association of Theological Schools. The Department of External Studies (DES) was launched in 1980 as a video-based external program and today offers more than fifty courses each year. Courses are delivered using videotapes of both on-campus and predesigned curricula. DES also offers, in conjunction with the Institute of Theological Studies, a series of audio-based courses taught by evangelical faculty at institutions across the country. Certificate courses have been approved by the Association of Christian Schools International (ACSI) for use toward teacher certification in Christian institutions. Diploma courses may later be applied to the on-campus master's programs. Individual classes are open to enrollment on an enrichment basis at a lower tuition rate than is charged for academic credits.

WHEATON COLLEGE GRADUATE SCHOOL

Extension & Continuing Education
Masters Program for Persons in Ministry (MPPM)
Wheaton, IL 60187-5593
630-752-5944
800-325-8718
E-mail: gradexten@wheaton.edu
URL: http://www.wheaton.edu

Campus Visits

The final semester is spent in residence along with two one-week on-campus intensive seminars while the degree is in progress. Residency exceptions may be granted for learners residing outside North America.

Admissions

A bachelor's degree from an accredited college with a minimum 2.75 GPA and ministry experience is required. The special Master's Program for Persons in Ministry (MPPM) is designed to allow those in the church or para-church ministry to earn their Master of Arts in Theology with limited residency.

Programs

36 credits
Master of Arts in Theology

Tuition & Fees

Basic Tuition: $165 per credit
Master's Tuition: $5,940
Financial Aid: Billy Graham scholarships, half-tuition for extension study compared to on-campus instruction rates

Notes

Wheaton College is a comprehensive private Christian university, founded in 1860 for "Christ and His Kingdom." The Wheaton College Graduate School was founded in 1937 as part of a graduate system that offers on-campus master's degrees in seven disciplines as well as a Doctoral Program in Clinical Psychology (Psy.D.). Extension courses are delivered using audiocassette tapes of class lectures and course manuals. E-mail may also be used to facilitate communication with faculty.

WORCESTER POLYTECHNIC INSTITUTE

Department of Management
Advanced Distance Learning Network (ADLN)
100 Institute Road
Worcester, MA 01609-2280
508-831-5218
E-mail: nwilkins@wpi.edu (Norm Wilkinson, Director)
URL: http://mgnt.wpi.edu/graduate.htm

Campus Visits

No campus or site visits are required. Applicants may complete degrees or certificates by either attending interactive broadcast and group study sites in Cambridge, Clinton, Waltham, Worcester, Westboro, or New Bedford, Massachusetts, or by studying independently from any location worldwide using videotapes and the Internet.

Admissions

Applicants are required to submit undergraduate transcripts, three letters of recommendation, and GMAT or GRE scores. The GMAT is required for the MBA, with the GRE acceptable for the MS degree. Applicants should possess the equivalent of a four-year American bachelor's degree and have the necessary mathematical and business study background to complete advanced study in a technology-oriented management degree program. Distance learners are required to have a computer, modem, and Internet access as well as access to a fax machine and a VCR. Some courses may require access to a video camera to tape class presentations. TOEFL scores are required for international applicants.

Programs

12–15 credits
Certificate in Information Technology
Certificate in Management of Technology
Certificate in Technology Marketing

30 credits
Master of Science in Management/Marketing & Technology Innovation
Master of Science in Management/Operations & Information Technology

31–55 credits
Master of Business Administration/Management of Technology

Tuition & Fees

Basic Tuition:	$612 per credit
Certificate Tuition:	$7,344–$9,180
Master's Tuition:	$18,360–$33,660
Financial Aid:	Government loans, Xerox Graduate Management Fellowships, Robert H. Goddard Graduate Research Fellowships

Notes

Worcester Polytechnic Institute (WPI) is a private university founded in 1865. WPI is the nation's third oldest college of science, engineering, and management. The MBA was first offered on campus in 1970. Courses have been offered via distance learning since 1979. Courses are delivered worldwide via the Advanced Distance Learning Network (ADLN) using mailed video cassettes of lectures, E-mail, and conferencing via the World Wide Web. The standard MBA requires completion of forty-nine credits; however those who enter with a business foundations background may complete the degree in as few as thirty-one-credits, while those wishing to earn specialties may be required to complete as many as fifty-five-credits. Applicants should have taken three semesters of undergraduate mathematics or at least two semesters of calculus to be adequately prepared for advanced study. WPI management and business programs emphasize the link between management and technology and strive to integrate project-based learning and global applications into the curriculum. A final qualifying capstone project, which emphasizes hands-on learning, is completed by all degree candidates.

BIBLIOGRAPHY/REFERENCES

Albright, Michael J., and David L. Graf, eds. *Teaching in the Information Age: The Role of Educational Technology*. San Francisco, CA: Jossey Bass, 1992.

Cookson, Peter S., ed. *Recruiting and Retaining Adult Students*. San Francisco, CA: Jossey-Bass, 1989.

Dillman, Don A., et. al. *What the Public Wants from Higher Education: Workforce Implications from a 1995 National Survey: Technical Report #95-52*. Pullman, WA: Social and Economic Sciences Research Center, 1995.

El-Khawas, Elaine, and Linda Knopp. *Campus Trends: 1996*. Washington, DC: American Council on Education, 1997.

Jones, Glenn R. *Cyberschools: An Education Renaissance*. Englewood, CO: Jones Digital Century, Inc., 1997.

Life After 40: A New Portrait of Today's & Tomorrow's Postsecondary Students. Boston, MA: The Education Resources Institute, 1996.

Mandell, Alan, and Elana Michelson. *Portfolio Development & Adult Learning: Purposes & Strategies*. Chicago, IL: Council for Adult and Experiential Learning (CAEL), 1990.

Markwood, Richard A., and Sally M. Johnstone, eds. *New Pathways to a Degree: Technology Opens the College*. Boulder, CO: Western Interstate Commission for Higher Education (WICHE), 1994.

National University Continuing Education Association. *Lifelong Learning Trends*. Washington, DC: NUCEA, 1996.

Phillips, Vicky. "Earn Your Master's Virtually." *Internet World,* Sept. 1996, pp. 67–70.

Phillips, Vicky. "Five Essential Rules for Designing Distance Degree Outreach Materials for Adult Learners." *Adult Learning,* Jan./Feb. 1995, pp. 10–11.

Phillips, Vicky. "Modem Cum Laude: College Life Is a Screen." *Connect-Time*, Mar. 1997, pp. 7–8.

Rossman, Mark. H., and Maxine E. Rossman, eds. *Facilitating Distance Education*. San Francisco, CA: Jossey-Bass, 1995.

Schuemer, Rudolf. *Some Psychological Aspects of Distance Education: ERIC Clearinghouse on Information Resources Report # ED 357-266*. Hagen, Germany: Fern Universitat, 1993.

Statistics in Brief: Forty Percent of Adults Participate in Adult Education Activities: 1994-1995. Washington, DC: National Center for Education Statistics, 1995.

Verduin, John R., and Thomas A. Clark. *Distance Education: The Foundations of Effective Practice*. San Francisco, CA: Jossey-Bass, 1991.

INDEXES

Alphabetical List of School Profiles

Area of Study Index

A
Accounting & Taxation Studies
Adult Education & Vocational Training
Advertising
Aerospace & Aviation
Agriculture
Art

B
Biology
Business Administration

C
Careers
Chemistry
Communication & Journalism
Computer Science & Information Systems
Counseling
Creative Writing
Criminal & Correctional Justice
Curriculum & Instruction

D
Distance Education & Training

E
Economics
Education & Teaching
Engineering
Environmental Studies

F
Finance & Banking
Forestry & Horticulture

G
Geography

H
Health Care
Historical Studies
Human & Social Services
Human Resources
Humanities

I
Illustration
Individualized
Industrial Technology & Manufacturing
Instructional & Educational Technology
International, Multicultural, & Peace Relations

L
Labor Relations & Social Policy Resolution
Leadership
Liberal Arts, Liberal Studies, & Interdisciplinary
Library & Informational Science
Literature & English

M
Management
Marketing
Mathematics
Military Studies
Ministry, Biblical Studies, & Theology
Museum Studies
Music

N
Nursing
Nutrition

O
Organizational Development

P
Pharmacy
Philosophy
Physical & Occupational Therapy
Political Science & Government
Psychology
Public Health
Public Policy & Administration

Q
Quality Studies

R
Religion
Rural Development

S
Social Science
Sociology & Social Work
Sports & Physical Education

T
Telecommunications
Theater
Transpersonal Studies

W
Women's & Feminist Studies

Major Area of Study Index

Key: Asterisk Programs may be completed with no campus or extension site visits.
C = Certificate, Diploma, or Career Credential
M = Master's Degree
D = Doctoral Degree

BIOLOGY

BUSINESS ADMINISTRATION

Key: Asterisk Programs may be completed with no campus or extension site visits.
C = Certificate, Diploma, or Career Credential
M = Master's Degree
D = Doctoral Degree

CAREERS

CHEMISTRY

Key: Asterisk Programs may be completed with no campus or extension site visits.
C = Certificate, Diploma, or Career Credential
M = Master's Degree
D = Doctoral Degree

COMMUNICATION & JOURNALISM

COMPUTER SCIENCE & INFORMATION SYSTEMS

Key: Asterisk Programs may be completed with no campus or extension site visits.
C = Certificate, Diploma, or Career Credential
M = Master's Degree
D = Doctoral Degree

Key: Asterisk Programs may be completed with no campus or extension site visits.
C = Certificate, Diploma, or Career Credential
M = Master's Degree
D = Doctoral Degree

Key: Asterisk Programs may be completed with no campus or extension site visits.
C = Certificate, Diploma, or Career Credential
M = Master's Degree
D = Doctoral Degree

ENGINEERING

Key: Asterisk Programs may be completed with no campus or extension site visits.
C = Certificate, Diploma, or Career Credential
M = Master's Degree
D = Doctoral Degree

Key: Asterisk Programs may be completed with no campus or extension site visits.
C = Certificate, Diploma, or Career Credential
M = Master's Degree
D = Doctoral Degree

ENVIRONMENTAL STUDIES

FINANCE & BANKING

FORESTRY & HORTICULTURE

Key: Asterisk Programs may be completed with no campus or extension site visits.
C = Certificate, Diploma, or Career Credential
M = Master's Degree
D = Doctoral Degree

Key: Asterisk Programs may be completed with no campus or extension site visits.
C = Certificate, Diploma, or Career Credential
M = Master's Degree
D = Doctoral Degree

Key: Asterisk Programs may be completed with no campus or extension site visits.

C = Certificate, Diploma, or Career Credential

M = Master's Degree

D = Doctoral Degree

Key: Asterisk Programs may be completed with no campus or extension site visits.
C = Certificate, Diploma, or Career Credential
M = Master's Degree
D = Doctoral Degree

Key: Asterisk Programs may be completed with no campus or extension site visits.
C = Certificate, Diploma, or Career Credential
M = Master's Degree
D = Doctoral Degree

MANAGEMENT

Key: Asterisk Programs may be completed with no campus or extension site visits.
C = Certificate, Diploma, or Career Credential
M = Master's Degree
D = Doctoral Degree

Key: Asterisk Programs may be completed with no campus or extension site visits.
C = Certificate, Diploma, or Career Credential
M = Master's Degree
D = Doctoral Degree

Key: Asterisk Programs may be completed with no campus or extension site visits.
C = Certificate, Diploma, or Career Credential
M = Master's Degree
D = Doctoral Degree

Key: Asterisk Programs may be completed with no campus or extension site visits.

C = Certificate, Diploma, or Career Credential
M = Master's Degree
D = Doctoral Degree

Key: Asterisk Programs may be completed with no campus or extension site visits.
C = Certificate, Diploma, or Career Credential
M = Master's Degree
D = Doctoral Degree

Key: Asterisk Programs may be completed with no campus or extension site visits.
C = Certificate, Diploma, or Career Credential
M = Master's Degree
D = Doctoral Degree

Key: Asterisk Programs may be completed with no campus or extension site visits.
C = Certificate, Diploma, or Career Credential
M = Master's Degree
D = Doctoral Degree

ABOUT THE AUTHORS

Vicky Phillips designed and directed America's first online counseling center for distance learners for the Electronic University Network on America Online. She has counseled and instructed more than 7,000 adult learners using innovative online means. In the 1980s Vicky served as Director of Academic Services, psychology faculty, and distance degree mentor for Antioch University's innovative San Francisco Center. One of America's pioneering experts on adult education, her articles on online education and training have appeared in *Internet World*, *Home Office Computing*, *Training Magazine*, and scores of other publications. She has authored multimedia and online curriculum for Simon & Schuster's award-winning Computer Curriculum Corporation, the Electronic University Network, and the Canadian Government.

Cindy Yager, a licensed special education teacher in the State of New York, served as founding coordinator of the Computer Learning Center for Business and Industry Training at Ivy Tech State College in Bloomington, Indiana. She is currently a member of the Systems and Network Support team at Saint Michael's College in Colchester, Vermont. In addition to her interests in distance education, Cindy is a Certified Novell Administrator (CNA) who teaches computer courses for the Emerging Technologies Center at Saint Michael's College.

Vicky and Cindy are partners in the adult education consulting firm, Lifelong Learning. They maintain the Adult Education & Distance Learner's Resource Center on the World Wide Web, and publish the *Virtual University Gazette*, a newsletter for distance learning professionals.

Lifelong Learning
170 South Main Street
Waterbury, VT 05676

Adult Education & Distance Learner's Resource Center
http://www.geteducated.com
info@geteducated.com

NOTES

University of Sarasota
p. 269

Univ. of Nebraska-Lincoln
259

*California Institute of Integral
Studies p. 90

Fielding Institute p. 116
(California)

Grambling p. 131
Louisiana

Nova 179

NOTES

NOTES

NOTES

Expert Advice

www.review.com

Talk About It

www.review.com

Pop Surveys

Paying for it

www.review.com

THE
PRINCETON
REVIEW

www.review.com

Getting in

Word du Jour

www.review.com

Find-O-Rama School & Career Search

www.review.com

Best Schools

Finding it

www.review.com

FIND US...

International

Hong Kong
4/F Sun Hung Kai Centre
30 Harbour Road, Wan Chai,
Hong Kong
Tel: (011)85-2-517-3016

Japan
Fuji Building 40, 15-14
Sakuragaokacho, Shibuya Ku,
Tokyo 150, Japan
Tel: (011)81-3-3463-1343

Korea
Tae Young Bldg, 944-24,
Daechi- Dong, Kangnam-Ku
The Princeton Review- ANC
Seoul, Korea 135-280,
South Korea
Tel: (011)82-2-554-7763

Mexico City
PR Mex S De RL De Cv
Guanajuato 228 Col. Roma
06700 Mexico D.F., Mexico
Tel: 525-564-9468

Montreal
666 Sherbrooke St.
West, Suite 202
Montreal, QC H3A 1E7 Canada
Tel: (514) 499-0870

Pakistan
1 Bawa Park - 90 Upper Mall
Lahore, Pakistan
Tel: (011)92-42-571-2315

Spain
Pza. Castilla, 3 - 5° A, 28046
Madrid, Spain
Tel: (011)341-323-4212

Taiwan
155 Chung Hsiao East Road
Section 4 - 4th Floor,
Taipei R.O.C., Taiwan
Tel: (011)886-2-751-1243

Thailand
Building One, 99 Wireless Road
Bangkok, Thailand 10330
Tel: (662) 256-7080

Toronto
1240 Bay Street, Suite 300
Toronto M5R 2A7 Canada
Tel: (800) 495-7737
Tel: (716) 839-4391

Vancouver
4212 University Way NE,
Suite 204
Seattle, WA 98105
Tel: (206) 548-1100

National (U.S.)

We have over 60 offices around the U.S. and
run courses in over 400 sites. For courses and locations
within the U.S. call 1 (800) 2/Review and you will be
routed to the nearest office.

WHERE DO I GO FROM HERE?

EFFECTIVE RESUMES • INTERVIEWS

• NEGOTIATING JOB OFFERS • NETWORKING • PORTFOLIOS •

INTERNET JOB SEARCH • CONVINCING COVER LETTERS

THE PRINCETON REVIEW

JOB SMART

What You Need to Know to Get the Job You Want

■ Use network contacts to get you started
■ Create the right resume for any job search
■ Conduct an impressive job interview
■ Learn to write cover letters for every situation

Named one of the Ten Best Career/Job Search Books by the Chicago Tribune

Michelle Tullier, Tim Haft, Marci Taub, and Meg Heenehan

THE PRINCETON REVIEW

GUIDE TO YOUR

CAREER

How to Turn Your Interests Into a Career You Love

Third Edition

Aerospace Engineer   Economist
Webmaster   Ad Executive
Mathematician   Art Dealer

Anthropologist   Animator
Film Editor   Editor
Financial Planner   Landscape Architect

TM

"This is an emotionally intelligent guide to career planning—an original, genuinely helpful handbook to planning your life."
Daniel Goleman, author of Emotional Intelligence

Alan B. Bernstein, C.S.W., P.C., and Nicholas R. Schaffzin

We can help you answer that question, whether you're just getting out of college, have a graduate degree, or simply want to change your career path.

THE PRINCETON REVIEW GUIDE TO YOUR CAREER
3RD EDITION
0-375-75156-4 • $21.00

JOB NOTES: COVER LETTERS
0-679-77873-X • $4.95

JOB NOTES: INTERVIEWS
0-679-77875-6 • $4.95

JOB NOTES: NETWORKING
0-679-77877-2 • $4.95

JOB NOTES: RESUMES
0-679-77872-1 • $4.95

JOB SMART
JOB HUNTING MADE EASY
0-679-77355-X • $12.00

TRASHPROOF RESUMES
YOUR GUIDE TO CRACKING THE JOB MARKET
0-679-75911-5 • $12.00

NEGOTIATE SMART
0-679-77871-3 • $12.00

SPEAK SMART
0-679-77868-3 • $10.00

NO EXPERIENCE NECESSARY
THE YOUNG ENTREPRENEUR'S GUIDE TO STARTING A BUSINESS
0-679-77883-7 • $12.00

WORK SMART
0-679-78388-1 • $12.00

Available at bookstores, or call (800) 733-3000